TWENTIETH CENTURY PARIS

TWENTIETH CENTURY PARIS

A Literary Guide for Travellers
(1900–1950)

MARIE-JOSÉ GRANSARD

TAURIS PARKE
Bloomsbury Publishing Plc
50 Bedford Square, London, WC1B 3DP, UK

BLOOMSBURY, TAURIS PARKE and the TAURIS PARKE logo are trademarks
of Bloomsbury Publishing Plc

First published in Great Britain in 2020

A catalogue record for this book is available from the British Library

ISBN: HB: 978-0-7556-0175-2; eBook: 978-0-7556-0177-6

2 4 6 8 10 9 7 5 3 1

Typeset in Adobe Garamond Pro by Deanta Global Publishing Services, Chennai, India
Printed and bound in Great Britain by CPI Group (UK) Ltd, Croydon, CR0 4YY

To find out more about our authors and books visit www.bloomsbury.com
and sign up for our newsletters

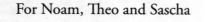

For Noam, Theo and Sascha

Contents

List of Illustrations

Author's Note

Paris has always acted as a magnet for artists and writers from outside France, particularly during the period covered by this literary guide, 1900 to 1950, marked by so many avant-garde movements and so much political and social change. The guide looks at some of those who came to Paris, seeking freedom from oppression or the freedom to live their lives without constraint, as well as at tourists and travellers of all kinds. It explores where they lived, what they wrote, what was written about them and whom they met. They are introduced through their literary legacy in diaries, memoirs, autobiographies, letters, poetry, theatre and fiction.

I chose to include also French writers and artists connected with them sentimentally or professionally. The creative community in Paris embraced all artistic and literary forms from fashion, photography, choreography, music, painting and sculpture to writing. The art dealer Daniel H. Kahnweiler stressed that painters during the first half of the twentieth century, particularly Cubists, were also writers: 'They came to discover that painting was in fact a form of writing.' Gertrude Stein considered her writing a literary form of Cubist painting. I include the familiar figures who dominated the period, but my selection also introduces lesser-known figures who have been unfairly ignored or forgotten, including many women.

Names in bold in the text indicate those who have left a written record. Visitors to Paris will have access to a city plan or a digital street map, so I have included an overview of the arrondissements for orientation. Artists and writers lived and socialised mainly in two locations, Montmartre (18) up to 1910, attractive for its cheapness and village atmosphere (and where Picasso settled when he arrived in Paris in 1904, following in the footsteps of painters like Renoir), and then the Left Bank, which by 1910 had superseded Montmartre, with the Latin Quarter (6) and Montparnasse (14) described by the writer Jean Giraudoux as 'the centre of the world'. I have included a reference list with addresses of locations mentioned in the text, as well as a short glossary, a chronology of key cultural and historical events dominating the period, and suggested reading for those who wish to explore further.

Map of Arrondissements

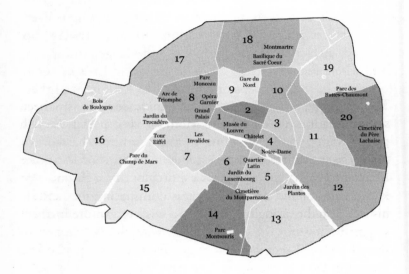

Acknowledgements

The challenge of writing a literary guide to Paris has been simplified a little by limiting myself to the very specific but rich period from 1900 to 1950. My research has been carried out mainly in the British Library in London, in Paris, and also at the Marciana Library in Venice. I am grateful to Eric Hazan, who knows Paris *comme sa poche*, for some of my initial ideas, and for his views on the changing city he knows so well and cares about so greatly. Towards the end of her life Mary Keen (Blumenau) shared personal memories of James Baldwin, whom she had known in Paris in the 1950s, and gave me a number of useful books. Her encouragement made the project a reality. John Venning guided me through an intensive and illuminating reading of T. S. Eliot's *The Waste Land*. I benefited from discussions with Michael Clarke on Modernism, and consulted David Budgen on the Russian entries. My son Sebastian Budgen has again encouraged me and given me valuable professional advice. Most of the photographs were taken by my grandson Noam, and by Jean-Jacques Gransard, and I am grateful to Martin Kamer for allowing me to use some from his collection. Jack Holmes drew the map of the Paris arrondissements. Above all I would like to thank Jenifer Ball, who has once more stood by from the start to suggest, translate and correct, and without whom this book could not have been written.

1

Introduction

*Paris was a free city, an open city. The entire revolution in
art happened at that time.*

(Jean Cocteau)

By 1900 the Belle Époque was at its height. The city of Paris
had been transformed by major projects like Haussmann's
controversial Grands Boulevards. The Eiffel Tower had
been constructed on the Champ-de-Mars for the *Exposition
universelle* of 1889, which was the start of an exciting period,
seeing the birth of art forms like cinema and photography.
The *Exposition universelle* of 1900 in which countries from
all around the world participated was visited by millions.
There were wonderful waterworks which created a fairy-tale
atmosphere by the river at night. Never had Paris looked
so good. Further major exhibitions followed over the next
decades. The 1925 *Exposition des arts décoratifs et industriels
modernes* was exceptional, and gave its name to *Art Déco*, a
modern style influenced by, amongst others, Africa, jazz and
Josephine Baker. Then in 1931 came the *Exposition coloniale*,
with thirty million visitors, and at the Trocadéro Palace

in 1937 the *Exposition internationale des arts et techniques appliqués à la vie moderne.*

The French capital, which was by 1900 the centre of international culture, was a magnet for artists, enrolling to study painting at Académie Julian, or sculpture at the studios of Bourdelle and Rodin. For Picasso's compatriot Joan Miró: 'My formation was in Paris.'

Photo 1   The Eiffel Tower: symbol of the Belle Époque

The giants of French literature had long been drawing writers from all over the world to Paris. For Walter Benjamin, Charles Baudelaire was the ultimate '*flâneur*, whose way of life still conceals behind a mitigating nimbus the coming desolation of the big-city dweller'. The novelist Turgenev left Russia for Paris in order to be close to fellow writers, as well as to the singer Pauline Viardot. Yeats hoped to meet Paul Verlaine, but was drawn to Paris from Ireland also because of his interest in the occult and Theosophy. Verlaine inspired Modernist poets including T. S. Eliot and Ezra Pound, as did Arthur Rimbaud, Jules Laforgue and Gérard de Nerval. The admiration was reciprocal. Edgar Allan Poe never visited Paris but set two short stories there, 'The Murders in the Rue Morgue' and 'The Mystery of Marie Rogêt'. Alain-Fournier's novel *Le grand Meaulnes* (The Great Meaulnes), published in 1913, was Scott Fitzgerald's inspiration for his title *The Great Gatsby* (1925). The contemporary giants Sartre, de Beauvoir and Camus were fascinated by their American counterparts, and Camus wrote that his novel *L'Étranger* (1942) was influenced by Ernest Hemingway's style.

After the French Revolution in 1789 the introduction of the Napoleonic (civil) code granted French citizens rights and freedoms earlier than in most other countries. As a result, France attracted political refugees and many seeking respite from religious persecution. The German writer Heinrich Heine spent the later part of his life in Paris until his death in 1856. Friedrich Engels came in 1844, possibly because Parisians 'join, as no other people have done, a passion for enjoying life with a passion for taking historical action'. There he collaborated with Karl Marx, who had arrived in 1843. Antisemitism, racial prejudice, revolutions in Russia, the Spanish Civil War and two world wars brought new waves of exiles to Paris in the twentieth century.

It was possible in France to act outside established conventions and enjoy a life with fewer constraints, allowing sexual freedom for those who wanted to live differently. Radclyffe Hall's 1928 novel *The Well of Loneliness*, dealing with the sensitive theme of lesbian experience, was banned in England and condemned in America, but could be published in France, as was James Joyce's *Ulysses* (1922). Press freedom and myriad magazines and reviews were also a great attraction for writers.

During the extraordinarily creative period between 1900 and 1950, culture embraced all artistic and literary forms. The trend, particularly after World War I, was for all things modern, especially in décor and haute couture. Oscar Wilde was horrified by the bourgeois decoration of Proust's home. Guillaume Apollinaire summarises the mood of the time in his poem 'Zone' (1913):

> At last you're tired of this elderly world
> Shepherdess O Eiffel Tower this morning the bridges are
>   bleating
> You're fed up with living in ancient Greece and Rome
> Here even the automobiles seem old-fashioned …

Paris from 1910 became a centre for new artistic and literary movements combining African, European and American culture, and inspiring ventures like Diaghilev's Ballets Russes, supported and encouraged by wealthy patrons and fashionable salons.

The city could now be reached easily. Its first aerodrome, Le Bourget, was built between 1919 and 1924. Most people however arrived by boat and train, crossing the Atlantic on Cunard Line ships. The luxurious Art Deco-style liner *Île de France* was launched in 1926, followed by *Paris* and *L'Atlantique*. Those seeking the lower cost of living in Paris could take the cheaper tickets introduced from 1924 by the steamship companies. For just a dollar you could almost live for a week, it was said, even if survival remained problematic for many.

Paris offered the attraction of freedom, but reality was not always rosy. For many fleeing racism and antisemitism the harsh realities they had left behind were not entirely absent in Paris, where xenophobia was widespread. The Dreyfus affair had divided the country from 1894 to 1906, and when war broke out in 1914 anti-German propaganda and sentiment created an unpleasant climate of suspicion towards all foreigners. The war left its mark on those who stayed and had to put up with the hardships of a city under siege and constant bombardment. Artists and writers who had been on the front and survived were traumatised, some maimed for life. It was hardly a paradise for those plagued by hunger, illness or depression. World War I also created a cultural mood in which conventional (academic) art no longer made sense. Art was dead. For the Dadaist Tristan Tzara new values could be created only through destruction. A decade of euphoria followed. The Roaring Twenties, the Jazz Age, *les années folles*, ended abruptly with the 1929 economic crash, which affected many expatriates and forced them to return home or adopt a less extravagant way of life. By 1932 the idea of Paris as a city of enjoyment was largely gone. More were affected by the Spanish Civil War and then World War II. The Nazi occupation caused humiliation in France. Some French accepted defeat and even collaborated with the

PHOTO 2 *Les années folles*

occupiers, while some joined the Resistance movement. For
many there was no choice but to leave Paris to escape arrest,
deportation or even death. When survivors returned after the
liberation, the city had changed and was attracting a different
crowd. After a slow recovery, a period of energy, expectation
and innovation followed, and the arts, cinema and literature
began to flourish again. Americans fleeing McCarthyism
arrived, as well as those seeking refuge from the lack of civil
rights in post-war America.

2

Gay Paree

*Even the pigeons are dancing, kissing, going in circles,
mounting each other. Paris is the city of love, even
for the birds.*
(Samantha Schutz)

The myth of Paris as a romantic city survives. The early twentieth-century idea that the French capital was a place for indulgence, '*la capitale de l'amour*', derives directly from the less savoury image of Paris as the capital of prostitution, the '*bordel de l'Europe*'. By the beginning of the twentieth century the many artists and writers visiting Paris had a different idea of fun. They went there to enjoy the beauty of the city which had become Europe's cultural centre, as well as to experience the sense of excitement and freedom it offered. 'Gay Paree' suggested a certain insouciance and joy. There was certainly also a sexual frisson. Paris in the early twentieth century dealt less repressively with 'deviance' or homosexuality than England or the US, attracting those suffering from discrimination. Paris was also easier to get to now, thanks largely to the relatively efficient and affordable

railway services: 'Going abroad ... getting out at the Gare du
Nord and smelling that combination of coffee and garlic and
French cigarettes and drains which is forever Paris – one of
the best smells in life,' wrote Ethel Mannin in her memoirs
Young in the Twenties (1971). She was one of the many young
people, artists and writers longing to travel: 'We loved to
write sitting at pavement cafés, to show how assimilated we
had become into life abroad; words like *bistro*, *demi-bière*,
vin ordinaire, were precious to us ...' Everything seemed
cheaper: '... in congested Paris ... an English pound went
three times as far as it did in London'. But not all was so rosy:
'It was all completely crazy. We all had perfectly good homes
but there we were ... in Paris, in dark Left Bank hotels with
frightful wallpaper and abominable plumbing.'

Paris was an indispensable step for artists and writers,
hoping to achieve fame by attending the city's prestigious
art schools, or by rubbing shoulders with established artists,
writers and musicians. The city was throbbing with avant-
garde ideas and new art forms like cinema, but you could also
be there to learn French or cooking, or just to hang around:
'it was the "Bohemian" thing to do, and we followed each
other around, in Paris at the Dôme, the Select, the Flore, and
in the cheap restaurants of Montparnasse and St. Germain
de Près [*sic*]'.

The Grands Boulevards and their great department stores
had made Paris the capital of fashion, and the place where
one went to have one's wedding dress made, to buy evening
wear or to imitate the elegance of *la Parisienne*. Young
girls were sent to complete their education, their mothers
hoping the experience would transform them into polished,
sophisticated young women, and their daughters hoping to
find romance.

Margery Sharp (1905–91) is remembered mainly as an author of children's books. Her lightweight novel *Martha in Paris* (1962) is set partly in 1940s Paris, and follows the adventures of Martha, who goes to Paris to learn how to paint, as well as to learn some facts of life. Martha joins an art studio where art is taken seriously, and spends every possible moment drawing and painting: 'To not a single gay party was Martha invited. Nor did she learn to frequent such cafés as Le Dôme or La Rotonde. All the red wine she ever consumed was consumed at table in the rue de Vaugirard' (where she has a room in a *pension*).

Her life in the City of Light is limited to a work routine until she meets a very English young man in the Tuileries Gardens. 'A neat suit and close hair-cut placed him securely within the resident Anglo-Saxon pale ...' Eric lives with his mother, and the comfort-loving and ever-practical Martha starts weekly visits to them, principally to get a good hot meal and a bath with unlimited hot water, both lacking in her digs. While Eric's mother is away in England, Martha and Eric sleep together, with predictable consequences. The final section of the novel tells how Martha deals in her very special way with the pregnancy and the birth of a baby.

This is the second of Margery Sharp's three books with Martha as the main character. She is far from a conventional romantic heroine as she is plain, loves her food and is 'fat' and 'stocky'. She is totally and exclusively focused on herself and her art, and pursues her own goals single-mindedly, not allowing domesticity and convention to interfere.

The final book in the trilogy, *Martha, Eric and George* (1964), picks up Martha's story again. Now a successful painter, she returns from Richmond in the suburbs of London to Paris, and finally meets the son she had deposited on Eric's doorstep ten years before. She is in Paris to attend an exhibition of her work, but she must also face some unfinished business. Her ten-year-old son George, who has been raised in Paris by his grandmother and Eric, attends his mother's exhibition. Like *Martha in Paris* it is a witty story, but also poignant, as it explores the deep bond between a mother and her child. The Martha novels are partly autobiographical and are very evocative of post-war Paris, a city associated with dangers. Martha's aunt Dolores warns before she leaves: 'in Gay Paree Martha might get raped. Not sordidly and horridly … but after some gay party when they'd all been drinking red wine.' Dolores shares the preconception that Gay Paree is a place of moral turpitude, but it is also perceived as an elegant city where a young girl can learn sophistication. When Martha returns to Richmond for Christmas, Dolores is disappointed that Paris has not had the expected effect: 'It was an additional disappointment to her that three months in Paris had so little improved Martha's personal appearance. Whatever Martha wore still looked like a pup-tent; no trace of make-up … "You might just as well never have gone to Paris at all," cried Dolores despairingly.' Some of Margery Sharp's books were turned into successful films, but the Martha novels never left the page.

Countless films have been shot in Gay Paree since the invention of the cinema, but one of the most famous is certainly the musical comedy *Gentlemen Prefer Blondes* (1953), based on a book by the American scriptwriter **Anita Loos** (1889–1981), and directed by Howard Hawks. It had previously been adapted for a 1949 Broadway musical, following a 1928 silent film directed by Mal St Clair and co-written by Loos.

Gentlemen Prefer Blondes: The Illuminating Diary of a Professional Lady started in 1924 as a series of short sketches in six monthly episodes for *Harper's Bazaar* magazine, known as the 'Lorelei' stories, or *Blondes*. Lorelei is the narrator, who relates her adventures as a young attractive woman fending for herself in a man's world. Anita Loos's message was very clear at the time. She 'wanted Lorelei to be a symbol of the lowest possible mentality of our nation'. Lorelei's stories were so popular that the magazine's circulation quadrupled overnight. Pressure was put on Anita Loos to publish them in book form in 1925; it immediately became a bestseller, praised by William Faulkner, Aldous Huxley and Edith Wharton. *Blondes* was reprinted three times in the same year and saw eighty-five editions.

Lorelei Lee, the heroine, is a bold, confidently ambitious flapper, secure in her fresh good looks which she uses shamelessly to exploit men. In spite of her apparent ignorance and naïveté she is practical and single-minded, and has no doubt that a young woman has limited time to make the most of her youth, a clear message in one of the film's songs, 'Diamonds Are a Girl's Best Friend':

> The French are glad to die for love
> They delight in fighting duels
> But I prefer a man who lives
> And gives expensive jewels
> A kiss on the hand may be quite continental
> But diamonds are a girl's best friend
> A kiss may be grand but it won't pay the rental
> On your humble flat, or help you at the automat
> Men grow cold as girls grow old
> And we all lose our charms in the end …

Anita Loos had spent the summer of 1919 in Paris with friends, and that stay was the inspiration for her articles and subsequent book. The gold-digger Lorelei is 'under the protection' of millionaire Gus Eisman, a Chicago button manufacturer, who somewhat unwisely sends her for her 'education' on a European tour chaperoned by her friend Dorothy (a brunette loosely based on Loos). Quickly bored with London, despite a dance with the Prince of Wales, they head for 'devine' [*sic*] Paris with its expensive shops in rue de la Paix and place Vendôme and its most famous sights, especially 'the Eyefull Tower', which Lorelei finds far superior to the Tower of London, as it can be seen from everywhere. Her sentimental 'education' takes shape as she quickly realises that however charming, 'devine' and helpful French men are, they are no match for rich Americans: 'I really think that American gentlemen are the best after all, because kissing your hand may make you feel very, very good but a diamond-and-safire bracelet lasts for ever.'

The girls naturally stay at the Ritz and spend an evening in 'Momart' where they feel perfectly at home. As Lorelei points out: '... in Momart they have genuine American jazz bands

PHOTO 3   Of course Lorelei stayed at the Ritz

and quite a lot of New York people which we knew and you really would think you were in New York and it was divine.'

She consequently does not bother to learn French, as '… I always seem to think it is better to leave French to those that cannot do anything else but talk French.' French might have been useful after all since, as the plot thickens, a French lawyer, Robert Broussard, and his son Louie, are pursuing her to retrieve a diamond tiara illegally in her possession. Through Leon, a French waiter (who thankfully speaks English), Lorelei learns that Robert and Louie are plotting to take her around the Paris sights, waiting for an opportunity to regain the tiara and return it to its rightful owner, Lady Beekman. They visit Fontainebleau (Fontaineblo), the Folies Bergère (Foley Bergere), and the Palace of Versailles (Versay). Lorelei has a copy made of the tiara so that she can keep the original and palm them off with the fake article: 'I can be smart when I want to, but I've noticed most men don't like it.'

Edith Wharton, doubtless tongue-in-cheek, hailed the book as 'the great American novel' and Loos claimed that James Joyce, despite his failing sight, saved his reading for Lorelei Lee's adventures.

The iconic film *Gentlemen Prefer Blondes*, which launched Marilyn Monroe's career, also starred Jane Russell, then a better-known and better-paid actress. Generally considered slight, a poor adaptation of the original stage play, which was more knowing, satirical and sharp below its frothy surface, the film is nevertheless great fun, with Marilyn Monroe glowing in some stunning clothes, particularly the famous pink dress she wore for her performance in the 'Foley Bergere'.

Many other escapist films shot in 1950s Paris adopt a similar view of the city. In *Funny Face* (1957), Audrey Hepburn co-stars and dances through a real Paris, with

Fred Astaire's role based on a famous photographer, Richard Avedon. Hepburn too wears wonderful clothes, and is magically transformed in Paris, confirming what the French writer Balzac had claimed in 1830: 'Whoever does not visit Paris regularly will never really be elegant.'

Love in the Afternoon (1957) and *Sabrina* (1954) also show a naïve young American heroine going to Paris to get 'an education'. Audrey Hepburn as Sabrina is sent to a cookery school, the prestigious Le Cordon Bleu in rue Léon Delhomme in the fifteenth arrondissement. After a couple of years she returns home, not necessarily a good cook, but dramatically transformed into an elegant, confident woman ready to find true love. As she summarises the effect Paris has had on her, she says: 'Paris isn't for changing planes, it's for changing your outlook! For throwing open the windows and letting in *la vie en rose*.'

Audrey Hepburn was truly in love with Paris and with the elegant outfits Hubert de Givenchy created for her in his workshop at 3 avenue Georges V in the eighth arrondissement. She is glowing again in Givenchy in the unforgettable witty thriller *Charade* (1963), co-starring with Cary Grant. In *Paris When It Sizzles* (1964) she co-stars with William Holden, playing the assistant of an irresponsible Hollywood screenwriter, who has been too busy drinking and partying to find time to write a script, due in two days' time.

One of the very few female writers in Hollywood, and having fought for her career in a predominantly male world, Anita Loos was well placed to focus on the position of women in her scripts, which included in 1951 the stage adaptation of Colette's popular novel *Gigi* (1945), produced on Broadway with Audrey Hepburn in the title role. It follows quite closely Colette's original story of a young Parisian girl being

groomed for a career as a courtesan by her aunt, while living
with her mother and grandmother. It centres once again on
a young girl's 'education' and transformation, but allows her
to make her own choices.

A recent Broadway revival of *Gigi* was less of a success.
The *New York Times* considered it 'scrubbed of anything even
remotely naughty or distasteful'. (The 1958 film starring
Leslie Caron had already removed much of the novel's
original sexuality.)

In the song 'The Parisians' from the 1958 film, Gigi
expresses her boredom with the current obsession with love
and money, a rather different message from 'Diamonds Are
a Girl's Best Friend':

A necklace is love
A ring is love
A rock from some obnoxious little king is love
A sapphire with a star is love ...
You would think it would embarrass all the people here
    in Paris
To be thinking every minute of love!
...
I don't understand how Parisians
Never tire of walking hand in hand
But they seem to love it
And speak highly of it
I don't understand the Parisians!

For the producer Jenna Segal, the ultimate message is that
Gigi becomes her own person. 'Gigi shows the triumph of
women over circumstance: that if you held onto your ideals,
the ideal was achievable.'

Josephine Baker (Freda Josephine McDonald) (1906–75) arrived in Paris in 1925. She and many African-American musicians, writers and artists generally found it a welcoming, tolerant and congenial place, away from the discrimination and humiliation they often endured in their own country, with real change still lying more than thirty years away.

It is no wonder that, as the dancer Mildred Hudgens enthused, 'Paris was like Christmas every day. People so crazy about you, you forgot you were black.' Josephine Baker and many African-Americans left the US to get away from the ghetto as well as from unemployment and prohibition, to move to a city where the music and prevailing Modernist movements acknowledged their debt to Africa, as noted by the Parisian gallery owner Paul Guillaume: 'The modern movement in art gets its inspiration undoubtedly from African art, and it could not be otherwise.' Jazz music, brought by American forces to Europe at the end of World War I, was in full swing, rivalling classical and popular music.

'The Black Venus' singer and dancer was born in St Louis, Missouri, which she left for New York aged thirteen, to escape a life of deep poverty, cruelty and racial discrimination. Joining a dance company as a chorus girl in 1925, she was encouraged by its director, Caroline Dudley, to leave for Paris with a group of twelve musicians (one of them Sidney Bechet), and eight dancers. Staying in a hotel in rue Campagne-Première they took the Parisian audience by storm with their exotic and erotic musical show, the *Revue nègre*, at the Théâtre des Champs-Élysées. Baker appeared almost nude in her *Danse sauvage*, her costume amounting to little more than a few feathers.

In the undisputed capital of modernity and freedom, many artists like Picasso, Calder, Matisse and Léger were

PHOTO 4 Théâtre des Champs-Élysées, where Josephine Baker created a stir

showing an interest in primitivism, African art and jazz, so the timing of Baker's meteoric success as an African goddess was perfect: 'I was the wild idol Paris needed. After four years of violence, I symbolised renewed freedom, the discovery of Negro art and jazz, I represented the freedom to bob my hair, to parade naked, to ditch all the constraints, including the corset.' Adrienne Monnier was enthusiastic: '... doesn't Josephine Baker all by herself give the liveliest pleasure, the most amazing that can be imagined? With her get-ups, her

grimaces, her contortions she kicks up a shindy that swarms
with mocking enticements ...' Janet Flanner reported:

> She made her entry entirely nude except for a pink
> flamingo feather between her limbs; she was being carried
> upside down and doing the splits on the shoulder of a
> black giant. ... She was an unforgettable female ebony
> statue. Whatever happened next was unimportant. The
> two specific elements had been established and were
> unforgettable – her magnificent dark body, a new model
> that to the French proved for the first time that black was
> beautiful, and the acute response of the white masculine
> public in the capital of hedonism of all Europe – Paris.
> The music is tuneless and stunningly orchestrated and the
> end of the show is dull, but never Miss Baker's part.

Like most of the audience, Flanner must have been amused
by Miss Baker's sexy but self-deprecating clownish act, as
she crossed her eyes and grimaced at the audience. For
Hemingway she was 'the most sensational woman anybody
ever saw, or ever will,' and he described a night spent with her:

> ... Le Jockey, a classy nightclub in Montparnasse –
> wonderful jazz, great black musicians who were shut out
> in the States but welcomed in Paris. I'd sit at the bar ...
> One of those nights, I couldn't take my eyes off a beautiful
> woman on the dance floor – tall, coffee skin, ebony eyes,
> long, seductive legs ... Her name was Josephine Baker,
> an American, to my surprise. Said she was about to open
> at the Folies Bergère, that she'd just come from rehearsal.
> I asked why the fur on a warm night in June. She
> slid open her coat for a moment to show she was naked.

'I just threw something on,' she said; 'we don't wear much at the Folies.'

Not everyone however was so bewitched, and the conservative French Academician Robert de Flers reported in *Le Figaro* the 'dreadful transatlantic exhibitionism which seems to be taking us back to the apes in less time than it took us to evolve from them'. Nevertheless the company enjoyed a huge success, and in 1926 departed for a European tour which Baker (her name now French: Joséphine) abandoned, enticed by a well-paid offer to perform at the Folies Bergère, wearing the now legendary 'skirt' of fake bananas. She could afford to move out of the Hôtel Fournet at 23 boulevard des Batignolles into an elegant flat in rue Beaujon near the Étoile, a long way from the slums she had left in St Louis and New York.

Baker took singing and etiquette lessons, learned some French and trained with Diaghilev's choreographer George Balanchine, and became a muse and fashion icon, as women copied her *garçonne* haircut and striking make-up, and tanned their own skin. She started to wear elegant Poiret clothes and, following the example of the dancer Ida Rubinstein, would take her pet cheetah Chiquita for walks on a leash in the city.

She added singing and acting to her dance repertoire, and was the first African-American to star in films with titles like *Siren of the Tropics* (1927), the story of Papitou, an Antillean woman who falls in love with a Frenchman whom she follows to Paris, *Zouzou* (1934) and *Princess Tam Tam* (1935). She was also later seen in *Moulin rouge* (1939), *Fausse alerte* (The French Way, 1945), *An Jedem Finger Zehn* (Ten on Every Finger, 1954) and *Carosello del varietà* (Carousel of Variety, 1955).

Her countless admirers included authors, painters, designers and sculptors. Scott Fitzgerald had her in mind for Daisy Buchanan, the sexually liberated flapper in *The Great Gatsby*. The French writer Colette and fashion designer Christian Dior were enthralled, as was Pablo Picasso, who praised her 'legs of paradise'. Jean Cocteau may have been the designer of her famous stage outfit, the banana skirt, and Georges Simenon, a young and then still unknown Belgian writer, fell under her spell after meeting her after a show at the Théâtre des Champs-Élysées on 7 October 1925. For two years he was officially her 'secretary', as he was married and had to keep up appearances. Thousands of others would have liked to marry her, and she received many love letters and proposals. In April 1927 Simenon even launched a review, *Joséphine Baker's Magazine*, dedicated entirely to her, which did not however continue beyond the first issue.

Baker was focused on her career and in 1927 opened a nightclub, *Chez Joséphine*, in rue Fontaine in the Pigalle district, which closed a year later when she left on a world tour. Back in Paris in 1930, she appeared in a costume consisting mainly of a spectacular headdress for a show, *Paris qui remue* (Swinging Paris), at the Casino de Paris at 16 rue de Clichy.

She became a French citizen in 1937, marrying a French businessman, and she stayed in the city at the outbreak of World War II, singing and dancing at Christmas 1939 for the wounded at the American Hospital. In spring 1940 she reopened her nightclub in occupied Paris and joined the French actor/singer Maurice Chevalier in a revue. She was then recruited by French Intelligence to provide information on Germans attending the theatres and nightclubs where she was performing. She left her work in Paris to join the Red Cross to help refugees, and she used her fame, and the special status which allowed her to travel, to work for the Resistance. She was later rewarded by the French Government for the risks she took during those years, and was made *Chevalier de la légion d'honneur* and awarded the *Croix de guerre*.

Apart from a few trips to the US, where she became an active supporter of civil rights, she spent the rest of her life in France, either at her little château in the Dordogne, Les Milandes, or in Paris. She constantly praised her adoptive home in songs with titles like '*Sous le ciel de Paris*', '*Ça c'est Paris!*' and '*Paris mes amours*':

In her last concert at the Bobino Theatre in 1975 shortly before she died, she included her most memorable piece, '*J'ai deux amours*' (composed by Vincent Scotto):

> I have two loves
> My country and Paris
> By both always
> My heart is thrilled
> My savannah is lovely
> But why deny it
> What bewitches me
> Is Paris, all of Paris

She published her autobiography, *Les mémoires de Joséphine Baker*, in 1927, and one of her many foster children, Jean-Claude Baker, wrote a story of her life, *Josephine: The Hungry Heart* in 1976. Much has been written about her, and even Luigi Pirandello planned to write a play about her. More recently *Josephine Baker*, a graphic biography by Edward Gauvin, was published in 2017. Paris remembers her through place Joséphine Baker in Montparnasse, and her name has been given to a swimming pool near the Seine. She died in Paris, but is buried in Monaco.

Cole Porter, George Antheil and George Gershwin were three young American musicians who went independently to Paris during the 1920s, drawn by the free lifestyle and a chance to study with prestigious composers like Ravel, Nadia Boulanger and Stravinsky. They are now remembered as the first serious composers successfully to bridge classical, jazz and popular music.

In Paris in November 1917 the French writer Paul Morand, invited to the elegant home of the music lover and patron Winnaretta Singer, Princesse de Polignac, found himself in the company of American guests, one of whom was twenty-six-year-old **Cole Porter** (1891–1964), newly arrived in the city. It is not clear whether he was, like so many young Americans, in the army in Europe at the end of World War I, and in addition he claimed he had served in the Foreign Legion. Nothing is certain, but he was now in Paris to work with a relief organisation. Porter was a dedicated musician who was said to have travelled to Europe with a portable piano on his back. His original plan was to study with the French composer Vincent d'Indy. He also attempted to study with Igor Stravinsky, to whom he was presented as '... a very nice young man, intelligent and gifted, and a multi-millionaire'. The arrangement fell through, however, as they disagreed on financial arrangements. This is surprising, as Porter was indeed wealthy, having inherited a substantial sum of family money. In 1919 he met and married Linda Lee Thomas (in Paris), and they moved into a luxurious house at 13 rue Monsieur in the elegant district of Les Invalides. Money was clearly no object, and visitors described a house lavishly decorated, with walls covered with platinum wallpaper, marble floors, and chairs upholstered in zebra skin. Memorable parties hosted high society, as well as talented writers and artists. Wine flowed and recreational drugs were consumed. Although seemingly happily married, Cole Porter, who was bisexual and promiscuous, had also found the ideal environment for his indulgent private life: 'I wanted every kind of love that was available, but I could never find them in the same person, or the same sex.' In Gay Paree he found the justification for his lifestyle, and wrote one of his first musical comedies, *Fifty Million Frenchmen*.

... Paree, Paree
Oh what did you do to me?
I am not the respectable person I used to be ...

The boy-meets-girl musical opened on Broadway in 1929 and was adapted for film two years later. The title is a reference to the hit 1927 song 'Fifty Million Frenchmen Can't Be Wrong', which compared freedoms in 1920s Paris with censorship and prohibition in the US:

They say the French are naughty
They say the French are bad
They all declare that over there
The French are going mad.
They have a reputation of being very gay
I just got back from Paris, and I just want to say ...

Through his friend Gerald Murphy, whom he knew from his student years at Yale University, Porter met Diaghilev, the Russian impresario of the Ballets Russes. Porter was keen to work with the Russian company, which was perpetually in need of cash, and he subsidised some of its famous productions.

He also became infatuated with Diaghilev's former lover and secretary Boris Kochno, to whom he sent lovesick letters: 'I miss you so much that I am falling apart and if this continues, this utter silence, I don't dare think what I could do.' Cole Porter was however enjoying to the full the swinging 1920s in Paris, which inspired many of his carefree, risqué, witty, pleasure-loving lyrics, such as the famous 'Let's Misbehave', one of the songs he wrote for *Paris*, his 1928 Broadway hit:

> We're all alone,
> No chaperone …
> Let's be outrageous
> Let's misbehave.

Porter was fortunate enough to avoid the effects of the 1929 financial crash which so affected many of his compatriots, and he managed to maintain his extravagant lifestyle well into the 1930s. *The Battle of Paris* (1929) was followed by *Paree Paree*, another 1934 Paris hit.

Disaster struck in 1937. A serious riding accident put an end to his hedonistic lifestyle, but it did not put an end to his love affair with Paris. *Can-Can* was composed in 1950, with its famous elegy to Paris, 'I Love Paris':

> … I love Paris in the springtime.
> I love Paris in the fall.
> I love Paris in the winter when it drizzles,
> I love Paris in the summer when it sizzles.
> I love Paris every moment,
> Every moment of the year.
> I love Paris, why, oh why do I love Paris?
> Because my love is near.

Cole Porter is unflatteringly portrayed as the drunken pianist Abe North in the film adaptation of Scott Fitzgerald's novel *Tender is the Night*. In a 1946 biopic, *Night and Day*, Cary Grant plays a rather tame heterosexual Cole Porter. A more recent film, *De-Lovely*, directed by Irwin Winkler in 2004, attempts to portray a more complex character. Porter's appearance in Woody Allen's *Midnight in Paris* (2011) naturally continues to delight.

The second of the three young American composers was **George Antheil** (1900–59), who arrived in Paris in June 1923, in time to attend the premiere of the Ballets Russes production of *Les Noces* with music by Stravinsky, whom he greatly admired and who for a time was a friend. Antheil and his wife moved into rooms on the second floor above Sylvia Beach's bookshop Shakespeare and Company at 12 rue de l'Odéon. He used to scale the front of the building to enter by the window when his wife was out. Beach, who took him under her wing, described him as 'a fellow with bangs, a squished nose and a big mouth with a grin in it. A regular American high school boy …' In fact Antheil had come to Europe absolutely determined to become the 'bad boy' of music in the exciting French capital, which seemed to him as refreshing as a 'green, tender morning'. Through Beach he was introduced to an influential circle including James Joyce, Ezra Pound, Virgil Thomson, Ernest Hemingway and Erik Satie. Joyce, both a fan and a friend, attended the recital he had been invited to give before the prestigious opening in October 1923 of the Ballets Suédois. A riot broke out halfway through the performance of his work 'Mechanisms', much to Antheil's later delight. As it continued into the street, the police were called and there were arrests. Cultural

Paris had not seen so much excitement since the premiere of Stravinsky's *Le Sacre du printemps* (The Rite of Spring) in 1913. The incident had probably been engineered, since the riot was filmed, in order to provide a much-needed scene for the French filmmaker Marcel L'Herbier's 1924 film *L'Inhumaine*, which included a sequence in a concert hall. It is suitably entitled '*Chaotic Concert Scene*' and included as members of the audience Erik Satie, Darius Milhaud, Man Ray, Pablo Picasso, Francis Picabia, James Joyce and Ezra Pound, as well as many Surrealist writers and artists.

Antheil exploited his new fame to compose the music which was to accompany the daring *Ballet mécanique* (1924), a film commissioned by Natalie Barney and conceived by the American experimental filmmaker Dudley Murphy and the Modernist painter Fernand Léger. Considered a masterpiece of early experimental film-making, *Ballet mécanique* also included creative input from Man Ray and Ezra Pound. There was one problem, as George Antheil's music initially ran close to thirty minutes, while the film itself was seventeen minutes, half as long as the score.

The *Ballet* music was performed several times in Paris salons, but Antheil was never able to realise his original vision, which was to include sixteen synchronised pianos playing four parts, two grand pianos, seven electronic bells, three xylophones, four bass drums, a gong, a siren and three aeroplane propellers. Antheil called it 'by far my most radical work ... It is the rhythm of machinery, presented as beautifully as an artist knows how.' In 1926 he rewrote the piece, creating the version that would make it to America a year later. This one made do with a single pianola (electrically amplified), when four were originally planned, and two pianos played by humans, plus the percussion and the noisemakers. By the time he got to the 1953 version, he had dispensed with the pianola.

The official Paris premiere took place in June 1926 at the Théâtre des Champs-Élysées, at which Natalie Barney was reportedly tossed in a blanket by three baronesses and a duke. The experimental work shocked and enraged many, but their objections were drowned out by the cacophonous music and the noisy supporters of the work.

It was a *succès de scandale*. Many were less amused, and were shocked by its daring novelty, always the intention of its ambitious young composer who explained that it was: 'Scored for countless numbers of player pianos. All percussive. Like machines. All efficiency. NO LOVE. Written without sympathy. Written cold as an army operates. Revolutionary as nothing has been revolutionary.'

Joyce and Pound proposed an opera collaboration with Antheil, but nothing concrete came of it. Joyce wanted the opera to be based on the play *Cain: A Mystery*, a dramatisation of the biblical story of Cain and Abel written by Lord Byron in 1821. Antheil himself was interested in composing an opera based on Joyce's *Ulysses*, but he managed to tackle only the Cyclops episode.

Ezra Pound, his greatest admirer, compared Antheil to Stravinsky and commissioned him to write three violin sonatas for his companion, Olga Rudge. He introduced him to Jean Cocteau, who in turn introduced him to the musical salons. In 1924 the ever-supportive Ezra Pound published *Antheil and the Treatise on Harmony* to promote the composer's work. At the end of the 1920s, Antheil moved to Germany and then to the US, where he spent much of the rest of his life composing music for films. Antheil has been unjustifiably ignored, unlike Cole Porter and George

Gershwin, and his music deserves wider recognition. Even less well known is his scientific invention, on which he collaborated with the actress Hedy Lamarr, the system known as 'frequency hopping', first intended to render underwater missiles undetectable, and the foundation of modern wireless technology. Both inventors were rightly but belatedly included in the US National Inventors Hall of Fame in 2014 for this important contribution.

George Gershwin (1898–1937), born in Brooklyn as Jakob Gershowitz, is our third American composer. Already successful and famous, Gershwin first travelled to Paris in April 1923. Like his two compatriots he was attracted by the prospect of learning from European composers such as Ravel, Stravinsky, Schoenberg and Bartók, who were in the musical vanguard.

After another short week spent in Paris in 1926, he was urged to return by Ravel, and was back for three months in March 1928, this time accompanied by his sister Frankie, his brother and collaborator Ira, and his sister-in-law, all staying in the sixteenth arrondissement at the Majestic Hotel at 29 rue Dumont d'Urville. His plans to study with Ravel, Prokofiev and Nadia Boulanger came to nothing, as they refused to teach him. Ravel famously said to him 'Why should you be a second-rate Ravel when you can be a first-rate Gershwin?' He was unique.

In 1927 the dancer Anton Dolin produced a ballet using *Rhapsody in Blue* at the Théâtre des Champs-Élysées, and Gershwin's *Concerto in F* was performed at the Paris Opéra. It was a heady time, and the Parisian atmosphere encouraged a creative mood. During and after his visit to Paris Gershwin composed a fragment of music called 'Very Parisienne' as a gift for his hosts. This was to lead ultimately to the ballet suite, *An American in Paris* (1928), influenced by early jazz. Diaghilev begged Gershwin to allow him to stage it for the Ballets Russes, but it had already been promised to the conductor Walter Damrosch. It was to include saxophones and the novelty of automobile horns (perhaps to emulate George Antheil and his use of machine noises). The composer was inspired by the sound of taxis he heard along the Paris boulevards, and went shopping for those horns in the automobile shops along the avenue de la Grande Armée, to use when he returned home for his 'rhapsodic ballet', which had its debut at Carnegie Hall in December 1928.

Modernism was at its height in Paris and had an impact on Gershwin's music: 'I tried to express our manner of living, the tempo of our modern life with its speed and chaos and vitality.' Strongly influenced by Claude Debussy and Maurice Ravel (whose reputation he promoted in the US), Gershwin sought to reflect the excitement of Paris as well as his nostalgia for home. In a 1929 radio show the composer discussed his most famous piece, *An American in Paris*:

> My purpose here is to portray the impressions of an American visitor in Paris as he strolls about the city, listens to the various street noises and absorbs the French atmosphere. I thought of a walk on the Champs Elysées, of the honking taxi, of passing a building which I believed was a church ... There is a meeting with a friend, and after a second fit of blues [a] decision that in Paris one may as well do as the Parisians do.

A cinema adaptation followed in 1951, directed by Vincente Minnelli, and choreographed by Gene Kelly, who shared the main dancing parts with the young Leslie Caron. Kelly plays Jerry Mulligan, a former soldier, who wants to build up his career as a painter. The long ballet sequence at the end of the film refers through the sets and costumes to paintings by Renoir, Toulouse-Lautrec, Rousseau, Van Gogh and Dufy, and recreates the spirit of artistic wonder in the main character of Jerry. Both Gershwin brothers had toyed with the idea of becoming painters before launching their musical careers; George was a gifted painter, and some of his portraits were outstanding, like the one he made of the composer Arnold Schoenberg in 1934. He was also a keen collector, and could afford Impressionist and Post-Impressionist paintings, as well as works by Picasso, Chagall and his favourite painter Rouault.

A stage musical version of *An American in Paris* was premiered in 2014 at the Théâtre du Châtelet in Paris. Here the main character is a struggling pianist, Adam Hochberg, a Jewish composer who dreams one day of conducting Gershwin's *Concerto in F* in a concert hall. This production of the musical places a conventional plot in a more serious historical context; swastika posters are hung around the set together with tricolour banners, to remind us that it is the end of World War II and that Paris has just been liberated. Life is hard for its inhabitants, including the poor struggling artists who join bread queues in the otherwise welcoming, vibrant city. The sets are perhaps a tribute to Gershwin the artist and collector, as Paris is presented as a vast Impressionist painting dominated by the primary colours of Matisse and Picasso.

Kiki de Montparnasse (1901–53), the 'Queen of Montparnasse', was a female model, singer, painter and for a short time a writer, who played an important part in bohemian artistic life in Paris during the 1920s. She was born Alice Ernestine Prin to a very poor family in Châtillon-sur-Seine in Burgundy, and brought up by her grandmother. As a child she would do chores for neighbours in return for food, or steal vegetables from neighbouring gardens. She left for Paris aged twelve to join her mother, finding work in a bakery. After a fight with the baker's wife in which she demonstrated her fighting spirit: 'I jumped on her and gave her a good beating,' she started modelling for an elderly sculptor. This caused a permanent rift with her mother, who saw the work as immoral. In 1920 Alice took to the streets, often sleeping rough near the Gare Montparnasse, and exploiting her looks to earn a pittance: 'they often ask me to show my breasts for ten sous'. She also recalled being forced to wash in the cloakrooms of Montparnasse cafés, including La Rotonde: 'The cook heated hot water for me and I take my bath in the washrooms ... it is just like home there.' It was there that she met the artists who reinvented her. With her striking looks, she was in great demand as an artists' model, and started to earn a living posing for Utrillo, Foujita, Soutine (who named her Kiki), and for Modigliani. In 1921, she met the American photographer Man Ray, who later wrote in his *Self-Portrait* (1963):

I was sitting in a café one day chatting with Marie Vassilieff, a painter who eked out a living by making leather dolls which caricatured celebrities. She was one of the institutions of the quarter, friend of all the painters, and her Cossack dancing was the life of our improvised studio parties. Across the room sat two young women, girls under twenty, I thought, but trying to look older with heavy make-up and the hairdo then in fashion among the smart women, short cut with bangs low on the forehead. The prettier one had curls coming down on her cheeks ... She waved a greeting to Marie, who told me it was Kiki, favourite model of the painters.

PHOTO 5   La Rotonde in Montparnasse, favourite haunt of Kiki

It was love at first sight, and Kiki and Man Ray were together for seven years, during which time he made hundreds of photos of her, and was influential in creating her image. Kay Boyle, a contemporary Paris-based American novelist, wrote that 'Man Ray had designed Kiki's face for her ... and painted it on with his own hand. He would begin by shaving her eyebrows off ... and then putting other eyebrows back, in any colour he might have selected for her mask that day ... Her heavy eyelids might be done in copper one day and in royal blue another, or else in silver or jade.' Thus made up, she became the subject of many of his most famous photographs. She acted in his experimental 1928 Surrealist film *L'Étoile de mer* (The Starfish), and can also be seen in Fernand Léger's *Ballet mécanique*, the experimental film made with George Antheil's musical collaboration.

Kiki went to live with Man Ray in his studio, an Art Nouveau building at 31 bis rue Campagne-Première in

Montparnasse. She remained volatile. Things often went too far, she would get into fights and occasionally ended up in jail; on one occasion she could be released only by producing a doctor's certificate stating that she was mentally unfit. Man Ray opted for a quieter life when he left Kiki, who had been unfaithful, for his young American protégée, the photographer Lee Miller. When he broke the news to Kiki in a café, he was forced to take shelter under a table while she hurled plates at him.

She sang with great gusto in popular cabarets like Le Jockey as well as in Cocteau's favourite bar, Le Boeuf sur le Toit, in rue Boissy d'Anglas. Her repertoire consisted of traditional French songs, as well as bawdy ones like '*Les filles de Camaret*', some written by her friend, the poet Robert Desnos. She was an outspoken, independent, liberated woman and once declared: 'All I need is an onion, a bit of bread, and a bottle of red. And I will always find somebody to offer me that.'

By the late 1920s, Kiki was at her peak. She had her own cabaret, *Chez Kiki*, and a reserved table at Le Dôme. She had also begun to paint primitive narrative scenes, and in 1927 had a sell-out exhibition which included a portrait of Cocteau. Although practically illiterate when she arrived in Paris in 1929, her memoirs (perhaps written with the help of Robert Desnos) were published by Titus in 1929, and in English translation under the title *The Education of a French Model*. Although Ernest Hemingway had thought Kiki's French untranslatable, he wrote a preface. He had met her at the Dingo bar: 'This is the only book I have ever written an introduction for and ... the only one I ever will.' (In fact he did write another preface, for Jimmie Charters, the Dingo barman). The introduction hailed her as 'a monument to herself and to the era of Montparnasse', and he continues to praise Kiki to the skies:

> It was also very pleasant after working to see Kiki. She was very wonderful to look at. Having a very fine face to start with, she had made of it a work of art. She had a wonderfully beautiful body and a fine voice, talking voice, not singing voice, and she certainly dominated the era of Montparnasse, more than Queen Victoria ever dominated the Victorian era ... It is written by a woman who, as far as I know, never had a Room of Her Own ... a woman who was never a lady at any time. For about ten years she was as close as people get nowadays to being a Queen, but that, of course, is very different from being a lady.

Kiki's memoir was banned in the US on the grounds of obscenity, probably because it contained so many nude photos of the author. Praised by Hemingway also for its simplicity, it is divided into thirty-nine short chapters. A revised version appeared in 1996, where she describes her beloved Montparnasse: 'Montparnasse, so picturesque, so colourful! All the people of the earth have come here to pitch their tents, and yet it's all just like one big family.'

The big family was extended to everyone who was anyone on the Left Bank at the time: 'We hang out with a crowd called Dadaists, and some called Surrealists. I don't see much difference between them. There is Tristan Tzara, Breton, Philippe Soupault, Aragon, Max Ernst, Paul Eluard etc.' Her relationship with the Surrealists soured after Man Ray left her.

In 1940 she joined the exodus as the German army approached, but she was back in Paris at the end of the war. By that time, damaged by alcohol and drug abuse, and having lost her stunning looks, she had also lost most of the artist friends who had once packed Le Jockey to see and hear her sing in her inimitable fashion. She will be remembered as the model for Man Ray's stunning photographs, the most famous of which is '*Le violon d'Ingres*' ('Ingres's violin', 1924), showing a naked Kiki wearing only a turban. On her bare back the two 'f' holes of a violin have been drawn. It is a celebration of her famous curves, 'a work of art,' as Hemingway was well qualified to observe. She features in Man Ray's memoirs and in other works including Jean Rhys's novel *Quartet* (1928), where she is described as Cri-Cri:

> ... a bold spirit and a good sort ... a small, plump girl with astonishingly accurate make-up, a make-up which never varied, day in and day out, week in and week out. Her round cheeks were painted orange-red, her lips vermilion, her green eyes shadowed with kohl, her pointed nose dead white.

Largely and unfairly forgotten, her life story has been told more recently in 2007 as *Kiki de Montparnasse*, in a comic strip by Catel & Bocquet. She was only fifty-two when she collapsed and died, a destitute human wreck. Deserted by her former friends, her funeral was paid for by her 'family', the café-owners of Montparnasse. Her tomb has now been moved to the Montparnasse Cemetery.

Bernice Abbott (1898–1991), an American poet and photographer, was born in Springfield, Ohio, and moved to New York to study theatre and sculpture. There she met Marcel Duchamp, who introduced her to Man Ray. In March 1921 she set sail for France, arriving in April 1921 'possessing six dollars, a slight knowledge of French and a few friends'. At the suggestion of Djuna Barnes she adopted the French spelling 'Berenice' of her first name, Bernice. She studied with the sculptor Antoine Bourdelle at Académie de la Grande-Chaumière at 14 rue de la Grande-Chaumière, but was struggling financially, so she undertook odd jobs, sometimes posing for artists. In 1923, short of money and starving, *'mourant de faim'*, she met Man Ray again, and despite her inexperience and the added complication of Kiki de Montparnasse's presence, he hired her as a darkroom assistant in his studio. It was a godsend: 'I took to photography like a duck to water. I never wanted to do anything else.' Ray was impressed by her quick learning and allowed her to use his studio for her own work. She would work in his studio for the next three years: 'Man Ray did not teach me photographic technique. He took the portraits on the balcony in his studio while I worked in the darkroom. One day he did, however, suggest that I ought to take some myself; he showed me how the camera worked and I soon began taking some on my lunch break.' Her first photo was shot from his balcony and she found out that she was quite good at it: 'I would ask friends to come by and I'd take pictures of them … I had no idea of becoming a photographer, but the pictures kept coming out and most of them were good. Some were very good and I decided perhaps I could charge something for my work. Soon I started to build up a little business and I paid Man Ray for the supplies I used, but eventually I was paying him more than he was paying me and that's when it started to become a problem.'

The crunch came when in 1926 the wealthy patron Peggy Guggenheim telephoned Man Ray to arrange a studio appointment to have her portrait taken, not by Man Ray himself, but by his assistant. Man Ray was not happy, realising

that his apprentice had become a business rival, and Abbott
was fired. Thanks to the financial help of Peggy Guggenheim,
Robert McAlmon and other friends, Abbott managed to settle
in her own studio at 44 rue du Bac, 'up the second stairway
to the left,' which she kept until 1928. With Guggenheim's
money she also purchased a view camera (a camera that exposed
one photograph at a time on a 4" x 5" negative), from which
prints were made. As partial repayment, Abbott photographed
Peggy's children, as recalled by Peggy Guggenheim in her
memoirs: 'While I was in Paris Berenice Abbott had asked me
to lend her 5,000 francs to buy a camera. She said she wanted
to start photography on her own. To pay me back ... she took
the most beautiful photographs of Sindbad and Pegeen and
me. I certainly was well reimbursed.'

Many of Abbott's subjects were people from the artistic
and literary worlds, some French, including Jean Cocteau
and André Gide, others expatriates like James Joyce, Djuna
Barnes, Janet Flanner and Sylvia Beach; according to the
latter 'to be done by Man Ray or Berenice Abbott meant you
rated as somebody'. Abbott took two sets of photographs of
James Joyce, one at his home and the other at her studio at
18 rue Servandoni, to which she moved in January 1928. He
would immortalise the occasion in *Finnegans Wake* (1939):

> Talk about lowness! Any dog's quantity of it visibly oozed
> out thickly from this dirty little blacking beetle for the
> very fourth snap the Tulloch-Turnbull girl with coldblood
> kodak shotted the as yet unremunderanded national
> apostate, who was cowardly gun and camera shy.

Commissioned by Sylvia Beach, Joyce had sat for Man Ray
in 1922 to mark the publication of *Ulysses*. Abbott's intimate

portraits are very distinct from Man Ray's approach. *Paris Vogue* and other magazines hired her as a part-time photographer and published her fashion shots. On 8 June 1926 she had her first solo exhibition at the *Galerie Au Sacre du Printemps* at 5 rue du Cherche-Midi.

She exhibited her work again in April 1928, this time in the company of Man Ray, André Kertész and others. The venue was the First Salon of Independent Photographers at the *Salon de l'Escalier*, on the staircase of the Théâtre des Champs-Élysées. 'I was not in any way competing with Man Ray, but the papers made out I was.' Man Ray was furious that she was included, and it is no wonder that she does not appear in his 400-page autobiography *Self-Portrait* (1963).

In 1925, Man Ray had introduced Abbott to Eugène Atget's Paris photographs, and she was immediately attracted by his minimalist realist style: 'The first time I saw photographs by Eugène Atget was in 1925 in the studio of Man Ray in Paris.' Now largely forgotten, the French photographer who recorded everyday life in and about Paris kept a studio near Ray's at 17 bis rue Campagne-Première. Abbott persuaded him to sit for a stunning portrait, shot a few months before he died in 1927, and after his death she acquired the 8,000 prints and 1,500 glass-plate negatives left in his studio and started to champion his work. Janet Flanner in a letter from Paris in 1929 supported the work Berenice Abbott was undertaking to promote him, referring to Atget as 'the most remarkable photographic documentor of his day ... now featured in all the avant-garde European reviews – his plates having been saved from destruction by the American photographer Berenice Abbott.' Later that year Abbott, now famous, returned to New York for good. In 1930 she published a collection of Atget's work, *Atget, photographe de*

Paris (Atget, Paris Photographer), with a preface by the French poet Pierre MacOrlan. In her introduction to *The World of Atget* (1964) she recalls the effect his photographs had on her: 'Their impact was immediate and tremendous. There was a sudden flash of recognition – the shock of realism unadorned. The subjects were not sensational, but nevertheless shocking in their very familiarity.' Thanks to her sustained efforts Atget finally gained the international recognition he deserved.

Paul Gallico (1897–1976) was a prolific writer. He was born in New York, where he worked as a journalist. After earning a large sum of money in 1936 for a film script, he moved to Europe, ultimately settling in England at Salcombe on the south Devon coast, where he wrote popular novels. One of his most likeable characters, Mrs Harris, appears in four of his books. *Flowers For Mrs Harris*, now better known as *Mrs Harris Goes to Paris*, was published in 1958, but set in 1940s Paris. Mrs 'arris, the ''orny-'anded' heroine, a twentieth-century Cinderella, is a London charwoman who travels to Paris to pursue her dream of owning a Dior dress. Most of her life she has cleaned other people's houses. She has taken pride in her work, and she and her good friend Mrs Butterfield can pick and choose their clients. In spite of her reduced means she loves beautiful things: 'Drab and colourless as her existence would seem to have been, Mrs Harris had always felt a craving for beauty and colour which up to this moment had manifested itself in a love for flowers.' She is also an optimist, and has no doubt that she will achieve her aim against all odds as 'she scrimps and syves' to own the object of her dreams:

It had all begun that day several years back when during the course of her duties at Lady Dant's house, Mrs. Harris had opened a wardrobe to tidy it and had come upon the two dresses hanging there. One was a bit of heaven in cream, ivory, lace, and chiffon, the other an explosion in crimson satin and taffeta, adorned with great red bows and a huge red flower. She stood there as though struck dumb, for never in all her life had she seen anything quite as thrilling and beautiful.

Having managed eventually to raise the huge sum of money she needs to buy the dress, she makes her way to Paris, but on arrival she experiences a moment of panic: 'Standing alone now in a foreign city, assailed by the foreign roar of foreign traffic and the foreign bustle of foreign passers-by … Mrs Harris suddenly felt lonely, frightened and forlorn …' She is luckily rescued by a group of friendly locals, who help her to acquire the dress and guide her around the city. After her initial fears, thanks to her new friends she launches fully into her discovery of Gay Paree: 'Thus Mrs Harris saw Paris by twilight from the second landing of the Tour Eiffel, by milky moonlight from Le Sacré-Coeur, and waking up in the morning at dawn when the market bustle at Les Halles began.'

By the time she goes home with her prize, she has transformed the lives of everyone she has met, including those in the prestigious salons of Dior. Although her Paris adventures are light-hearted, funny and often clichéd, the book makes a serious point, as her Paris experience has been life-changing for her too. Apart from acquiring the dress, she has learned to overcome her deep-rooted prejudices and to trust the dreaded foreigner: 'For it had not been a dress she had bought so much as an adventure and an experience that would last her to the end of her days. She would never again feel lonely, or unwanted. She had ventured into a foreign country and a foreign people whom she had been taught to suspect and despise. She had found them to be warm and human.' The novel was first adapted for the stage in 1958 by Studio One theatre, with the British comedian Gracie Fields playing Mrs Harris in an American TV version, *Mrs 'arris Goes to Paris*. Negotiations for a film adaptation began in 1960, and the film of the same name came out as a TV movie in 1992, with Angela Lansbury as Mrs Harris. Directed by Anthony Shaw, it is not a faithful adaptation, as it is set in the 1960s instead of the 1950s, which alters the story. Diana Rigg as the Dior employee Madame Colbert, and Omar Sharif as French aristocrat the Marquis de Chassange are nevertheless fun to watch, as is the magnificent scene portraying a Dior fashion show. The stage adaptation, *Flowers for Mrs Harris*, by Richard Taylor and Rachel Wagstaff, is more faithful to the original, receiving warm reviews, including praise for a 'five-star fairytale'.

The once popular but now somewhat outmoded writer **William Somerset Maugham** (1874–1965) was born in the British Embassy at 35 rue du Faubourg Saint-Honoré in the eighth arrondissement, where his father was a lawyer. The family rented a flat at 25 avenue d'Antin (now avenue Franklin Roosevelt) until Maugham returned to live in England in 1885 after the death of his parents, but all his life he kept a strong bond with the French city, particularly as his interest in art developed:

> On one of my vacations I took a trip over to Paris ...
> I had read, re-read and read again Walter Pater's essay
> on the Mona Lisa and on my first visit to the Louvre I
> hurried, full of excitement, past the pictures, till I came to
> Leonardo's famous portrait. I was bitterly disappointed.

Was this the picture Pater had written about with such eloquence and in prose so ornate? I spent my mornings in the Louvre. I had no one to guide me. One young man, whom I met somewhere, an aesthete, said to me: 'There's only one picture worth looking at in the Louvre, the Chardin. Don't waste your time on all that rubbish they've got there. You'll get much more art in the Folies Bergère.'

In 1892 Maugham was a medical student in London. Medical practice in the London slums gave him material for his first novel, *Liza of Lambeth*, in 1897 and for his autobiographical novel *Of Human Bondage* (1915), which included a sequence in the bohemian Paris which his character Philip Carey experiences when he decides to become a painter. Maugham spent four years in Paris from 1901 to 1905, learning how to become a writer. During that period he started a number of plays which would run in London from 1908. One of the apartments he occupied in Montparnasse in the fourteenth arrondissement was at 3 rue Victor Considérant. As he recalled in *Purely for My Pleasure* (1962):

Time passed. I had abandoned medicine and was an impecunious author. I left London and took a tiny flat in Paris near the 'Lion de Belfort'. An intimate friend of mine, Gerald Kelly, one day to be President of the Royal Academy, took me to dine at a restaurant where painters, their wives or mistresses, dined every night at small cost in a room that was kept for them.

Deeply interested in the visual arts, once he could afford it Maugham started to build his own art collection. At that time he met many painters in Paris, mostly impoverished, and all too pleased to sell him their work. By the end of his life he owned a remarkable number of Impressionist, Post-Impressionist and Modernist paintings. He recalled buying a painting from Fernand Léger whom he found 'a jovial, friendly man, but, like all painters then, desperately hard up. I bought an abstract picture which Léger called *Les Toits de Paris*.'

Maugham was very proud of his collection, and particularly of two paintings by Henri Matisse, whom he had met: 'I bought two pictures by Matisse. One is known as *The Yellow Chair*. It is one of the most engaging pictures he had ever painted. It gave one the impression that a happy inspiration had enabled him to paint it in a single morning.'

A few years later on the outbreak of World War I, the forty-year-old Maugham joined a British Red Cross ambulance unit attached to the French Army, as did so many others, including Hemingway. The twenty-four well-known, mainly American 'Ambulance Driver' writers included John Dos Passos and e e cummings. From October 1914 to February 1915 Maugham served as an interpreter and driver in France and Flanders, where he met his lifelong companion Gerald Haxton. He was recruited in 1916 into the British Secret Intelligence Service and started a parallel career as a spy.

Some of Maugham's novels like *Of Human Bondage* follow the tribulations of naïve heroes who, on their journey of self-discovery, stop briefly in Paris. In this extended, partly autobiographical novel, Philip Carey, in Paris on a business trip, decides to give up his comfortable but tedious life in England to study art in France: 'If I'm going in for painting I must do it thoroughly, and it's only in Paris that you can get the real thing.'

The section on Paris focuses on the harsh realities faced by his fellow art students, leading a sometimes nightmarish

hand-to-mouth existence. Many do not make it, like Fanny
Price, who is desperately poor and driven to suicide. Their life is
not much brighter even when they go out to join the dancers at
the popular Bal Bullier: 'The air was heavy with the musty smell
of humanity. But they danced furiously as though impelled by
some strange power within them, and it seemed to Philip as if
they were driven forward by a rage for enjoyment. They were
seeking desperately to escape from a world of horror.' Accepting
that he will never be a good painter, Philip returns to England
to train as a doctor. The experience has been tough but has also
been one of essential self-discovery: 'He thought the best thing
he had gained in Paris was a complete liberty of spirit, and he
felt himself at last absolutely free.'

The novel was adapted for a 1934 film version which opens
with a short Paris sequence. Back in England and studying
medicine, Philip launches into 'human bondage' and a
disastrous love affair with a waitress, whose part is taken by a
young and impressively fiery Bette Davis, rather ill-matched
by Leslie Howard as Philip.

Pursuing the theme of the artist possessed, in 1919
Maugham wrote *The Moon and Sixpence*, a novel based
loosely on the tragic life of the painter Paul Gauguin, who
also renounced everything to become a painter, spending
many hard years of apprenticeship in Paris and achieving
fame only after his death. The film adaptation, directed
by Albert Lewin in 1942, has George Sanders as the lead
actor playing the tormented artist Charles Strickland, but
includes Herbert Marshall as Geoffrey Wolfe, an urbane
writer interested in the artist's life, just as Maugham became
interested in Gauguin's.

In *Christmas Holiday (Stranger in Paris)* (1939) the young
hero's father encourages him to go on a trip to Paris as a rite of

passage. On his first night Charley visits Le Sérail, a brothel in which he encounters a mysterious young woman whose story changes his life. What was intended as a pleasurable weekend proves a nightmare. Charley discovers that his best friend Simon has become a political extremist, and the young woman, Lydia, tells him the story of how the Russian Revolution forced her family into a desperate life of exile, and how she ended up marrying a murderer. When they visit the Louvre together, Lydia passes quickly in front of countless 'masterpieces' and stops before a small still life by Chardin. She proceeds to explain the painting in emotional religious terms, with references to the Passion of Christ: 'It's so humble, so natural, so friendly; it's the bread and wine of the poor who ask no more than that they should be left in peace, allowed to work and eat their simple food in freedom. It's the cry of the despised and rejected.' When Charley leaves Paris, his eyes have finally been opened to the tragedies and the dramas of the city's miseries and its underworld: 'It was a fact that he had done nothing; his father thought he had had a devil of a time and was afraid he had contracted venereal disease, and he hadn't even had a woman; only one thing had happened to him ... the bottom had fallen out of his world.'

Paris appears again in a sombre light in one of the major scenes of *The Razor's Edge*, a bestseller Maugham wrote in 1944. 'The sharp edge of a razor is difficult to pass over; thus the wise say the path to salvation is hard.' The path to salvation for Maugham's characters includes Paris. Larry has been traumatised by his experiences in World War I, and has become restless and unwilling to settle into a normal life. He wishes instead to go on a long quest around the world in pursuit of self-knowledge. He has been living modestly in Paris but Isabel, to whom he is engaged, is not prepared to share a life of poverty with him, and is determined to make him change his mind:

> Larry had reserved a table at Maxim's. We had lovely things to eat, all the things I particularly liked, and we had champagne. ... We danced. When we'd had enough of that we went on the Château de Madrid. We found some people we knew and joined them and we had more champagne. Then we went to the Acacia. Larry dances quite well, and we fit. The heat and the music and the wine – I was getting a bit light-headed. I felt absolutely reckless.

Despite the evening at Maxim's, they break off their engagement.

Maugham wrote the screenplay of the 1946 film adaptation with Tyrone Power cast as Larry, who explains to Isabel (Gene Tierney) why he chose to live in Paris: 'I came over here looking for answers to a lot of questions and because my mind was muddled.' The actor Herbert Marshall appears again as a writer, this time Maugham. We are treated to typical Gay Paree scenes with restaurants, cabarets, dance halls and fights. Maugham's Paris can also be dangerous, however, particularly for his female characters, like Fanny in *Of Human Bondage* and Blanche in *The Moon and Sixpence*, both of whom commit suicide. Sophie in *The Razor's Edge* becomes an alcoholic and addict, meeting a violent end. In spite of this, for Maugham and his several fictional alter egos, Paris is a necessary step on the journey which will lead Philip back to London, Strickland/Gauguin to Tahiti, and Larry to India and beyond.

3

Down and Out

I understood why it is that Paris attracts the tortured, the hallucinated, the great maniacs of love.
(Henry Miller)

It was often far from easy for those who traded stability and home comforts for the excitement Paris offered. Living in Paris was cheap, but some could hardly afford the most basic rented accommodation, hot in the summer and freezing in winter. Hygiene conditions were often appalling. The legendary Bateau-Lavoir in Montmartre which Picasso and many other artists and writers occupied was little more than a slum tenement.

Conditions were even worse for those forced to be in Paris, who just about made ends meet by taking menial jobs. George Orwell describes their plight well. Both he and the Lithuanian Jewish artist Chaïm Soutine use their working milieu as a resource, a world of cooks, waiters and bellboys in uniform. Working below stairs at Maxim's or one of the great hotels meant rubbing shoulders with wealthy clients, a source of satire, and occasionally of a future patron. Aspiring writers needed a patron if their work was to be published at all.

Some arrivals from Russia had nothing. Gazdanov survived by driving a taxi at night so that he could write by day. Some became destitute. Money was borrowed but not always repaid; in 1915 Marie Vassilieff opened a canteen for the impoverished to which Trotsky, Lenin and Modigliani came to eat. Meals were often paid for with a drawing or a painting.

Conditions for women were similar, but exacerbated by social expectations. There were fewer openings and opportunities for work. Language barriers meant office work was out of reach; entertainment in clubs and cabarets was a possibility, and prostitution the last resort. That in turn often meant abortions and the harsh world of hospitals.

The Italian artist **Amedeo Modigliani** (1884–1920) was sometimes called Modi, from *le maudit*, 'the accursed', by his contemporaries. The reputation of this most colourful artist in exile in Paris at the end of the Belle Époque was owed to a combination of genius, stunning good looks and womanising. Biographies, novels, films and a play have tried to retrace his eventful life, but for many he remains a fascinating and tragic mystery. The 'Prince of Montparnasse', as he was also dubbed, was born into a Jewish family from Livorno in Italy. He suffered from ill health early in his life, and was diagnosed with tuberculosis at the age of sixteen. He consequently spent much time reading at home, and was known always to carry a book in his pocket. The Russian poet Ilya Ehrenburg was impressed by his literary knowledge: 'I do not think I have ever met a painter who loved poetry so much. He could recite Dante,

Villon, Leopardi, Baudelaire and Rimbaud from memory.'
He recalled Modigliani in a poem:

> You were sitting on a narrow staircase,
> Modigliani.
> Your cries were those of a storm bird ...
> The oily clarity of a dimmed lamp
> And the blue of your burning hair!
> And suddenly I heard the terrible Dante,
> The dark words rang out, burst forth ...

Having chosen initially to study sculpture in Florence and
Venice, Modigliani moved to Paris in 1906 after inheriting
family money. After a short stay in a hotel near La Madeleine,
he was drawn to the colony of artists in bohemian Montmartre
who clustered around an artist he particularly admired, Pablo
Picasso, then working in his studio at the Bateau-Lavoir in
rue Ravignan. In this legendary place artists mixed with poets
like Apollinaire, Max Jacob and Francis Carco. The French
poet André Salmon recalled that 'Modi was beautiful ... not
tall, but muscular ... with a magnificent head, well-defined
features, his eyes dark and burning, his hair a dense crown,
slightly waved.'

By 1909 the bohemian crowd had moved to Montparnasse,
driven away by intensive building work in Montmartre. A
friend, the Romanian sculptor Brancusi, found Modigliani
a studio at the Cité Falguière, next to his own place, and
Modigliani spent time with fellow artists at La Ruche (the
beehive), or hanging around in neighbouring cafés like
La Rotonde, Le Dôme and La Closerie des Lilas. Gino
Severini, a painter and one of the few Italians he mixed with,
remembered their time together: '... Modigliani and I really

knew Paris, for we endured real suffering there. He died in that city …' It was indeed a tough life for those who had little money. Inspired by Brancusi, but unable to afford marble, Modigliani would look for discarded cuts of limestone on building sites. Poor health, exacerbated by the dust irritating his lungs, forced him to give up sculpture and concentrate on painting, which was also cheaper.

In 1910 he fell in love with **Anna Akhmatova** (1889–1966). The young Russian poet, born Anna Andreyevna Gorenko, was visiting Paris on honeymoon with her poet husband, Nikolai Gumilev. At the time Modigliani was interested in the Egyptian sculptures he had seen in the Louvre. In her memoirs Akhmatova noted that 'Modigliani was infatuated with things Egyptian. He used to take me to the Louvre, to the Egyptian wing, assuring me that everything else, *tout le reste*, was unworthy of attention. He sketched my head in the style of decorative motifs portraying Egyptian queens and dancers.'

They spent time together during the long walks they took in the Jardin du Luxembourg discussing their favourite French poets, Baudelaire, Verlaine and Mallarmé.

She refers to him in a poem *Without a Hero* (published posthumously):

Paris in a bluish haze
And probably again Modigliani
Wanders unnoticed behind me
He has the sad ability
To distress even in my sleep
And is behind many a calamity.

She was besotted with him: '… everything that was divine in Modigliani simply sparkled through some kind of gloom. He

PHOTO 6 Modigliani and Akhmatova walked and talked in the Jardin du Luxembourg

was unlike anyone else in the world.' On a second, longer stay in Paris in 1911, she came without her husband and rented an apartment near the church of St Sulpice. She and Modigliani resumed their long walks in the city even when it rained:

> When it was drizzling (it very often rains in Paris), Modigliani walked with an enormous and very old black umbrella. We sat sometimes under this umbrella on the bench in the Luxembourg Gardens. There was a warm summer rain; nearby dozed *le vieux palais à l'italien* [sic], while we in two voices recited from Verlaine, whom we knew well by heart, and we rejoiced that we both remembered the same work of his ...
> One day there was a misunderstanding about our appointment and when I called for Modigliani, I found

him out – but I decided to wait for him for a few minutes. I held an armful of red roses. The window, which was above the locked gates of the studio, was open. To while away the time, I started to throw the flowers into the studio. Modigliani didn't come and I left.

Their relationship was special: 'Modigliani liked to wander about Paris at night and often when I heard his steps in the sleepy silence of the streets I came to the window and through the blinds watched his shadow, which lingered under my windows.' The artist was struck by her hieratic beauty, like the Egyptian queens, which, according to some art critics, had a profound effect on his work. 'He drew me not in his studio, from nature, but at his home, from memory. He gave these drawings to me – there were sixteen of them. He asked me to frame them in *passe-partout* and hang them in my room at Tsarskoye Selo.' Until the end of her life she managed to keep a black crayon sketch of her drawn in 1911 in a low-cut dress reclining on a bed. She used it much later for the dust jacket of one of her poetry collections. Their brief affair seems to have been happy, as she does not refer to the dissipation with which he is usually associated, even mentioning in her memoirs that she never saw him drunk. In the same memoir she gives a vivid account of pre-war Paris:

The Paris of that time was already in the early Twenties being called '*vieux Paris et Paris d'avant guerre*'. Fiacres still flourished in great numbers. The coachmen had their taverns, which were called '*Rendez-vous des cochers*'. My young contemporaries were still alive – shortly afterward they were killed on the Marne and at Verdun. All the left-wing artists, except Modigliani, were called up. Picasso was as famous then as he is now, but then the people said: 'Picasso and Braque'. Ida Rubinstein acted Salome. Diaghilev's Ballets russes grew to become a cultural tradition (Stravinsky, Nijinsky, Pavlova, Karsavina, Bakst). … The building of the new boulevards on the living body of Paris (which was described by Zola) was not yet completely finished (Boulevard Raspail). In the Taverne de Panthéon, Verner, who was Edison's friend, showed me two tables and told me: 'These are your social-democrats, here Bolsheviks and there Mensheviks.' With varying success women sometimes tried to wear trousers *(jupes-culottes)*, sometimes they almost swaddled their legs *(jupes entravées)*.

On a last trip to Paris at the end of her life she recalled those heady days, mentioning the barrel-organ playing against the 'roar of Paris, like that of a subterranean sea'.

In 1914 Modigliani met another writer, **Beatrice Hastings** (Emily Alice Haigh) (1879–1943). By then his reputation had changed. Many described him as erratic, violent and often high on the drugs and alcohol to which he resorted, according to some to hide the fact that he was suffering from tuberculosis, which caused him to be shunned in society as infectious; perhaps twice a pariah, as he reacted angrily whenever he encountered any kind of antisemitism. Beautiful and intelligent, born in England and raised in South Africa, '*la poétesse anglaise*' had arrived in Paris aged thirty-five after two failed marriages, a false start on the stage in New York with a theatre group, a child who died in infancy, a suicide attempt and more. Her life resembles to a certain extent that of contemporary self-destructive female writers who also chose to live in Paris, like her close friend Katherine

Mansfield (born in New Zealand) and later Jean Rhys (born in Dominica). Her Pygmalion was A. E. Orage, editor of *The New Age*, a London review promoting Modernist literature and Socialism, whom she had met in London in 1907. He became her partner, and she his co-editor. In 1914 when she moved to Paris she was connected with formidable figures like Ezra Pound and Max Jacob, and she started writing columns for *The New Age*, providing vivid descriptions of Parisian cultural and social life; she submitted her *Impressions de Paris* under the name of Alice Morning. Sharp and strong-minded, she could be openly critical about fellow writers and friends like Ezra Pound: 'The state of things in Art which Mr Pound deplores is somewhat due to just such florid, pedantic, obscurantist critics as himself.'

Her meeting with Modigliani happened at Café de la Rotonde through a common friend, the sculptor Zadkine. It was not auspicious: 'A complex character. *Perle et pourceau* (both swine and pearl). Met him in 1914 at a *crémerie*. I sat opposite him. Hashish and brandy. Not at all impressed. Didn't know who he was. He looked ugly, ferocious and greedy.' But the second meeting was more promising: 'Met him again at the Café Rotonde. He shaved and was charming. Raised his cap with a pretty gesture, blushed and asked me to come and see his work. And I went. He always had a book in his pocket ... He had no respect for anyone except Picasso and Max Jacob. Detested Cocteau. Never completed anything good under the influence of hashish.'

They shared her house at 13 rue Norvins in Montmartre where life was stormy, particularly when he was high on wine and hashish, while she drank whisky. Both were unfaithful and jealous, and their fights in public became legendary. It was a passionate two-year relationship which was productive for him; during the time they were together he painted her fourteen times, representing her in the eccentric outfits she favoured, and in one she is carrying a basket of live ducks. It was Dante Gabriel Rossetti which led her to change her name from Alice to Beatrice, his *Beata Beatrix*.

Modigliani also appeared in her regular column for *The New Age* as well as in her diary, published as *Madame Six*, and in her unfinished novella (written in French) *Minnie Pinnikin*. She described his mood swings, his fits of rage and their legendary public fights, but when he started locking her out of her house they separated acrimoniously. She then had various affairs including with, among others, the precocious French writer Raymond Radiguet, Jean Cocteau's young lover. She also became quite close to Katherine Mansfield, whom she helped to publish and with whom she also became sentimentally involved. Beatrice appears in *Les innocents* (1916), a novel by Mansfield's lover Francis Carco.

In early 1917 in the canteen at 21 avenue du Maine Modigliani's Russian friend and fellow artist Marie Vassilieff threw a grand party, '*le banquet de Braque*', to celebrate Georges Braque's safe return from the Front. The thirty-five invited guests included Picasso, Matisse, Beatrice Hastings and her new lover, the Italian sculptor Alfredo Pina. Modigliani had not been invited, to avoid an unpleasant confrontation. He was often excluded from such gatherings because of his unpredictable drunken behaviour. He did turn up however, and was on the verge of spoiling the party, when Picasso, brandishing a pistol, locked him out. The memorable event, retold in various versions, is recorded in a drawing by Marie Vassilieff, where all the guests are easily recognisable, including the gate-crasher Modigliani.

During that year Modigliani was becoming better known, particularly when the Berthe Weill gallery put on a solo exhibition of his nudes. They created a stir, and the police closed the gallery for 'outrage to public decency'. It was a great pity, as the paintings remained unsold when the artist badly needed money. On a visit to Paris at the time, Roger Fry wrote in the *Burlington Magazine*: 'The beautiful variety and play of his surfaces is one of the remarkable things about Modigliani's art, and shows that his sculptor's sense of formal unity is crossed with a painter's feelings for surfaces.'

Modigliani had recently met **Jeanne Hébuterne** (1898–1920), a young art student. They left for the South of France in April 1918 because of his failing health, and to escape German air raids on Paris. They returned in May 1919 together with their baby daughter to a studio in Montparnasse at 8 rue de la Grande-Chaumière.

Soon after their return to Paris Modigliani's health deteriorated through abuse of alcohol, opium, hashish and ether. Having refused to see a doctor, he died of tubercular meningitis in the Hôpital Broussais Charité at 96 rue Didot in Montparnasse, aged only thirty-five. Two days later, and just before his funeral, Jeanne, twenty-one and pregnant with their second child, committed suicide by throwing herself out of a window of her parents' house at 8 bis rue Amyot. Modigliani was buried in Père Lachaise Cemetery. His friend the sculptor Lipchitz wrote movingly: 'I will never forget Modigliani's funeral. So many friends, so many flowers, the sidewalks crowded with people bowing their heads in grief and respect. Everyone felt deeply that we had lost something precious, something very essential.'

Modigliani is mentioned in Jean Rhys's *After Leaving Mr Mackenzie* (1930): '… I was looking at a rum picture she had on the wall – a reproduction of a picture by a man called Modigliani. Have you ever heard of him? This picture is of a woman lying on a couch, a woman with a lovely, lovely body. Oh utterly lovely. ... A sort of proud body, like an utterly lovely proud animal. And a face like a mask, a long, dark face, and very big eyes.'

Down and Out in Paris and London (1933) was the first published book by **George Orwell** (Eric Arthur Blair) (1903–50). As the title indicates, the first part concentrates on the two years the writer spent in Paris at the end of the 1920s, sharing the life of impoverished people in the French capital at the time, immigrants and asylum-seekers, sleeping rough or sharing dirty rooms in slummy hotels, scraping a living doing menial jobs.

As a young man George Orwell had a short career as a policeman in Burma before deciding in 1927 to be a writer. He was obsessed with poverty, and started writing as P. S. Burton, working in London as an investigative journalist, dressed as a tramp to write about the plight of the poor, resulting in his first substantial essay, 'The Spike' (1931). It is this environment he chose when he moved to Paris in early 1928. In the aftermath of World War I and the 1917 Russian Revolution, thousands of immigrants had arrived in Paris. Boris, one of the main protagonists of *Down and Out in Paris and London*, is a desperate Russian who had lost everything: 'The only things left to Boris by the Revolution were his medals and some photographs of his old regiment.'

Orwell had initially gone to the French capital to write for *Le Monde*, but instead of attending literary salons or spending time discussing artistic or literary matters, had chosen to focus on the exhausting life of the down-and-outs, observing, reporting and taking a sympathetic and active approach to their plight: 'Poverty is what I am writing about and I had my first contact with poverty in this slum.'

He had taken lodgings at 6 rue du Pot de Fer in the Latin Quarter. 'My hotel was called the Hotel des Trois Moineaux ... Near the ceiling long lines of bugs marched all day like columns of soldiers ...' The area was popular with bohemian American writers such as Ernest Hemingway, who lived around the corner in rue du Cardinal Lemoine. Hemingway's situation was different, as he had an income from the articles he wrote and was partly supported by his wife. For him life in Paris was 'a moveable feast' and the characters in his novel *The Sun Also Rises* inhabit another world. Orwell's characters are condemned irrevocably to extreme poverty, even when they are lucky enough to get a job. He did not seem interested in the busy intellectual and artistic life which made Paris so famous. The only experience he mentions is a possible sighting of James Joyce in the street.

This restless, committed writer was searching for something totally different. Paris was a way to break away from Britain and look for an environment less restricted by censorship. Life was not necessarily freer in Paris, as the police were 'very hard on Communists, especially if they are foreigners, and I was already under suspicion'.

Down and Out in Paris and London is based on Orwell's first-hand experience. In the introduction to the 1935 French edition he wrote: '... I think I can say that I have exaggerated nothing except in so far as all writers exaggerate by selecting. I did not feel I had to describe events in the exact order in which they happened, but everything I have described did take place at one time or another.' He focuses on the lives and practical problems of the destitute, exploited immigrants and prostitutes, describing in graphic and accurate detail their precarious survival on pitiful payment for working seventeen hours a day, seven days a week. They are exhausted and sleep-deprived, their cheap hotel rooms filthy and bug-ridden. Originally titled *A Scullion's Diary*, it was completed in October 1930, and describes the same world of cooks, dishwashers, waiters, bellboys, hustlers and chambermaids painted by the Lithuanian Jewish artist **Chaïm Soutine** (1893–1943). As an exile in Paris in 1913, Soutine also lived in abject poverty until the rich American art collector Albert Barnes took a liking to his unusual choice of subjects and technique, and bought sixty of his pictures. Soutine became famous overnight, his talent recognised during his lifetime, unlike his friend Modigliani.

Life was tough for Orwell. After finding himself penniless when his belongings were stolen shortly after his arrival, he tried giving English lessons, but lost his pupil and had to sell his clothes, going without food for a few days. When an employer did not pay him, he slept on a bench: 'It was very uncomfortable ... and much colder than I had expected.' In February 1929 he fell ill and experienced the horror of Parisian hospitals. He ended up earning a kind of living in autumn 1929 as a *plongeur* (dishwasher) in 'Hotel X', one of the most expensive hotels in rue de Rivoli. (This mystery luxury hotel was named by Sonia Orwell as the Hôtel de Crillon.) From the kitchen where he worked he reflected on the shocking contrast between rich and poor:

It was amusing to look round the filthy little scullery and think that only a double door was between us and the dining-room. There sat the customers in all their splendour ... and here, just a few feet away, we in our disgusting filth. For it really was disgusting filth. There was no time to sweep the floor till evening, and we slithered about in a compound of soapy water, lettuce-leaves, torn paper and trampled food. ... The room had a dirty mixed smell of food and sweat.

In chapter XXII Orwell muses on the life of the *plongeur*: 'For nothing could be simpler than the life of a *plongeur*. He lives in a rhythm between work and sleep, without time to think, hardly conscious of the exterior world; his Paris has shrunk to the hotel, the Métro, a few bistros and his bed.' It is a pointless job and he condemns their exploitation: 'I think one should start by saying that a *plongeur* is one of the slaves of the modern world. ... The question is, why does this slavery continue?'

And he concludes: 'I believe that this instinct to perpetuate useless work is, at bottom, simply fear of the mob.' Orwell's own introduction to the first French edition in 1935 stated that his characters are 'intended more as representative types', but are also to be individuals. One of these 'types' is the Russian émigré Boris who, 'like most Russian refugees, had had an adventurous life'. Another is Charlie, 'one of the local curiosities'; there is Roucolle the miser, and Henri 'who worked in the sewers'. He wonders at the extraordinary sense of solidarity he finds among them, as well as the hierarchy of the catering world, where he finds himself at the bottom of the ladder.

When the book was published in 1933 he used the name George Orwell for the first time, possibly to spare his family. He did not return to live in Paris, as he was drawn into the Spanish Civil War. Orwell was preoccupied with the fate of the down-and-outs in Paris in the early 1920s. One of his protagonists, Boris, is a Russian who joins the White

Army during the Russian Revolution. He is one of 200,000 White Russians who left Russia after the Revolution heading towards Western Europe, many of whom settled in France. Declared stateless by the Bolsheviks who had taken power in their country, life in exile is for them a struggle for survival. As Russian émigrés, many could not find properly paid jobs. Fiction is very closely reflected in reality.

One such exile was the Russian writer **Gaito Gazdanov** (1903–71), born in St Petersburg, who joined the White Army aged just sixteen. He was barely twenty when he arrived in Paris in 1923. He worked first as a labourer, managed to study for a time, and then found a job in a car factory. By 1928 his life had improved somewhat. He drove a taxi at night, and wrote during the day. His short stories and novels like *An Evening with Claire* (1929) (where the narrator meets his former girlfriend in Paris) were admired by Gorky and other recognised Russian writers, who even compared him to Proust and Nabokov. The latter wrote in English, which gave him access to a reading public. Émigré writers like Gazdanov who wrote only in Russian had their works banned in the Soviet Union, and generally had little contact with the French literary world. Their readership could therefore be limited to the Russian community in exile.

Night Roads was written between 1939 and 1941 and published in Russian in 1952, not translated into French until 1991 and into English in 2009 by Justin Doherty. Gazdanov's book is in many ways similar to *Down and Out in Paris and London*, as it too concentrates on the daily life of the destitute, the Parisian poor and prostitutes, and the shell-shocked immigrants he describes during their descent into alcoholism, madness and despair in 'this sinister and fantastical' Paris. During the 1920s and 1930s it was common to see former Russian aristocrats and members of the Russian intelligentsia working as doormen or waiters, and taxis were often driven by former White Army officers.

Driven by curiosity, 'that insatiable and immediate urge to know and try to understand the lives of all manners of strangers,' Gazdanov sets out to describe in this book the people he comes across while driving his cab at night, listening to their stories. He keeps his distance, his compassion tinged with humour, despite the desperation he witnesses. Very little is revealed about the narrator; like Gazdanov, he has fought against the Red Army, has worked as a labourer in Paris and now drives a taxi at night. He meets all sorts of people, rich and poor, tramps, alcoholics, prostitutes and 'once-influential people who were now labourers or drivers,' like him. 'I was forced to lead several different lives and at the same time to meet with people who differed markedly from one another in every way, beginning with the language they spoke ... the inhabitants of nocturnal Paris differed sharply from its daytime population and consisted of several categories of people whose nature and profession more often than not rendered them doomed from the start.'

He gives a depressing description of the so-called City of Light: '... I know of nothing more dismal or piercingly depressing than the working-class Paris suburbs, where it seems as if even the air itself is filled with centuries-old, desperate poverty.' It is, for him, and for his compatriots, a hostile place: 'In this nocturnal Paris I felt myself to be like a traveller who finds himself in an alien environment ...' But he is fascinated by its inhabitants and their plight: 'My constant curiosity kept drawing me to these places, and many times I would wander around all the districts of Paris where this frightful poverty, this human carrion resides.'

One protagonist is the old courtesan Jeanne Raldy, who during her 'splendour' had been mistress of a duke and a king, but now that she has lost her looks is reduced to a miserable life and ultimately a lonely death. He also meets Alice, the beautiful heartless prostitute, the tormented, obsessive Fedorchenko, and Katia, the cabaret artiste 'singing of regrets and farewells, and about lost possibilities of happiness – and … distant Russia, along with … snow, and coachmen and sleigh bells.'

This dispossessed community congregates in the seventeenth arrondissement and around the Russian Orthodox church at 12 rue Daru in the eighth arrondissement. A sense of loss and nostalgia prevails. Everyone wants to return home, but by the late 1920s there was no going back to Soviet Russia. As the Depression bit, most Russians became unwelcome in France, and the coming of World War II prompted many to leave for the US. Gazdanov stayed in Paris, but stopped taxi-driving in 1953, when he started working for Radio Liberty, an anti-communist radio station.

A compatriot from St Petersburg, **Nina Berberova** (1901–93) had arrived in France in 1924. She also described in her autobiography *C'est moi qui souligne* (The Italics are Mine, 1969) the dire situation of the immigrant in Paris: 'This is where our Parisian life began and where we received our "stateless" passports. This document, intended for people who no longer belong to a state, did not give us the right to work professionally, as a labourer or in an office. We had no choice but to work for ourselves.' She was a member of the Russian intelligentsia in exile, and now made a meagre living from her writing, supplemented by embroidery, making necklaces and decorating Christmas cards. Other women in her situation worked as milliners or seamstresses, a few went into show business, and for some survival was through prostitution.

Although a gifted poet and writer (she was the author of a biography on Tchaikovsky), Berberova found it difficult to make ends meet, and often went hungry. Her autobiography and short story collections, *Billancourt Tales* (1928–40), *The Tattered Cloak* (1991) and *The Book of Happiness* (1936) describe the hard life she experienced, and provide an account of antisemitism in occupied France, including the arrest of Jewish compatriots and their fate in the concentration camps. The expatriate Russian community was itself riven by bitterness and suspicion, as Bolsheviks had infiltrated White Russian organisations. Returning to Russia was out of the question. Prominent White Russians had been lured back to Russia, where they had been arrested and executed.

Berberova's life improved once she decided in 1950 to move to the US, where she had a successful career as a writer and university lecturer, having learned English from scratch. She is now remembered mainly for her biography of Tchaikovsky and *The Accompanist* (1987), a short novel about an impoverished pianist who, to escape hunger and deprivation, takes a job with a famous classical singer. It was successfully adapted for the screen by Claude Miller in 1992.

Perhaps the most famous of the Russian émigré writers is **Vladimir Nabokov** (1899–1977), also born in St Petersburg, where at the outbreak of the Russian Revolution in 1917 his father held a prominent position in the Provisional Government. After the Bolsheviks took control, the family was forced to leave St Petersburg, wandering as exiles round Europe and finally settling in Paris in 1937. They left just before the Germans occupied the city. Nabokov, like Berberova, later had a career in the US as a university lecturer and writer. His most famous book, *Lolita*, was published there in 1955, but its origin was during his two-year stay in Paris, when he was contributing to Adrienne Monnier's Surrealist magazine *Mesures*, and mixed with writers like the artist Salvador Dalí, Paul Éluard and André Breton. Nabokov, as improbable as it may seem, enjoyed recounting that the 'initial shiver of inspiration' for *Lolita* came from a newspaper account of an ape in the zoo at the Jardin des Plantes which had made the first ever drawing by an animal. Berberova noted: 'Nabokov is the only Russian writer, émigré or not, to belong to Russia and the whole of the Western world. Indeed, for people like him, having a nationality or a particular language does not play a fundamental role.' In 1936, in the second issue of *Mesures*, Nabokov published a piece called 'Mademoiselle O', written in French, about his French governess. He had written it in two weeks, and after a reading in Paris, the French writer Jean Paulhan asked the unknown Russian novelist if he might publish the piece in *Mesures*, which Paulhan helped to edit.

Marie Vassilieff (1884–1957), the 'Mother Courage of Montparnasse', was born to a prosperous family in Smolensk in Russia, and first went to Paris in 1905. She returned in 1907, having decided to continue her painting studies as a pupil of Henri Matisse. Her paintings show a very personal style, mixing Cubism with traditional religious Russian art. She founded her own art academy which was to become the Académie Vassilieff, at 21 avenue du Maine in Montparnasse.

She attracted painters and writers, and hosted talks and cultural events.

Taking pity on impoverished and starving fellow artists and writers, she opened a cheap canteen in her studio in 1915, frequented by Modigliani, Chagall, Matisse, Picasso and Cocteau, and by compatriots in exile including Trotsky, Diaghilev and Lenin. She may especially have pitied the latter, as she recalled in her memoirs that 'Lenin was living a very isolated life in Paris'. She was better off than most, as she made a reasonable living using recycled materials to make dolls for the French couturier Paul Poiret and designs for the Ballets Suédois. She also danced Cossack-style and sang at Le Jockey, a popular cabaret at 127 boulevard du Montparnasse.

She returned to Russia in the winter, but was back in Paris in 1916, when she revived her popular canteen. On 14 January 1917 she organised the legendary banquet to celebrate her friend Georges Braque's return to Paris. On 7 June 1917 her son Pierre was born. Some doubt remains about the identity of his father. He was perhaps one Amar Chrouat, of whom little is known, or it may have been Trotsky. If it was indeed he, she was probably right to keep the secret for the future safety of her child. At the end of the year she was denounced as a Bolshevik spy and an intimate of Trotsky. She was incarcerated near Paris in Melun with Pierre. During the ensuing trial she defended herself courageously, and was allowed to return home, although life remained difficult, as she was initially denied an identity card.

In 1934, she moved to 54 avenue du Maine where she founded the Vassilieff Museum, and in 1937 she showed her work in the Paris International Exhibition. Two columns she painted (one with an African in a top hat with a monocle) can still be seen in the Montparnasse café, La Coupole.

Matisse, Léger and Kisling were also approached to paint the columns. An exhibition was organised in Paris in 1969, *Hommage à Marie Vassilieff, L'âme de Montparnasse*. Her Musée Vassilieff became in 1951 the petit Musée du Montparnasse, but was sadly closed in 2015. Although she is now largely forgotten she features in Dan Franck's novels *Nu couché* (1998) and *Le temps des bohèmes* (2015) as well as in many of her contemporaries' testimonies including Man Ray's memoir, *Self-Portrait*.

The Russian political exiles Leon Trotsky and Vladimir Lenin both found refuge in Paris at the beginning of the twentieth century and, however improbable it may seem, both also found love there. During his life, spent mainly in exile, **Leon Davidovich Trotsky** (1879–1940), born Lev Davidovitch Bronstein, stayed in Paris on various occasions, but records his first or second time there after meeting Lenin in London. Just after he arrived in 1902 he met the woman with whom he would spend the rest of his life, **Natalia Sedova** (1882–1962), a student and participant of the *Iskra* group which published a Russian revolutionary newspaper. Trotsky had left his wife and fellow anarchist, Aleksandra Sokolovskaya, with whom he had two daughters, when he escaped from exile in Siberia. The meeting with Natalia took place at 4 rue Lalande on the stairs of a building where she usually went to eat. The moment is recorded briefly in *My Life: An Attempt at an Autobiography* (1930): 'I fell in love with a young exiled revolutionary who studied art history at the Sorbonne.' Later with some nostalgia he remembers the first heady days of their relationship in his *Journal d'exil* dated March 1935: 'How I regretted our youth, her youth … We ran at night from the Paris Opéra, hand in hand, bounding along, back to where we lived at 46 rue Gassendi … It was

PHOTO 7 46 rue Gassendi, where the young Trotsky lived for a while

1903 ... our combined age was forty-six. My God, N. was the more tireless.'

Natalia recalls their time together in notes given to Victor Serge later in life:

In 1902 I used to take my meals in a flat in rue Lalande where, to live more cheaply we pooled our meagre resources to save money. Leon Davidovitch came to rue Lalande on the day he arrived in Paris. He was twenty-three and had just spent three years in exile in Eastern

Siberia. His vitality, his keen mind and his capacity for hard work already set him apart as a forceful and mature figure. He took little interest in Paris then. He used to joke that Odessa was better. He had come to Paris to make contact with the Russian émigré socialist movement, but we did go together to the Montparnasse cemetery to look at Baudelaire's tomb ... From that time on our lives were inseparable ...

Trotsky recalled that she tried hard to make him share her interest in art and museums, and in turn she attempts to explain why Trotsky was so disparaging about Paris and its cultural life: 'L.D. was utterly absorbed in political life, and could see something else only when it forced itself upon him. He reacted to it as if it were a bother, something unavoidable. I did not agree with him in his estimate of Paris, and twitted him a little for this.' Another set of reminiscences gives more details of their first meeting:

The autumn of 1902 was marked by frequent lectures in the Russian colony in Paris ... In our group there was some talk about the arrival of a young comrade who had escaped from Siberia ... When the young contributor to the *Iskra* made his appearance in Paris, Ekaterina Mikhailovna bade me find out if there was a vacant room nearby. There happened to be one in the house where I lived. The rent for it was 12 francs a month, but the room was small, dark and narrow, just like a prison cell. ... After the young comrade (whose name was not revealed to us) established himself in the room, Ekaterina Mikhailovna asked me: 'Is he preparing for his lecture?' 'I don't know, I suppose so,' I answered. 'Last night as I was coming upstairs I heard him whistling in his room.' 'Then tell him to work hard and not whistle.'

Trotsky (as Pero) remembers nevertheless in *My Life* how crucial his stay in Paris was, not only politically but also culturally:

> I was much more interested in learning about Paris than I had been about London. This was because of the influence of N.I. Sedova. I was born and brought up in the country, but it was in Paris that I began to draw close to nature. And there, too, I came face to face with real art. I learned to appreciate painting, as well as nature, with great difficulty. Yes, it was just like that. I was entering the atmosphere of a world centre with an obstinate and antagonistic attitude. At first, I 'denied' Paris, and even tried to ignore it. Rightly considered, it was the case of a barbarian struggling for self-preservation. I felt that in order to get close to Paris and understand it fully, I would have to spend a great deal of mental energy.

He also recalls that on one occasion she did drag him to the opera, in the company of Lenin: 'Once we decided to take Lenin to the opera. All arrangements were entrusted to Sedova. Lenin went to the Opéra Comique with the same briefcase that accompanied him to his lectures.' Trotsky and Natalia, who shared the political struggle, went on to spend the rest of their lives together. After two years in Paris they were on the move again, but by 1910 Trotsky is reported to have been seen playing chess with Lenin and Apollinaire at the Closerie des Lilas, at 171 boulevard du Montparnasse.

Then came a return to Russia, another prison sentence and more wandering in Europe, but the couple was back in Paris again in 1914, this time with two young sons. A short stay in suburban Sèvres was followed by a move to 23 rue de l'Amiral Mouchez near Parc Montsouris and then to 27 rue Oudry in the Gobelins area. Trotsky, who spoke good French, had been sent to Paris this time as a war correspondent for a pacifist newspaper, *Kievskaya Mysl*. He was to view the war 'from the Eiffel Tower'. A committed anti-war activist, he describes the sad state of the French capital: 'Paris was growing more and more deserted. One by one, the street clocks stopped. The Lion de Belfort, for some reason, had dirty straw sticking out of its mouth. The war went on digging farther and farther into the ground. Let us get out of the trenches, out of this stagnation, this immobility!' Bleak days were spent in the stricken French capital, recalled by Natalia: 'Paris experienced the terrible war in all the fibres of its being, in its very stones and in all the shadows of its nights.'

It is during that stay that the couple struck up a friendship with the Mexican painter Diego Rivera at the Café de la Rotonde, at 105 boulevard du Montparnasse. Rivera would offer them shelter in Mexico City at the end of their life in exile. In Paris both sons attended a Russian school in boulevard Auguste Blanqui, but after a short time at 27 rue Oudry, in 1916 Trotsky was expelled from France, probably because of his openly anti-war views. As persona non grata practically everywhere in Europe, he was escorted to the Spanish border. Soon afterwards he became a major Bolshevik figure in the Russian Revolution, but with the rise of Stalinism he was expelled from the Communist Party and from the Soviet Union in 1928, and after a spell in Turkey he was offered asylum in France. While in Paris in December

1933 the fugitive and his bodyguards stayed for one night with the young philosopher Simone Weil in her parents' flat at 3 rue Auguste Comte in the sixth arrondissement. According to Simone Pétrement, Weil, who did not agree with some of Trotsky's ideas, argued passionately with him through the night. Trotsky and Natalia would finally leave France for good in 1935. Six months before his assassination in February 1940 he writes warmly in his will: 'In addition to the happiness of being a fighter for the cause of socialism, fate gave me the happiness of being [Natalia's] husband. During the almost forty years of our life together she remained an inexhaustible source of love, magnanimity and tenderness.'

Their elder son **Lev Lvovich Sedov** (1906–38) remained in Paris, where he had spent most of his adult life working on his father's behalf. In 1938, he reported in his letters to his father, who had reached his final place of exile in Mexico, that the GPU (Soviet secret police) was after him. He took the threat so seriously that he published in a French newspaper a statement warning that if he died suddenly, it would be because of Stalin's pursuers. His mother wrote that 'he knew he was being shadowed by the GPU and the French police had proof that he was being watched more closely than he ever realised'. In February 1938 after an attack of appendicitis he checked into the small Clinique Mirabeau at 7 rue Narcisse-Diaz, run by a Russian émigré. A few days after what seemed to have been a successful operation Lev died unexpectedly in the hospital. His partner Jeanne Martin claimed that he had been poisoned by the GPU. It would appear that he was murdered inside the clinic. The French police investigated the matter, but never came to any definite conclusions. He was buried in the Thiais cemetery outside

Paris, where every year on 20 August two Trotskyist groups
visit his tomb to commemorate his father's death.

For many political refugees at the turn of the twentieth
century Paris was a safe and desirable place to be, and it is not
surprising that the Russian political exile **Vladimir Ilyich
Ulyanov (Lenin)** (1870–1924) chose to go there. Arrested
by the Tsarist regime, Lenin had spent 1895–96 in a Russian
prison, followed by four years in exile in Siberia. He spent the
next sixteen years wandering in Europe, mainly in London
and Geneva, 'an awful hole', and finally reached Paris. He
arrived on 3 December 1908 and spent the following four
years there. It seemed the perfect place to work on political
meetings and publications. According to Eric Hazan in *A
Walk Through Paris*: 'The Union Printing Work (the Printing
Office of the Russian Social Democratic Party, which Lenin
set up at 8 rue Antoine-Chantin to produce *Proletary* (*The
Proletarian*)) has a whole story attached to it. Founded in
1910 by two Russian immigrants, Chalit and Snégaroff,
it initially served the very active Russian community in
Paris, and was supposedly used by Plekhanov and Lenin.'
Accompanied by his wife Nadezhda Krupskaya, sister Marie
and mother-in-law, Lenin first took a room in the Hôtel
des Gobelins at 57 boulevard Saint-Marcel, and the family
then moved into a three-room flat at 24 rue Beaunier in the
fourteenth arrondissement, where a plaque records Lenin's
stay. They settled finally in July 1909 at 4 rue Marie-Rose
near the carrefour d'Alésia. The small flat on the second floor
had central heating, and the quiet neighbourhood suited
them better. Lenin met his Russian friends in the nearby Parc
Montsouris in Montparnasse, and at Porte d'Orléans.

Lenin used his bicycle to go daily to the Bibliothèque
Nationale, where he seems to have resented the time he

spent waiting for requested books. Despite having left it in the safe proximity of the library he was outraged on one occasion to find that his precious bicycle had been stolen. He and Nadezhda were keen cyclists, spending their weekends exploring the suburbs. Lenin once rode twenty kilometres outside the city to see an air show at Juvisy-sur-Orge, but on his way there he was unfortunately run into by a car. He was not seriously hurt, but there was little left of that bicycle. Thanks to some helpful witnesses, Lenin managed to get compensation from the driver, who happened to be a Vicomte. Every Sunday morning Lenin would spend a couple of hours on the pavement outside his flat cleaning his bicycle, surrounded by local children learning some practical skills from the future leader of the Russian Revolution. It seems that Lenin loved being in the company of children, perhaps because he and Nadezhda were unable to have their own. They led a simple life, and Lenin spent much time in the warmth of cafés like La Rotonde nursing a single drink all evening and meeting revolutionaries, as well as artists, writers and poets, including Max Jacob, Apollinaire, Picasso, Derain, Diego Rivera, Soutine and Brancusi. On one occasion Modigliani set fire to the newspaper which Lenin was reading as a joke. This infuriated Matisse, also present, who snatched the flaming newspaper from Lenin's hands who, unperturbed, laughed it off.

Lenin used his knowledge of French, German and Russian to attend and to give political talks. In 1911, he spoke at the funeral of Laura, Karl Marx's daughter, who had committed suicide with her husband, the French writer Paul Lafargue. Lenin and his wife also helped many Russian immigrants who were barely surviving in the city. They lived frugally on bread, fish and cheese. Doctors' bills had to be paid, but they could afford to go to the theatre, as well as to occasional concerts. Although his interest in literature was mainly political, he reported in a letter to his sister that he had seen a play by the right-wing writer Paul Bourget: 'I have begun to pay more attention to the theatre; I have seen Bourget's new play *La Barricade*. Reactionary but interesting.'

In Paris Lenin met fellow revolutionary **Inessa Armand** (1874–1920) in the Café d'Orléans in avenue du Général Leclerc, a popular haunt of Russian militants. French born and half-Russian, intelligent and charismatic, she had arrived from Brussels where she was studying economics. Her wealthy husband, Alexander Armand, from whom she had separated, remained in Brussels looking after her children. They were to join her in Paris once she had settled as Lenin's close neighbour at 2 rue Marie-Rose. 'Inessa Armand arrived in Paris from Brussels in 1910,' wrote Nadezhda in her memoirs, 'and immediately became an active member of our Paris group. Together with Semanshko and Britman (Kasakov) she was elected to the presidium of the group and started an extensive correspondence with the other groups abroad. She had a family of two little girls and a boy. She was a hot Bolshevik, and before long our whole Paris crowd had gathered round her.' It has been claimed that Armand and Lenin had an affair, which Nadezhda seems to have tolerated. Nadezhda described Armand's political commitment, but omits to mention her radiant beauty, or her gifts as a pianist which the music-loving Lenin greatly appreciated. Armand's children brought delight to the Ulyanovs, who acted like uncle and aunt to them, not only in Paris but many years later in Moscow.

In summer 1911 Lenin organised the Party school for Russian workers at 17 Grande rue in Longjumeau on the outskirts of Paris with Armand's financial backing. She bought the house which was used as the school, and subsidised the canteen. Both keen on education and gender equality, Nadezhda and Armand worked together in the Party school. The Ulyanovs rented an apartment nearby at 91 Grande rue. A Turkish restaurant, Lénine Kebab, now occupies the site. Armand reminisces about this period in a letter to Lenin:

> At that time I was terribly scared of you. The desire existed to see you, but it seemed better to drop dead on the spot than to come into your presence; and when for some reason you popped into N.K. [Krupskaya]'s room, I instantly lost control and behaved like a fool. Only in Longjumeau and in the following autumn in connection with translations and so on did I somewhat get used to you. I so much loved not only to listen to you but also to look at you as you spoke. Firstly, your face is so enlivened and, secondly, it was convenient to watch because you didn't notice at that time.

But everyone else noticed that the feelings were mutual and the French Marxist Charles Rappoport, who had seen them talking together in a café on the avenue d'Orléans, reported that Lenin 'could not take his Mongolian eyes off this little Frenchwoman'. She became an invaluable and totally dedicated collaborator: 'Almost all of my activity here in Paris was linked to my thoughts of you with a thousand threads,' she wrote to him in a letter in 1913.

The film *Lenin in Paris* by Yutkevitch, shot in 1981, was a Soviet production which could not allow the Russian leader to have an extramarital affair on screen. The film was censored and a love scene between Lenin and Armand was cut. Instead it shows her having an affair with a young Russian called Trofimov. Her part was taken by Claude Jade. The film also shows a cabaret scene (probably the cabaret in rue de la Gaîté in the fourteenth arrondissement, known as Bobino) where Lenin and Armand join in the anarchist song '*Braves soldats du 17ème*' (glorifying soldiers who refused to obey orders to shoot demonstrators). The singer and popular composer Montéhus, a great favourite of Lenin, is seen singing in the film. Since the opening of the Soviet archives the affair is no longer secret, so more will doubtless be heard about the alleged love story. New books have already come out, as well as a play by David Pinner, *Lenin in Love*, one of three political plays entitled *The Stalin Trilogy* (2000).

After four years Lenin was disillusioned with Paris. He had never expected much, and as early as 1910 he wrote: 'Paris is a rotten hole in many respects ... I am still unable to adapt myself *fully* to it (after living *here* for a year!) but I nevertheless feel that only extraordinary circumstances could drive me back to Geneva!'

In July 1912 Lenin's friends organised a dinner at Le Pavillon Montsouris before he left for Cracow with his family. Inessa Armand followed quickly. He had come to rely heavily on her for Party affairs and as he was not allowed to set foot again in France, he sent her to Paris in early 1916 to attend a meeting of anti-war activists, where she gave a speech on his behalf. The next year she took part in the October Revolution and became active in feminist issues in the Soviet government, where she held important posts. She died of exhaustion and cholera in 1920 and was buried in the Kremlin necropolis. Her death deeply affected Lenin, as recalled by Alexandra Kollontai: 'As we were following the coffin Lenin was barely recognisable. He was walking with his eyes shut tight and was hardly standing on his feet.' The plaque on the building at 4 rue Marie-Rose was removed about thirty years ago, and the small museum dedicated to Lenin was closed when locals rejected the plan to rename the street after its famous former inhabitant.

Katherine Mansfield (1888–1923) and **Jean Rhys** (1890–1979), both writers in Paris at the beginning of the century, led similar lives to some extent. Both were born outside Europe, Mansfield in New Zealand and Rhys on the island of Dominica. Both were encouraged to write, and each became sentimentally attached to a male literary figure who helped to launch her literary career. Both also adopted pseudonyms. Katherine Beauchamp was known from 1910 as Katherine Mansfield, and Ella Gwendolen Rees Williams wrote as Jean Rhys. Mansfield was briefly on the stage, while Rhys worked as a chorus girl. Having become pregnant by her lover in London, Mansfield rushed into an unsuitable marriage with another man, abandoned her new husband the same day, and then miscarried the child on her way to Germany. Ten years later in Paris Rhys suffered similarly after her marriage to Jean Lenglet, a Dutch writer and conman, from whom she was divorced in 1933. She gave birth in a Parisian hospital, where their child died after a few days. In December 1911 Mansfield met **John Middleton Murry** (1889–1957), editor of the Modernist review *Rhythm*, who took an interest in her writing. Their relationship, lasting thirteen years until her death, was punctuated by break-ups, reconciliations and infidelities, although they eventually married in 1918. When Jean Rhys visited Paris in 1924 she met the English editor of the *Transatlantic Review*, Ford Madox Ford, with whom she had an affair, and who encouraged her to write. Here the

parallels end, as Katherine Mansfield died in Fontainebleau
near Paris in 1923 from tuberculosis, while Jean Rhys left
Paris in 1937 to spend the rest of her much longer life in
England.

Once in Europe Mansfield never stayed anywhere for
much longer than a year, living in rented houses and rooms,
including in Paris. In London in 1911 she had started to
write short stories for *The New Age*. Her first collection, *Bliss
and Other Stories* (1920), was dedicated to Murry. Two of the
fourteen stories, 'Feuille d'album' and 'Je ne parle pas français',
are based in Paris, which she also describes at the beginning of
a later short story 'An Indiscreet Journey', as well as in what
survives of her letters and *Journal*. Mouse, the young woman
in 'Je ne parle pas français', appears to be fragile, vulnerable
and lonely in an alien city where much time is spent in sordid
cafés: 'I do not know why I have such a fancy for this little
café. It's dirty and sad, sad.' The waiter is grimy and behaves
strangely: 'He is grey, flat-footed and withered, with long,
brittle nails that set your nerves on edge while he scrapes up
your two sous. When he is not smearing over the table or
flicking at a dead fly or two, he stands with one hand on the
back of a chair … waiting to be photographed in connection
with some wretched murder. "Interior of Café where Body
was Found".' Life is also depressing for Raoul Duquette, the
French protagonist of 'Je ne parle pas français'.

Things are even worse for the young 'awfully clever' but
very shy painter, Ian French, in 'Feuille d'album'. He is stuck
in a lonely routine: 'Every day was much the same. While
the light was good he slaved at his painting, then cooked his
meals and tidied up the place. And in the evenings he went
off to the café, or sat at home reading or making out the
most complicated list of expenses headed: "What I ought to

be able to do it on," …' His flat is bleak: '… one of those buildings that smell so unromantic all the year round, and where the concierge lives in a glass cage on the ground floor, wrapped in a filthy shawl, stirring something in a saucepan and ladling out tit-bits to the swollen old dog lolling on a bead cushion.'

In 'Je ne parle pas français' it is Mouse's first visit to Paris. Excited on arrival, she ends up alone, a situation familiar to Katherine Mansfield, who nevertheless saw the city as a place of freedom, far from the repression of her early life. She first went with Murry in December 1912, and both returned a year later, staying in an hotel at 31 rue de Tournon. According to their friend, the French writer **Francis Carco** (1886–1958), it was *un modeste hôtel de la rue Gay-Lussac,* which will have been the setting for 'Je ne parle pas français'. In his affectionate *Souvenirs sur Katherine Mansfield* (Memories of Katherine Mansfield, 1934) he added: 'she herself refers to it in this wonderful short story 'Je ne parle pas français', where I recognise myself with her and her future husband, J.M.M. These pages have fantasy, verve and delicious colour.' His meeting with Katherine Mansfield inspired him to write a novel, *Les innocents* (The Innocents, 1916). According to him: 'I owe having written my best book to Katherine Mansfield, because to a certain extent she has provided me with all the elements of it.'

Murry introduced her to the Paris he knew, 'Murry's Paris', but through Francis Carco she discovered the bohemian Left Bank. She had met Carco through Murry, in circumstances very like those of the meeting between Raoul Duquette and Mouse. In the story Murry would have been Dick Harmon, who '… stayed in one place leaning against the wall, his hands in his pockets, that dreamy half smile on his lips, and

replying in excellent French in his low, soft voice to anybody
who spoke to him.'

In December 1913 Mansfield and Carco embarked on
a passionate affair while Murry was in London, 'an affair
dedicated to disaster,' according to Carco, but he must
have been the perfect guide to Paris, his beloved *Paname*,
and it was doubtless a treat for Mansfield to meet his
colourful friends, who included Utrillo, Modigliani and
Picasso, in cafés like the Lapin Agile. Carco also let her use
his flat at 13 quai aux Fleurs when she was alone in Paris
in February 1915. There she wrote 'An Indiscreet Journey'
(1915), the semi-autobiographical short story telling how
a female narrator joins her lover, 'the little corporal', in the
town of Gray near Dijon, where he was billeted during the
war. The story opens as she embarks on the journey from
his flat in Paris:

'You will never get there' said the concierge, watching me
turn up the collar. 'Never! Never!' I ran down the echoing
stairs – strange they sounded, like a piano flicked by a
sleepy housemaid – and on to the Quai. 'Why so fast,
ma mignonne?' said a lovely little boy in coloured socks,
dancing in front of the electric lotus buds that curve over
the entrance to the Métro. Alas! there was not even time
to blow him a kiss. When I arrived at the big station I
had only four minutes to spare, and the platform entrance
was crowded and packed with soldiers, their yellow papers
in one hand and big untidy bundles. The commissaire of
police stood on one side, a nameless official on the other.
Will he let me pass? Will he? He was an old man with
a fat swollen face covered with big warts. Horn-rimmed
spectacles squatted on his nose. Trembling, I made an

effort. I conjured up my sweetest early-morning smile and handed it with the papers. But the delicate thing fluttered against the horn spectacles and fell. Nevertheless, he let me pass, and I ran, ran in and out among the soldiers and up the high steps into the yellow-painted carriage.

Mansfield spent much time during the war in the city under siege, terrified during the constant bombardment and dealing with the grief caused by the death of her beloved brother. She was trapped in Paris in March 1918 by the bombing, described by Murry in his preface to her *Journal*: 'The authorities delayed for weeks before granting their permission; and on the very day she arrived in Paris [from Bandol in the South of France, where she had been to visit], weak and by this time very seriously ill, the long-range bombardment of Paris began, and all civilian traffic between England and France was suspended. The hardships of her journey in France turned her pleurisy into consumption.'

Her daily letters to Murry give much information about life in wartime Paris. Sometimes her views on Parisians sound uncharitable: 'I wonder if it is the war that has made the people here so hideous or if I am out of joint. They appear to me a nation of concierges. And the women look such drabs in their ugly mourning ...'

In a letter from November 1920 she described meeting Oscar Wilde in a dream: 'Oscar Wilde was very shabby. He wore a green overcoat. He kept tossing & tossing back his long greasy hair with the whitest hand. When he met me he said, "Oh *Katherine*!" – very affected. But I did find him a fascinating talker. So much so I asked him to come to my home. He said would 12.30 tonight do? ... He was fatuous & brilliant!' Living in Paris and meeting French writers affected her style; she writes in her correspondence of her admiration for French writers like Colette, another independent and adventurous female writer. She wrote simply, in a Modernist manner, rendering a daydream or stream of consciousness, watching and describing ironically and with humour a Paris which is far from charming, particularly when she mentions another awful concierge: '... the old spider. She was too quick for me. She let me run down the last little ladder of the web and then she pounced ... And she beckoned with a dripping soup ladle.'

Paris inspired mixed responses, as shown in her journal entry for 31 January 1922: 'We arrived in Paris late, but it was very beautiful – all emerging from water. In the night I looked out and saw *the men with lanterns*. The hotel all sordid again – fruit peelings, waste-paper, boots, grime, ill temper.' Her emotions were intensified by her situation and her own physical decline. Carco describes their last meeting in Café de l'Univers: 'Her beautiful dark eyes held the same passion, the same fever. They exerted a kind of magnetism, but she did not look well, and her poor little hands had become so pale, so thin, which upset me dreadfully. She hid her hands under the table.'

By October 1922 she was seriously ill with tuberculosis. 'Ever since I came to Paris I have been ill as ever. In fact, yesterday I thought I was dying. It is not imagination. My heart is so exhausted and so tied up that I can only walk to the taxi and back. I get up at midi and go to bed at 5.30 ... My spirit is nearly dead ... I am a cough – a living, walking or lying down cough.' She died on 9 January 1923, aged only thirty-four, in the Gurdjieff Institute in Fontainebleau near Paris, which practised alternative medicine. Although looked after by a former school friend, Ida Baker, who had become a dedicated carer, it must have been a lonely end. Her grave is now in Avon cemetery near Fontainebleau.

Their affair left its mark on Francis Carco, who recalls her fondly in his *Souvenirs sur Katherine Mansfield* (1934): 'In her presence, I sensed a sort of charm that I linked to her youth, and which rose from the very soul of her being, like the spring of life she bore within her.' It would be tempting to think he had her in mind also when he wrote the poem '*L'Ombre*' (1933):

> Your shadow still haunts the street
> By the bar where I have often waited for you
> But you are no more
> And even now your shadow is at the door.

Jean Rhys arrived in Paris in 1919 with her husband Jean Lenglet. In her short novel *After Leaving Mr Mackenzie* (1930) she explains how the city was the place to find some freedom: 'I wanted to get away. I wanted it like – like iron. Besides, I wasn't frightened of anything. So I did get away. I married to get away. It was a lovely autumn in Paris. When we sat eating spaghetti in the sun I felt I had got out of prison. Neither of us had any money but that didn't matter ... We got a room in a hotel in the rue Lamartine.'

All Rhys's semi-autobiographical novels centre on lonely young females who have been abandoned and lead life on the edge, spending time in cheap cafés and depressing lodgings or in smelly hotels plagued by bedbugs. Always in need of money, they fall into depression, dependency on men and heavy drinking. That was Jean Rhys's own experience in Paris. It was hard, without money. Her first child having died soon after birth, she became pregnant again, gave birth to a daughter and then found herself destitute when her husband got into trouble with the law, and was arrested and imprisoned for embezzlement.

In *Good Morning, Midnight* (1939) she recalls how her alter ego tried to cope, working as a guide, 'standing in the middle of the place de l'Opéra, losing my head and not knowing the way to the Rue de la Paix,' giving English lessons, or modelling clothes in a shop. The titles of her short stories are telling: 'Illusion', 'Mannequin', 'Tea with an Artist' and 'Hunger' (*The Left Bank and Other Stories*, 1927). Her writings focus on poverty, their characters looking for poorly paid work in order to eat and pay the rent in hotels with 'cockroaches crawling from underneath the carpet and crawling back again'. They long for 'A room. A nice room. A beautiful room. A beautiful room with bath. A very beautiful room with bath.'

Rhys had started writing about her life in notebooks, perhaps in order to make sense of it. Her breakthrough happened in 1924, when she met the wife of the *Times* correspondent in Paris, Mrs Adam, in rue Taitbout:

> I explained briefly how I came to be in Paris. While we were drinking tea she asked me, 'Have you ever written anything yourself?' I thought of the exercise books that I'd carried round without having looked at them for years. I hesitated because I still didn't want to show them to anybody. Then I told myself not to be such a fool, all that was finished and I never meant to go back to London … Next day I had a pneumatique saying she liked what I had written and would I come and see her again? When I saw her again she asked me if I'd mind if she typed it and sent it to a man called Mr Ford Madox Ford, who published a small magazine, *The Transatlantic Review*.

Ford Madox Ford was running the *Transatlantic Review*, publishing promising writers like Hemingway, Joyce and Stein. He was attracted by Rhys's vulnerable beauty, youth and talent, and took her under his wing. In early 1924, while her husband was in prison, she moved into the spare room of his house at 65 boulevard Arago, so that he could keep an eye on her writing and encourage her. It was Ford who gave her the name Jean Rhys (Jean was her husband's Christian name and Rhys her father's Welsh name), and it was Ford who taught her how to turn her experiences into publishable prose. He criticised the fact that she gave too few topographical details in her writings: '... she eliminated even such two or three words of descriptive matter as had crept into her work.' This seems unfair, as she used her good first-hand knowledge of Paris in her writing, as in her first novel, *Quartet*:

> [Marya] dined that night by herself in a little crémerie in the Rue St Jacques. After the meal ... she walked very quickly along the winding street, between two rows of gas-lamps, past the low doors of little buvettes, where a gramophone was playing gaily and workmen in caps stood drinking at the counters ... The street of homeless cats, she often thought. She never came into it without seeing several of them, prowling, thin vagabonds, furtive, aloof, but strangely proud.

This *roman à clef* is about the affair Rhys had with Ford, and tells the story of Marya, who finds herself alone when her Polish husband goes to prison, and is taken up by an English couple, the Heidlers. The story of the affair was also used by the others involved. In *Sous les verrous* (1933) Jean Lenglet, using the name of Édouard de Nève, tells the story of his wife's infidelity while he was in prison. Rhys translated the novel herself, heavily editing her husband's version, and publishing it as *Barred* in 1932. Ford's partner Stella Bowen reminisced on the affair in her autobiography *Drawn from Life* (1941), and Ford's *When the Wicked Man* (1931) portrays Jean Rhys rather unfavourably in the character of Lola Porter. The affair collapsed when Ford decided to put an end to it, possibly because Rhys chose not to let her husband down. At least that is how she tells the story in *Quartet*. Ford and Rhys must have stayed in touch, however, as in 1928 he asked her to translate *Perversité* by Francis Carco. She eventually divorced her husband in 1933.

After *Quartet* (first entitled *Postures*), which created quite a stir in literary circles, other books followed. *After Leaving Mr Mackenzie* also dealt with the theme of abandonment, *Voyage in the Dark* (1934) concentrated on her early career with a provincial travelling theatre company in England, and *Good Morning, Midnight* (1939) described her later years in Paris. Her portrayal of her down-at-heel life in Paris, her multiple love affairs and her drinking make depressing reading. She shows that it was not easy to be young and lonely in Paris, a victim of predatory men: 'That night, coming back from her meal, a man followed her. When she had turned from the Place Saint-Michel to the darkness of the quay he came up to her, muttering proposals in a low, slithery voice. She told him sharply to go away. But he caught hold of her arm, and squeezed it as hard as he could by way of answer.'

Nor is it easy to be a foreigner: '*Ah! Quelle plaie, les Anglais!*' ('What a pest the English are!') Loneliness and depression are dealt with by shopping and drinking: 'At lunch she drank a half-bottle of Burgundy and felt very hopeful ... she spent the whole afternoon in the Galeries Lafayette choosing a dress and a hat.'

She left Paris in 1937. *Good Morning, Midnight* was not well received, and her books went out of print. Women described as underdogs, exploited and exploiting their sexuality, were perhaps ahead of their time. Her lonely and disconsolate women in a male-dominated world and her powerless heroines were not appreciated, nor was the simplicity and originality of her style, often described as 'stream of consciousness technique'. She was practically forgotten until 1949, when the actress Selma Vaz Dias, who was working on an adaptation of her work for the BBC, tracked her down. Rhys was asked by the writer Francis Wyndham if she had written anything since her Paris years, and told him that a novel was under way – this would turn out to be *Wide Sargasso Sea* (1966). A collection of short stories, many reminiscing about Paris, was published as *Tigers are Better-Looking* (1968), and a successful film adaptation of *Quartet* by the film director James Ivory in 1981 helped to revive her literary reputation. *Smile Please!* (1979), an unfinished autobiography, although recalling her dealings with Mrs Adam, barely mentions Ford.

James Joyce (1882–1941) equipped with a degree in languages, arrived in Paris from Dublin in 1902 to study medicine. Not particularly inspired by the subject, the young Irishman chose to hang around Parisian cafés (and brothels, as he boasted in letters to friends in Dublin). Needing to rush home to see his dying mother in 1903, and at the start of a long series of demands for cash advances, he borrowed money for the return to Dublin from one of his adult students, a champagne dealer called Joseph Douce.

Joyce did not return to Paris for a while. Having decided to leave Ireland, he chose Trieste as his first place of exile, where he stayed until the outbreak of World War I. In his *Portrait of the Artist as a Young Man* (1916), Joyce's protagonist and alter ego Stephen Dedalus makes it clear why he has decided to turn his back on Ireland: 'I will not serve that in which I no longer believe, whether it call itself my home, my fatherland, or my church: and I will try to express myself in some mode of life or art as freely as I can and as wholly as I can, using for my defence the only arms I allow myself to use – silence, exile and cunning.' In order to find personal and artistic freedom Stephen/James Joyce chooses self-imposed exile.

James Joyce nevertheless remained obsessed with Dublin all his life, but he believed, like Stephen, that he could really gain a clear understanding of his fatherland only by seeing it from afar in a life of perpetual wandering. After a few years in Pola (today Pula) and Trieste earning a living through language teaching, during which time he became a friend of the Italian writer Italo Svevo, he left during World War I for neutral Zurich. Back in Trieste in 1919, he was encouraged to spend a few days in Paris by the young American poet, Ezra Pound. The French city must have been to his liking, as the few days grew into twenty years, and only World War II drove him back to Switzerland, where he died in 1941.

By the time he had moved to Paris, Joyce was already a well-known author: *Dubliners* had been published in 1914, *A Portrait of the Artist as a Young Man* in 1916 and his only play, *Exiles*, in 1918, and it was in Paris that he completed his most famous and controversial work, *Ulysses* (1922). The revolutionary approach and style repelled many readers, and the work was criticised for crude language and direct sexual elements. A few episodes which had appeared in *The Little*

Review were burned, and the book was banned for indecency in both England and in Ireland. Many saw it as pornographic and sometimes downright unreadable, going far beyond an accepted Modernist style, with its use of interior monologues, unique vocabulary and play on words.

It was a crime to be in possession of the book in the countries where it was banned, and it became legally available in the US only in 1934, in England in 1936 and in Ireland in the 1960s. Only the efforts of Sylvia Beach, the American owner of the bookshop Shakespeare and Company, and of her partner Adrienne Monnier, enabled the book to be published in Paris and translated into French. Joyce was introduced to the two women by Ezra Pound and they got on well. 'He was so simple and unassuming that, instead of being overcome in the presence of the writer who was undoubtedly the greatest of his time, I felt quite at ease with him. It was always that way. Ever conscious though I was of his genius, I knew no one so easy to talk with,' Beach wrote in her autobiographical account of the events. Despite her inexperience, she made it her mission to have the book published as, by all accounts, Joyce was not exactly easy to deal with. After a subscription had been set up, *Ulysses* finally came out in Paris on 2 February 1922 – the superstitious Joyce had insisted on launching the book on his birthday. He also insisted on white letters on the blue jacket of the book (the white island in the blue Greek sea) and had a tie made to match for the occasion. Scott Fitzgerald, Ernest Hemingway and Ford Madox Ford all loved it; however, envious of Joyce's fame as a Modernist writer, Gertrude Stein was unenthusiastic. Celebrations took place at Fouquet's, Joyce's favourite restaurant (when he could afford it).

PHOTO 8 Fouquet's, James Joyce's favourite restaurant

His financial situation had improved considerably, since money now flowed in regularly from his ever-generous patron, the feminist editor of *The Egoist*, Harriet Weaver. Joyce and his wife were never very good at managing their financial affairs but now, free from immediate worries, he could concentrate on his next major novel, *Finnegans Wake* (1939), and on enjoying life. He had arrived in the French capital wearing tired clothes and tatty tennis shoes, but was now going around as 'a dandy in a velvet jacket and many rings on his fingers'. He spent money extravagantly on accommodation, drinks and restaurants, and outings to the opera followed by lavish meals at Fouquet's, where he would leave exorbitant tips. He avoided bohemian Paris and preferred elegant venues in the Champs-Élysées, although he still visited brothels like Le Sphinx or cafés like Café Polidor at 41 rue Monsieur le Prince. He would meet friends at the

Brasserie Lutetia and was once interviewed at the café Les Deux Magots by Djuna Barnes.

Untypically, from 1925 to 1931 Joyce stayed in the same flat at 2 square Robiac near rue de Grenelle, but otherwise kept moving, living in hotels like the Victoria Palace Hotel at 6 rue Blaise Desgoffe and in more modest flats. He probably moved more than twenty times during the years he spent in Paris, generally favouring the sixth, eighth and sixteenth arrondissements. We can follow his various addresses in the city, as the letters he sent to friends and family discussing his health and publication issues always bore his present address. Obsessed by Ireland, he scoured the newspapers for news of his country, interrogating Irish visitors wherever he met them, generally in the area around the Odéon and the Latin Quarter. Joyce was the latest in a succession of Irishmen to favour the Grand Hôtel Corneille at 5 rue Corneille, where at the end of the nineteenth century W. B. Yeats and J. M. Synge had both been residents.

Unfortunately, in the 1940s Joyce's health declined. He became practically blind in spite of numerous eye operations. He continued however to take long walks holding someone's arm, but needed friends and family to act as amanuensis. The playwright Samuel Beckett on his arrival in Paris from Ireland in 1928 became a regular assistant, and was included in Joyce's circle until the mental breakdown of Joyce's daughter, Lucia.

Lucia Joyce (1907–82) had fallen in love with the handsome Irish writer on whom her father had become dependent, but Beckett made it clear that he visited the family for the sake of her father, and not for her. It has been assumed that this disappointment, followed by other unhappy love affairs (she had among others a brief relationship with her drawing teacher, the sculptor Alexander Calder), combined with lack of success in her dancing career, triggered a breakdown. Her mental health started to deteriorate when she was twenty-five and became an increasing preoccupation for Joyce, who was attached to her. He wrote to a doctor: 'Her case is cyclothymia, dating from the age of seven and a half. She is about thirty-three, speaks French fluently … Her character is gay, sweet and ironic, but she has bursts of anger over nothing when she is confined to a straitjacket.'

Lucia was close to her father, even sharing a private language with him, and this may have been instrumental in the writing of *Finnegans Wake*. As a young woman, she joined the dance school run by Raymond Duncan, the brother of the experimental dancer Isadora Duncan, but never made a career of it. The strain of a difficult childhood, travelling through Europe until her parents arrived in Paris, moving constantly from one home to another, might also have contributed to her neurotic traits, which were later diagnosed as schizophrenia. As an adult, tension between Lucia and her mother grew. She became increasingly violent and her father would refer to 'her King Lear scenes'. On his fiftieth birthday in 1932, she threw a chair at her mother, after which her older brother Giorgio decided to have her admitted to a psychiatric institution. There is no doubt that she was a challenge; on several occasions she tried to set fire to houses in which she was a guest, and would vomit intentionally at the dinner table. Only very reluctantly did Joyce allow her to be confined to institutions, at first inside Nazi-occupied France in the suburb of Ivry. Later she was moved to England to St Andrew's Clinic in Northampton, where she remained for the rest of her life, and where

Beckett visited her once, allegedly supporting some of her hospital costs after Joyce's death. In 1989 when Beckett died, a photograph of a dancer dressed as a mermaid was found among his belongings. It was a portrait of Lucia Joyce. Leaving Lucia in Ivry, Joyce and his wife Nora left Paris in 1939 at the outbreak of the war to take shelter in Zurich. Apart from his blindness Joyce had been in poor health for a while, drinking heavily, and he died there in 1941. It seems that for the forty years after his death Lucia's mother and brother never again visited her.

Lucia was the subject of a biography by Carol Loeb Shloss, *Lucia Joyce, To Dance in the Wake* (2003); a West End play, *Calico*, in 2004, written by Michael Hastings; and a graphic novel, *Dotter of Her Father's Eyes*, by Bryan and Mary M. Talbot (2012). In 2016, she was the subject of a biographical novel by Annabel Abbs, *The Joyce Girl*, and she appears in a chapter of Alan Moore's novel *Jerusalem* (2016), set at the Northampton clinic and written in the style of *Finnegans Wake*. A further work, *Lucia*, by Alex Pheby, appeared in 2018. It seems ironic that so much has now been written about her, when her diaries, poems and correspondence were destroyed for family reasons. James Joyce is remembered in Paris through the square James Joyce, 7 rue George Balanchine. It is one place where he never stayed.

After taking a degree in languages at Trinity College Dublin, **Samuel Beckett** (1906–89) went to Paris in October 1928 to work as a *lecteur* (university assistant teacher) at the prestigious École Normale Supérieure in rue d'Ulm in the sixth arrondissement, where he was allocated a room on the first floor, looking out over '… the bare tree, dripping; then, behind, smoke from the janitor's chimneypot, rising stiff like a pine of ashes; then, beyond, beyond the world, pouring a little light up the long gully of the street that westers to the Luxembourg ...'

His comfortably wealthy Protestant family could not understand why their academically brilliant son chose to be penniless in bohemian Paris; nevertheless he stayed until September 1930, when he returned to Dublin to work as a university lecturer, resigning after four terms in order to travel in Europe. Beckett moved back to the Left Bank in Paris in 1937, more or less for good. 'Nothing changes the relief at being back here,' he wrote, 'Like coming out of gaol in April.'

His first address in 1937 was 12 rue de la Grande-Chaumière (in the sixth arrondissement), the site of art academies at which numerous Irish artists had studied. Soon afterwards, Beckett took a room across the street in the Hôtel Libéria at no. 9. It proved too expensive for him, so he moved again to a studio at the top of 6 rue des Favorites (fifteenth arrondissement) in April 1938. His friends found the name of the street amusing.

Life in Paris was not however always peaceful. In January 1938 he was stabbed through the lung by a pimp named Prudent on the avenue d'Orléans (now avenue Général Leclerc, in the fourteenth arrondissement). Fortunately, James Joyce managed to have him put in a private room at the Broussais hospital, which he paid for. He accompanied the American heiress Peggy Guggenheim, with whom Beckett was having an affair at the time, on a visit to him. In her autobiography *Out of this Century* (1979) she describes how she heard of his stabbing: 'when ... the proprietor told me what had happened ... I nearly went mad. I rushed to all the hospitals in Paris but could not find him. Finally I phoned Nora Joyce, who told me where he was. I went to him at once ...'

During his first stay in Paris in 1928, Beckett had been introduced to James Joyce by fellow Irishman and lecturer Thomas MacGreevy, and he became a frequent visitor to Joyce's flat at 2 square Robiac. Peggy Guggenheim states that Beckett was not Joyce's secretary as was widely claimed, although there is no doubt that they spent much time together talking or working. Beckett said in an interview that Joyce dictated parts of *Finnegans Wake* to him and that he translated some fragments of it into French. According to Guggenheim '[Beckett] had little vitality and always believed in following the path of least resistance. However, he was prepared to do anything for Joyce, and he was always leaving me for his great idol. I was very jealous of Joyce. I think Joyce loved [Beckett] as a son.' Reflecting on this intense relationship with Joyce, Beckett realised that he had to develop his own style, which ultimately would be the opposite of Joyce's: 'I realised that Joyce had gone as far as one could in the direction of knowing more, [being] in control of one's material. He was always adding to it; you only have to look at his proofs to see that. I realised that my own way was in impoverishment, in lack of knowledge and in taking away, in subtracting rather than in adding.'

It was in hospital that Beckett also received visits from Suzanne Déchevaux-Dumesnil (1900–89), a pianist whom he had met ten years earlier. He broke off the affair with Peggy Guggenheim, and Suzanne became his companion until the end of his life, although their relationship remained unconventional, as Beckett continued to have a string of affairs. They eventually married in 1961. Beckett lived in France for fifty-two years and chose to remain when World War II broke out, preferring, as he put it, 'France at war to Ireland at peace'. He did, however, leave Paris for a time during the war. He and Suzanne had been working for a Resistance network, and, fearing the Gestapo, they fled to Roussillon in the Vaucluse, remaining in southern France until January 1945. When they returned to their Paris studio after the city's liberation, they found it miraculously more or less as they had left it. Beckett was awarded the *Croix de guerre* for his clandestine activities, which he minimised, calling them 'boy scout stuff'.

So far he had been managing on a small family allowance, but after his wartime experience and freed from Joyce's influence, he started writing successfully in his own style. Fame followed, and money came in from his writing. In 1953, with money inherited from his mother, he bought a plot of land to the east of Paris in Ussy-sur-Marne, building a small house of 'spartan simplicity', according to his friend and biographer James Knowlson. It became an ideal retreat, and had a magnificent view across the Marne valley. The house was far enough from Paris to be away from people, but near enough to attend to business. By the late 1950s, when Suzanne stopped visiting for a time, Beckett was left alone 'with the snow and the crows and the exercise-book that opens like a door and lets me far down into the now friendly dark'.

Beckett had written a piece in 1929 in defence of James Joyce, *Dante ... Bruno. Vico ... Joyce* (1929), but little else before 1945, when he began to write in French. The language offered greater clarity, forced him to think more fundamentally and to write with greater economy. His play *Krapp's Last Tape* (1958) was in English but *Waiting for Godot* (1953) was first written in French, as were *Endgame* (1957), *Happy Days* (1961) and *Play* (1963). The economy of his French will probably have been developed when he was inside the Resistance group conveying information to the Allies.

In October 1960 Beckett and Suzanne moved to a seventh-floor flat in a new apartment block at 38 boulevard Saint-Jacques in the fourteenth arrondissement. They led separate lives and had separate entrances, enabling Beckett and his guests to come and go without disturbing Suzanne. By the end of the 1970s he was meeting friends in the anonymous Petit Café PLM in the Hôtel Saint-Jacques on the boulevard Saint-Jacques. From the window of his flat he could look down on the Santé prison, and could almost see into the individual cells.

The success of *Waiting for Godot* finally allowed him to make a comfortable living from writing. Unlike Joyce, Beckett tended to live a modest, almost ascetic life, although he was known to be a heavy drinker. One of his favourite watering-holes was the Cochon de Lait (which no longer exists) in the rue Corneille, where earlier in 1930 he had spent much of the prize money for his long poem, *Whoroscope*. He indulged only in small pleasures, meeting friends and eating simply in restaurants such as Aux îles marquises on the rue de la Gaîté and Rosebud, around the corner on the rue Delambre. Other favourites were the Closerie des Lilas (in the boulevard du Montparnasse, sixth arrondissement), and the Coupole, which in those days stayed open most of the night, and where many gatherings of friends would stay until breakfast. He was known to be generous, helping anyone in need of money. Jameson whiskey remained his staple drink, even when he was eventually a resident of the nursing home on the rue Rémy-Dumoncel in which he spent his final months, dying there five months after Suzanne. They are buried together in Montparnasse Cemetery.

The one street in Paris named after Beckett is the allée Samuel Beckett (part of the avenue René-Coty). It was the

PHOTO 9 The simple tomb of Samuel Beckett in Montparnasse Cemetery

place where Beckett, during his time in the Resistance, would hand over documents he had translated, which were smuggled to the Special Operations Executive (SOE) headquarters in London.

Samuel Beckett and **Peggy Guggenheim** (1898–1979) had an affair in 1937–38. In 1937 the wealthy American heiress was planning to open an art gallery in London. Although she knew nothing about art at the time, she had help from her friend the artist Marcel Duchamp, with whom she was then conducting an affair: 'When I got to Paris, Brancusi was not there. But Marcel Duchamp and Agnes introduced me to Cocteau and we decided to give him the opening exhibition. ... At that time I couldn't distinguish one thing from another. Marcel tried to educate me. I don't know what I would have done without him. To begin with, he taught me the difference between Abstract and Surrealist art. Then he introduced me to all the artists. They all adored him and I was well received wherever I went. He planned shows for me and gave me lots of advice. I have him to thank for my whole life in the modern art world.' Brancusi may have been away, but she did meet Samuel Beckett:

> I must have gone to Paris expecting something to occur but I never dreamed for an instant what was in store for me. In spite of the fact that I took every consolation which crossed my path, I was entirely obsessed for over a year by the strange creature whom I shall call Oblomov [Beckett] ... I knew that he was a friend of James Joyce, that he had been engaged to his daughter and had caused her great unhappiness ... Beckett was not Joyce's secretary, as everyone has since claimed, though he was perpetually doing errands for him. Joyce had a Russian Jewish intellectual for secretary called Paul Léon ...

James Joyce introduced her to his protégé at Fouquet's, 'where Joyce gave us an excellent dinner'. That was the beginning of their affair. After the dinner Beckett escorted her home, where they enjoyed what she describes elsewhere as 'an intense marathon' in bed.

She was strongly attracted by his intellect and good looks: '[Beckett] was a tall, lanky Irishman of about thirty with enormous green eyes that never looked at you. He wore spectacles, and always seemed to be far away solving some intellectual problem; he spoke very seldom and never said anything stupid. He was excessively polite, but rather awkward. ... [Beckett] accepted life fatalistically, as he never seemed to think he could alter anything.' She was jealous of time he spent away from her: 'On the tenth day of our amours [Beckett] was untrue to me ... He had two passions besides James Joyce. One was Jack Yeats and the other a Dutch painter, Van Velde ...' They did not meet for a while, but then:

> One night I met him on a traffic island in the Boulevard Montparnasse. I must have been looking for him without realising it ... We went home to Agnes's house where we lived for twelve days. We were destined to be happy together only for this short period. Out of all the thirteen months I was in love with him, I remember this time with great emotion. To begin with he was in love with me as well, and we were both excited intellectually. ... The thing I liked best about our life together was that I never knew at what hour of the night or day he might return to me. His comings and goings were completely unpredictable, and I found that exciting.

Guggenheim called Beckett Oblomov after the eponymous hero of Ivan Goncharov's famous nineteenth-century Russian novel. Oblomov is incapable of action, and stays in bed most of the time. Beckett, who suffered from depression for much of his life, found it difficult to get up in the morning, and his view on life included deep pessimism, as far as human relationships and sentimental involvement were concerned, which Guggenheim found difficult to accept. 'He [was] saying he was dead and had no feelings that were human and that was why he had not been able to fall in love with Joyce's daughter.'

During the affair Beckett urged her to dedicate herself to modern art: 'I was happy to be with [Beckett], who really was an ideal companion as he loved to see beautiful things. It was a pleasure to visit the museums with him.' She launched her gallery Guggenheim Jeune in 1938, but the planned 'modern museum' in London, whose director was to be her friend (and lover) Herbert Read, was thwarted by the war. In 1941, she had to flee Nazi-occupied France with her soon-to-be second husband, the German artist Max Ernst. She remained in the US until 1947, when she returned to Europe, opening her famous art gallery in Venice in 1948.

Another of Beckett's close friends in Paris was **Alberto Giacometti** (1901–66). Giacometti had moved to Paris in 1922 to join Antoine Bourdelle's sculpture class. He settled in a studio in Montparnasse with his brother Diego, who served as both model and assistant. Soon they moved to 46 rue Hippolyte-Maindron, where Giacometti lived and worked until his death, despite the limited space.

Beckett and Giacometti were probably introduced by mutual artistic acquaintances in Paris in the autumn of 1937. It was an unlikely friendship, as Beckett was prone to long awkward, silences, whereas Giacometti was notoriously extrovert and loquacious. Their bond developed gradually, as a result of shared artistic concerns. At the time of their first meeting, Beckett was living at the small artists' hotel, Hôtel Libéria, located in a narrow alley and only a twenty-minute walk from Giacometti's studio. After they had finished work the two would repair to Café de Flore, Le Dôme or La Coupole, staying until the early hours when they set off on long walks around the city, sometimes ending up at Le Sphinx, a brothel behind Montparnasse station. During their nocturnal rambles they discussed work, although Giacometti is believed to have monopolised these conversations with anxieties about his art. It is during one of those walks in 1938 that Beckett was stabbed, and in the same year Giacometti was knocked down by a vehicle driven by a drunken American heiress at the place des Pyramides. He suffered a crushed foot and limped for the rest of his life.

After the war years, spent by Beckett in Roussillon and by Giacometti in Geneva, they met again, and their friendship strengthened between 1945 and 1960. Beckett returned to his apartment at 6 rue des Favorites, remaining deliberately close to the cafés and to Giacometti's studio, at a time when both artists were producing their most important work. The greatest photographers in Paris at the time, including Richard Avedon, Brassaï and Henri Cartier-Bresson, produced photographs of both of them, seemingly sharing a sartorial taste for conservative tweed and woollen suits. In 1961 Giacometti collaborated in the re-staging of *Waiting for Godot* at the Théâtre de l'Odéon. He had been in the audience for the original 1953 production of *Godot* at the Théâtre de Babylone, where the director Roger Blin had arranged a flimsy tree for the production, made of twisted wire coat hangers wrapped in tissue paper, stuck onto a piece of foam rubber. Giacometti designed a skinny plaster tree for the 1961 set; it was the best-known example of their collaboration and became an iconic stage set of the twentieth century. In an interview with the art critic Reinhold Hohl Giacometti recalled: 'We spent the whole night in the studio with that plaster tree, trying to make it sparser, smaller, the branches thinner. It never looked any good and neither [Beckett] nor I liked it. And we kept saying to each other: perhaps like this ...' Unfortunately the tree was destroyed in the May 1968 Paris riots when students occupied the Théâtre de l'Odéon, but photographs have survived. The pair also collaborated on a film entitled *Film* in 1965 and a series of television pieces beginning with *Eh Joe* in 1966.

Giacometti had many other friends among Left Bank artists and writers before and after World War II whom he used as models, including the French writer and convicted criminal Jean Genet, author of *The Studio of Giacometti* (1957). Jean-Paul Sartre also wrote on Giacometti in *The Search of the Absolute* (1948), and his companion Simone de Beauvoir's writing also includes pages on him. Giacometti inspired other contemporaries, such as Anna de Noailles and Michel Leiris. The American writer James Lord published *Giacometti: A Biography* (1985), a fifteen-year project drawing on his time spent with Giacometti in the 1950s. Isaku Yanaihara, a professor of philosophy, often sat for Giacometti, and in his *Together with Giacometti* (1969) described Giacometti's daily routine in Paris: 'He leads a very simple life in Montparnasse dressed in his plaster-spattered clothes, has breakfast at nearby Café-tabac Le Gaulois and eats at restaurant La Coupole.' In his memoirs *The Artists of My Life* (1982), the photographer Brassaï remembers him at Le Gaulois in 1963: 'Alberto, who was ravenous, downed a sandwich and some hard-boiled eggs that were set out on the bar. He lit one cigarette after another. I was upset to see that he wasn't taking better care of himself ... I was afraid he wouldn't be able to keep up his present pace for long.' He neglected his health and died in 1966 aged sixty-four, of heart disease and chronic bronchitis, most likely exacerbated by fatigue. Beckett was very affected by the death. 'Giacometti is dead,' he wrote, 'Yes, take me off to the Père Lachaise jumping all the red lights.' Giacometti is buried in Père Lachaise Cemetery.

4

City of Exiles

*Every time I look down on this timeless town / whether
blue or gray be her skies / whether loud be her cheers, or
whether soft be her tears / more and more do I realize that
I love Paris ...*

(Ella Fitzgerald)

*Paris at night is sad and alien,
Dear to the heart is madness gone!*

(Marina Ivanovna Tsvetaeva)

Paris is well known for welcoming political refugees like
Lenin and Trotsky, but the most famous exile was probably
Oscar Wilde, who spent the last two years of his life mainly
in self-imposed exile in Paris. He died penniless in 1900 in
room 16 of the Hôtel d'Alsace at 13 rue des Beaux-Arts. His
too had been a story of unpaid bills and frequent moves to
ever-cheaper lodgings, always spiced nevertheless by the wit
which never left him: 'My wallpaper and I are fighting a duel
to the death. One of us has got to go.'

The first decades of the twentieth century were marked
by turmoil in Europe, by revolutions in Russia and Latin

PHOTO 10 13 rue des Beaux-Arts, Wilde's Hôtel d'Alsace

America, civil war in Spain and the struggle for racial
equality in the US, and from all came men and women
seeking security and a future. Paris provided a melting pot of
creativity and opportunity.

Many exiles, especially from Russia, were stateless, with
no papers. Many missed their homeland, which they would
never see again. The privations of World War I made life
even harsher, but the outbreak of World War II in 1939 and
the German occupation of Paris forced émigré artists and
writers to leave France and become exiles for a second time
at great emotional cost. Some reached neutral countries like
Switzerland; many headed for the US via the Pyrenees escape
route to Spain. Others found a temporary haven in a rural
community and returned to Paris after the war.

The Italian war poet **Giuseppe Ungaretti** (1888–1970)
joined the exiles trying to survive in Paris at the beginning
of the twentieth century. Born in Alexandria in Egypt, his
formal education began in French at Alexandria's Swiss
school, where he became acquainted with the work of the

French poets Charles Baudelaire, Jules Laforgue, Stéphane Mallarmé and Arthur Rimbaud.

In 1912 Ungaretti went to Paris to study at the Sorbonne and at the Collège de France, attending lectures by the philosopher Henri Bergson. His friendship with Guillaume Apollinaire, a promoter of Cubism and forerunner of Surrealism, was crucial to his development, as was encountering Picasso and de Chirico. He was also in contact with Italian expatriates like Modigliani, and leading Futurist artists such as Carlo Carrà and Umberto Boccioni. It was a formative period for him. One of his first poems, 'In Memoria' (1916), is concerned with exile, and was dedicated to his friend Moammed Sceab, who had committed suicide in 1913 in the room they were sharing at 5 rue des Carmes, in the fifth arrondissement. The poem evokes poignantly their shared fate as exiles or *déracinés*:

> He was called
> Moammed Sceab
> descended
> from Emirs of the nomads
> he killed himself
> because he no longer had
> a homeland
> he loved France

Moammed, who had taken the French name of Marcel, was buried in the cemetery at Ivry.

> A suburb that always
> looks like the day
> when a funfair

has come down
And perhaps I alone
still know
that he was alive

'Nostalgia' was written in the trenches in February 1916, when Ungaretti was discovering the dark reality of World War I. As a follower of the Futurists he had desired the war, but was now discovering its insanity and horrors, his mind turning nostalgically to Paris:

When
night fades
a little before spring
and unusually
someone passes
over Paris closes
a dark colour
of weeping
in a poem
on a bridge
I contemplate
the limitless silence
of a slender
girl

The 'slender girl' was Marthe Roux. Ungaretti's experience in the Italian infantry in 1915 and then on the French front was traumatic, but made a poet of him. In 1917, he published a volume of free verse in which he describes the reality of war and friendship between soldiers. This was followed by *La guerre* (The War, 1919), written in French.

After the war he decided to stay in Paris, finding a flat in rue Campagne-Première and working as a correspondent for Mussolini's paper *Il Popolo d'Italia*. In 1920 Ungaretti married Jeanne Dupoix. He joined the anti-establishment and anti-art movements, among them Dada, led by the Romanian poet Tristan Tzara, and took part in the grotesque Dada mock trial of Maurice Barrès on 13 May 1921, with the right-wing French writer represented by a dummy, accused of 'crimes against the security of the mind'. The event triggered a split between Dada and Surrealism. Ungaretti then moved to Italy, a country he hardly knew. His life as an exile was to continue, as after involvement in Mussolini's Fascist Italy he left for Brazil in 1936 to assume an academic post and remained until 1942, returning to spend the rest of his life in Rome, his Fascist past never completely forgotten.

The Russian symbolist poet **Marina Tsvetaeva** (1892–1941), born to a well-to-do family in Moscow, joined thousands of desperate Russians taking refuge in Paris at the outbreak of the 1917 Russian Revolution. Her first visit to Paris had been a study trip in happier circumstances in 1909 when, as a great admirer of Napoleon, she had made a point of staying in rue Bonaparte in the Latin Quarter. She attended the theatre to see the famous French actress Sarah Bernhardt in the title role in Edmond Rostand's play *L'Aiglon*, based on the life of Napoleon's son. Her poem '*Paris*' was written during that stay:

As in far Moscow, my breast
Throbs to Rostand's poetry.
Paris at night, painful strangeness,
Dear the heart's ancient folly!
...

Rostand, *L'Aiglon* that martyr,
And Sarah – in dream I find them all!
In Paris, so vast and joyous,
I dream of clouds and grass,
Laughter, shadows, ominous,
And the pain that will not pass.

In 1922 Tsvetaeva fled Russia with her daughter Ariadna and was reunited with her husband in Berlin; the family finally ended up in Paris in 1925. Short of funds, they headed for the suburbs but had to keep moving from place to place, unable to afford the rent to settle in a proper home. In 1934, she described what it had been like: 'I write after the terrible move to a new place and still feel unsettled and disorganised. There is no gas in the house and no light; and I don't know when we will have them because there is no money.' Like many exiles she suffered from homesickness, as expressed in a 1923 poem:

Homesickness! That long
Exposure to misery!
It's all the same to me –
…
I won't let the milky call
Of my native language tempt me.
It's all the same to me in what
Tongue they misunderstand me!

She spent fourteen of her seventeen years of exile in France, mostly in the Paris suburbs, including Meudon in the Bellevue area, at 31 boulevard Verd de Saint-Julien, Clamart at 101 rue Condorcet, Vanves at 33 rue Jean-Baptiste Potin from 1934 to 1938, and back to Paris, living at the Hôtel Innova (now Hôtel Madrigal) at 32 boulevard Pasteur.

Her poem 'In the Luxemburg Garden' (1909) in a translation by Lyudmila Purgina sounds melancholic:

> The blossoming boughs lean low and near,
> The fountain's flows are bubbling in basin,
> In shadowy alleys there are children, children ...
> Oh children in grass, why are you not mine, any?

After the initial happy first year in exile Paris Tsvetaeva led a generally isolated life, but she did make a few friends, attended Natalie Barney's salons and, with excellent French and German, could earn badly needed money working on translations. Her poetry was not always fully appreciated by most of her unsympathetic compatriots in exile. Painfully aware that a return to Russia was problematic she wrote: 'Everyone is pushing me towards Russia, the place I can't return to. Here I feel useless.' The poem 'The Garden' (1934) also expresses her hopelessness:

> For this hell
> For this delirium
> Send me a garden
> In my old-age years.

The Russian writer Nina Berberova recalls seeing Tsvetaeva at the Paris funeral of another poet, before she left for Moscow in 1939, and gives a sad description of her: 'She had grey hair, her eyes were grey, and her face was grey. Her large hands, coarse and rough, a charwoman's hands, were folded on her stomach and she had a strange toothless smile.

And I, like everyone else, passed by without greeting her.'
Tsvetaeva sought refuge in her correspondence with other
writers, including Boris Pasternak (who had remained in his
homeland) and, although they never met, the Austrian poet
Rainer Maria Rilke until his death on 29 December 1926. At
the time she was living in Bellevue:

> I live in Bellevue. a little city
> of nests and branches, exchanging glances with the guide:
> Bellevue. the fortress with the perfect view
> of Paris – the chamber with the Gallic chimera –
> of Paris – and further still …

In 1938, we find her with her son in the Hôtel Innova, her
last Paris home. Life for both was grim, so they returned to
Russia in 1939 on the eve of war, where worse awaited them.
Within two years her estranged husband had been executed
by the Soviet regime, her daughter imprisoned, and she had
taken her own life.

The poet **Rainer Maria Rilke** (1875–1926) spent his early
years in Prague, coming to Paris for the first time in 1902.
He had been commissioned to write a monograph on the
French sculptor Auguste Rodin (1840–1917), with whom
his German sculptress wife Clara Westhoff had studied
in 1900. Arriving with little money, the young man, who
suffered from anxiety and who hated crowds, moved to a
cheap hotel in the Latin Quarter at 11 rue Toullier. He had
to face the alien, crowded city with its dirt and poverty: 'The
city is just too vast and overburdened with melancholy.' The
vicinity of hospitals reeking of illness and death depressed
him, as he noted in *The Notebooks of Malte Laurids Briggs*

(1910): 'So, people do come here to live. I would sooner have thought that this is where one dies.'

On 1 September he visited Rodin's studio in the Paris marble depot in rue de l'Université, and in spite of their age difference, language barriers and dissimilar temperaments and eating habits, they got on surprisingly well.

Like many others, Rilke fell under Rodin's spell: 'It was not only to do a study that I came to be with you, – it was to ask you: how must one live?' Rodin's answer was that, for them, living should be dedication to work and their art: '*Il faut travailler, rien que travailler.*'

Rilke did not waste time, studying at the Bibiliothèque Nationale and visiting the Louvre, where he must have found inspiration for his poem 'Archaic Torso of Apollo' (1918), or perhaps this came from Rodin's own headless figures? On Rodin's advice he made daily visits to the Paris Zoo, the Ménagerie du Jardin des Plantes, to observe the animals. One of his best-known poems, 'The Panther', dates from November 1902:

> His vision from the passing of the bars
> Is grown so weary that it holds no more.
> To him it seems there are a thousand bars
> And behind a thousand bars no world …

In spite of feeling himself caged 'behind a thousand bars', a month later Rilke had completed the monograph on Rodin, and was attending Rodin's Saturday open house at his studio. He behaved very much as an admiring disciple of the sculptor although he disapproved strongly of his attitude towards female students and assistants, including Camille Claudel, or his models, like the Welsh artist Gwen John, with whom he was having an affair as she sat for him.

Otherwise there was a deep understanding between both men, who were working towards similar ends. 'Rodin reverted again and again in his figures to this turning-inward-upon-oneself, this tense listening to inner depths', he noted on Rodin's sculpture *The Inner Voice (The Muse)* (1896–97). Clara joined him briefly in 1903, and they took separate rooms in a hostel in rue de l'Abbé de l'Epée. They were hoping to find work and settle in Paris, so their young daughter had been left with her grandparents.

In 1905 Rodin took pity on him, and employed him as a secretary in exchange for a small salary and accommodation in his house and studio at the Villa des Brillants in Meudon, just outside Paris. His two hours of daily duties included organising and filing Rodin's vast correspondence, but in 1906 the arrangement came to an abrupt end and Rilke was back in a cheap room in rue Cassette, and then in 1907 the Hôtel du quai Voltaire, at 19 quai Voltaire. It is not entirely clear what occurred, but it has been suggested that Rilke was accused of having answered a letter without Rodin's permission. The ensuing rift profoundly wounded Rilke, who felt treated like a 'thieving servant', but the friendship picked up again in 1908 when the poet, now more financially secure, moved into a spacious room in the Hôtel Biron at 77 rue de Varenne, which at the time offered accommodation to writers and artists in many disciplines, and which had originally been taken by Clara. The huge eighteenth-century building, formerly a disused convent school, housed Henri Matisse, Jean Cocteau and the dancer Isadora Duncan.

Rilke was delighted, and wrote enthusiastically to Rodin: 'My dear friend, you really ought to see this lovely building and the room I moved into this morning. Its three bays look out prodigiously across an abandoned garden, where from time to time one sees unsuspecting rabbits leap across trellises as if in an ancient tapestry.' As soon as Rodin saw it he requisitioned four ground-floor rooms and the garden to accommodate his sculptures, making a studio-workshop which he retained to the end of his life. Since 1919 the building has been the Musée Rodin in Paris.

Rilke was also interested in contemporary art, and it is in Paris that he discovered Cézanne's paintings at an exhibition at the 1907 Salon d'automné, held in honour of Cézanne who had died a year earlier. There was time for some social life, and in autumn 1908 at the Hôtel Liverpool he met Princess Marie von Thurn und Taxis, who would become one of his most admiring and supportive patrons.

From 1909 to 1914 Rilke returned regularly to Paris, staying in rue de Varenne, and in 1913 and 1914 just before the outbreak of World War I in rue Campagne-Première, which he left in a hurry, abandoning his notes, manuscripts and belongings; he was never able to retrieve them. They had disappeared by the time he returned in 1920, when he found the city transformed by the war. Many friends including Rodin were no more. There was a last trip in 1925 shortly before his death, when he stayed at the Hôtel Foyot at 33 rue de Tournon.

Rilke left more than seven thousand letters, corresponding with lovers like Lou Andreas-Salomé, and friends including Gwen John and his patron Princess Marie, as well as with his wife Clara. His novel *The Notebooks of Malte Laurids Briggs*, completed in 1910, is considered partly autobiographical, and is revealing about his life in Paris. In spite of his frequent stays he had mixed feelings about the city, which he considered a hostile place in which to work, with little room for play. His melancholy can be sensed in the first lines of his poem 'Herbst' ('Autumn', 1920):

> The leaves are falling, as if from far away,
> As if in the heavens distant gardens were wilting

But although Paris was often a terrifying city, 'where everything echoes and fades away differently because of the excessive noise that makes Things tremble ...', as he wrote in his *Letters to a Young Poet* (1929), he did return, and lived longer in Paris than in any of the many cities he visited.

The German Jewish thinker, art critic and philosopher **Walter Benjamin** (1892–1940) spent most of his adult life in exile. With the increase of antisemitism in Germany, his closest friend Gershom Scholem tried hard on several occasions to convince Benjamin to join him in Palestine. Many Jewish intellectuals and political refugees had moved there when their life in Germany became precarious and active Nazi persecution started. From the late 1920s Benjamin had found it impossible to secure a university position in Frankfurt, and Scholem could have organised a post for him at the Hebrew University in Jerusalem. Benjamin however opted for Paris, where he arrived in 1933. At the time his life was in disarray. He had gone through a bitter divorce from his wife Dora and separation from his young son Stefan. Barely surviving on a stipend from a New York foundation and earning little working as a freelance journalist, he lived from hand to mouth, particularly hard for someone who had been used to a comfortable family life. He was in bad health and the next seven years in Paris were spent in poverty and uncertainty.

Like many immigrants he was forced to move from place to place: in March 1933 he was at the cheap Hôtel Istria in rue Campagne-Première in Montparnasse, by October he was in the Hôtel Regina de Passy at 6 rue de la Tour, then the Palace Hotel at 1 rue du Four, followed by rooms at 25 rue Jasmin. The next place was Hôtel Floridor, at 28 place Denfert-Rochereau until August 1935, from where he moved successively to 7 villa Robert Lindet and 23 rue Bernard. Afterwards he shared his sister's flat at Villa Nicolo, in rue Nicolo. He was now stateless after the Nazis stripped German Jews of their citizenship in 1938; his application for French citizenship was unsuccessful.

In spite of constant moves there were compensations in France, which he describes in his letters as 'more like home' than Berlin. He records how happy he is: 'Besides, I can only feel lucky to have enjoyed such a welcome in France.' He was nevertheless arrested in 1939 by the French police and incarcerated for three months in a prison camp for 'voluntary labourers'. His Parisian friends Adrienne Monnier and Jules Romains procured his release in November 1939, and he moved to a modest flat at 10 rue Dombasle, where a plaque now commemorates his last two Parisian years. He resumed studies at the Bibliothèque Nationale and was delighted to renew his library membership on 11 January 1940: 'I had to renew my library card ... that was a small celebration for me ... I don't need to say exactly how attached I am to France for my life as much as for my work.'

In the meantime, his friends and his ex-wife Dora were urging him to leave Europe, where his life was at risk; despite recognising that his situation was precarious, he found it difficult to tear himself away from Paris. He compared himself to 'one who keeps afloat on a shipwreck by climbing to the top of the mast that is already crumbling. But from there he has a chance to give a signal leading to his rescue.'

In June 1940 he had made up his mind, and left for Lourdes with his sister, just one day before the Germans entered the capital. In August he had unexpectedly obtained a travel visa to the US, which he planned to reach via Francoist Spain and neutral Portugal, a route used by some of his compatriots. While waiting with fellow exiles in the Catalonian town of Portbou in northern Spain, the Spanish police threatened to return them to France. Fearing his chance of survival was slight, he took a fatal overdose of morphine tablets on 25 September in room no. 4 of the Hôtel de Francia. The official Portbou register records 26 September 1940 as the official date of his death. The rest of the party eventually made it to the US, after reaching Lisbon the following day. Benjamin was buried in the consecrated section of the local Roman Catholic cemetery (unusual for a suicide), where his tomb can be visited.

Benjamin's strong connection with Paris had started on a visit in 1913, when he encountered the poetry of Baudelaire. He started to translate it into German, as well as some of Marcel Proust's writing. Particularly impressed by Baudelaire, on whom he wrote a collection of essays, *Baudelaire, The Writer of Modern Life*, in 1923 he published a translation of *Tableaux parisiens* (Parisian Scenes), seventeen poems comprising the second section of Baudelaire's *Les Fleurs du Mal* (The Flowers of Evil, 1857). In 1925, he translated three volumes of Proust's *À la recherche du temps perdu* (In Search of Lost Time, 1913) with his friend Franz Hessel. On another trip to Paris in 1926, financed by the *Frankfurter Zeitung* for which he was writing articles, he met many compatriots in exile including Hessel, Ernst Bloch and Max Horkheimer. One of the first pieces he wrote on Paris at the time, '*Paris, ville dans le miroir*' (Paris, City in the Mirror), was published in *Vogue* in 1929.

PHOTO 11 Notre-Dame, the monument which has inspired masterpieces

For Benjamin Paris was the ultimate city of books: 'There isn't a single monument in this city which has not inspired a literary masterpiece', mentioning among others Victor Hugo's *Notre-Dame de Paris* (The Hunchback of Notre-Dame, 1831), the Eiffel Tower for Jean Cocteau and the Paris Opéra, which inspired Gaston Leroux's *Le Fantôme de l'Opéra* (The Phantom of the Opera, 1911).

In Paris Benjamin was mixing with Germans in exile, but was familiar also with local cultural life, particularly the work of Apollinaire, Jean Giraudoux and above all the Surrealists. Louis Aragon's *Le Paysan de Paris* (Paris Peasant, 1926) and André Breton's *Nadja* (1928) had a considerable impact on his writing. Their Paris as well as Benjamin's is a place of dreams. 'Too Close', a short story included in the collection *The Storyteller* (2016), opens with the lines: 'In the dream, on the left bank of the Seine in front of Notre Dame. I was standing there, but there was nothing that resembled Notre Dame. A brick building towered above a high fence made of wood, revealing the extremities of its highest echelons. I stood, though, overwhelmed, right in front of Notre Dame. And what overwhelmed me was longing. Longing for the same Paris in which I found myself in the dream ...'

Surrealism dominates his major work *Paris, Capital of the Nineteenth Century* (1939): 'The father of surrealism was Dada; its mother was an arcade.' In 1927 Benjamin started on a major work, *Passagen-Werk* (The Arcades Project), 'the theatre of all my struggles and all my ideas'. He considered the arcades, the iron and glass '*passages couverts*', a most important building type of nineteenth-century Paris, a symbol of consumer society, shops, fashion and advertisements.

His ambitious social and economic study of Parisian life, *Paris, Capital of the Nineteenth Century*, took shape painstakingly during daily visits to the Bibliothèque Nationale, then at 58 rue de Richelieu. There he examined key moments of the city's history which had left so many marks on the city and its topography. Benjamin notes the passage du Caire, erected after Napoleon's return from Egypt. He also discusses the Commune and the 1871 insurrection in Paris, and comments at length on the lasting effect the urban architect Baron Haussmann had on the city, which was partly demolished in the second half of the nineteenth century in order to build wide avenues, mainly intended to prevent civil unrest. Benjamin notes that: 'The true goal of Haussmann's projects was to secure the city against civil war.'

In Paris Benjamin, like Baudelaire, is a *flâneur*: 'It was Paris which taught me the art of losing one's way, Paris fulfilled the dream whose earliest signs were the labyrinths I drew on my school exercise books.' He is fascinated by the city's secrets, and quotes from Victor Hugo: 'Cities, like forests, have their dens in which all their vilest and most terrible monsters hide.' He proceeds to unveil the Paris underworld with its catacombs, cemeteries and brothels, and includes the '*passages couverts*' in his disapproval: 'The arcade is a street of lascivious commerce only; it is wholly adapted to arousing desires.'

Paris served him as 'the great reading room of a library which crosses the Seine'. Unfortunately *The Arcades Project* remained in note form. Benjamin never completed it, and it was not published in his lifetime. The importance of his writing was recognised only posthumously, by friends who survived him, including Hannah Arendt, Gershom Scholem, Bertolt Brecht and Theodor Adorno. Returning to Paris in 1949, Adorno retrieved the *Arcades* papers which Benjamin had entrusted to the Bibliothèque Nationale librarian Georges Bataille, and the work was finally published in the US in 1999.

It is speculated that during his flight towards Portbou Benjamin had a further manuscript in his suitcase, perhaps a final version of *The Arcades Project*, but it was never recovered. Other manuscripts had also been left with Theodor Adorno and Hannah Arendt, who then proceeded to publish everything. When *Illuminations*, a collection of essays including studies on Baudelaire and Proust, came out in 1968 in English, with a preface by Hannah Arendt, Benjamin, who had so far been largely unknown, became posthumously famous. Nowadays it is possible to read all his essays and surviving correspondence. He was a compulsive letter-writer and corresponded with Brecht, Adorno, Scholem and other friends and family members. Much has been written about him, starting with Adorno's *A Portrait of Walter Benjamin* (1950) republished in *Prisms* (1967). Works also include fictional versions of his life, like Bruno Arpaia's *L'Angelo della storia* (The Angel of History, 2001).

Born in Hanover, the Jewish theorist **Hannah Arendt** (1906–75) had married Günther Stern, a cousin of Walter Benjamin, in 1929. After being detained by the Gestapo in 1933, she fled to Paris via Geneva, accompanied by her mother. Shortly afterwards, in 1937, she was stripped of her German nationality. She was reunited with her husband in Paris, although their marriage did not last, and she stayed in the city until 1940, making a living by working for Jewish charities, helping exiles and rescuing young Jews. Arendt mixed with French writers and intellectuals and shared a particularly close friendship with the French-Jewish philosopher Raymond Aron. She was also strongly encouraged by Benji, as she affectionately called Benjamin, to complete her biography on Rahel Varnhagen, *The Life of a Jewess* (1957). In her essay 'We Refugees' (1943) she commented on the condition of exile as she experienced it:

> We lost our home, which means the familiarity of daily life. We lost our occupation, which means the confidence that we are of some use in this world. We lost our language, which means the naturalness of reactions, the simplicity

of gestures, the unaffected expression of feelings. We left
our relatives ... and our best friends have been killed ...
and that means the rupture of our private lives.

A survivor, she was practical and resourceful, unlike Benjamin,
whom she indulgently described as inept in his daily life:
'With a precision suggesting a sleepwalker his clumsiness
invariably guided him to the very centre of a misfortune.'

They were close, and during their exile often met at
Benjamin's apartment, where they would play chess. At one of
these evenings in 1936 Arendt met the poet and philosopher
Heinrich Blücher, whom she subsequently married in Paris.
The couple was forced to leave the city in 1940 but, unlike
Benjamin, they made it to New York via Portugal in 1941.
The political philosopher Arendt is remembered less as
a poet, although she wrote poetry all her life. In 1948 she
dedicated a poem to Walter Benjamin:

> Dusk will come again sometime. Night will come down
>   from the stars.
> We will rest our outstretched arms. In the nearness, in the
>   distances.
> Out of the darkness sound softly small archaic melodies.
>   Listening,
> Let us wear ourselves away let us at last break ranks.
> Distant voices, sadness nearby. Those are the voices and
>   these are the dead
> Whom we have sent as messengers, ahead, to lead us to
>   slumber.

A square in the nineteenth arrondissement in Paris, place
Hannah-Arendt, is named after her.

In 1938 Benjamin had paid a last visit to his friend **Bertolt Brecht** (1898–1956), who was still in exile in Denmark. They were introduced in Berlin in 1929. Benjamin was strongly influenced by Brecht's politics, and they developed a bond which endured after both were forced to leave Germany. When they met they would often play chess, a metaphor Brecht uses in a poem describing their creative impotence in exile:

> Tactics of attrition are what you enjoyed
> Sitting at the chess table in the pear tree's shade.
> The enemy who drove you from your books
> Will not be worn down by the likes of us.

Benjamin developed a keen interest in the new art form of photography, and in his 1931 essay '*Petite histoire de la photographie*' ('A short history of photography') he considered the work of various photographers including Eugène Atget. He also mentions a promising photographer named Germaine Krull, who took a well-known photo of him in Paris in 1925.

Gisèle Freund (1908–2000), another photographer, had become a friend of Benjamin in Germany and was now in exile in Paris. He encouraged her to pursue her doctoral studies at the Sorbonne, and her PhD dissertation on nineteenth-century French photography, '*La photographie en France au XIXe siècle*' was published in 1936 by Adrienne Monnier, who became an important mentor, and who introduced her to writers and cultural figures in Paris, including James Joyce. For a few years both women lived together in Monnier's flat. In 1937 she photographed Benjamin sitting at a table absorbed by work in the familiar surroundings of the Bibliothèque Nationale. The photo which brought Freund real fame was of the writer André Malraux, taken on a Paris rooftop in 1935. Malraux would later become a statesman, and in 1996 the French government used the image to create a postage stamp, notoriously editing out the cigarette dangling from Malraux's lip. When she was invited by Malraux to document the First International Congress of Writers in Defence of Culture, held in 1935 and attended by 250 writers from thirty-eight countries, her portrait photographs included Brecht, Pasternak, E. M. Forster, Aldous Huxley, Barbusse and Gide.

Freund favoured working with writers, and generally liked to know her subjects well. She discussed their books before taking their portraits, in order to establish the intimacy which shines through her photographs: 'I certainly didn't pretend to be making works of art or inventing new forms, I wanted to show what means the most to me: people, with their joys and sorrows, hopes and fears.' Her famous portrait of Joyce, a difficult subject who ultimately cooperated, appeared on the cover of *Time* magazine on 8 May 1939.

The Nazi invasion in 1940 forced Freund to leave Paris. She followed the familiar route across the Pyrenees out to safety. With Malraux's assistance she reached Buenos Aires in 1942, as her left-wing views made her unwelcome in the US. She was back in France for good in the early 1950s, and in 1981 she took the official portrait of the newly elected French president, François Mitterrand. She was made *Chevalier de la légion d'honneur* in 1983, and died in Paris, where she is buried in the Montparnasse Cemetery, located very near her home and studio at 12 rue Lalande. She is the author of *James Joyce in Paris: His Final Years* (1965), *Trois jours avec Joyce* (Three Days with Joyce, 1982) and a book of memoirs,

Itinéraires (1985). '*La Photographie en France*' appeared in a new edition in 2011. In Greta Schiller's 1996 documentary, *Paris was a Woman*, Freund is one of the ten women being interviewed, describing Paris in the 1930s.

The thirty-eight-year-old American **Henry Valentine Miller** (1891–1980) travelled with his second wife June to Paris in 1928. They stayed in an hotel at 24 rue Bonaparte, before going cycling in the South of France. In 1930 Miller returned alone to Paris from New York, with very little money, but with the manuscripts of two unpublished novels. He moved into the cheaper Hôtel Saint-Germain-des-Prés further along at 36 rue Bonaparte, from which he wrote euphorically to a friend: 'I love it here, I want to stay forever ... I will write here. I will live and quite alone. And each day I will see a little more of Paris, study it, learn it as I would a book ... The streets sing, the stones talk. The houses drip history, glory, romance.'

By the end of the year his mood had changed. When Richard Galen Osborn rescued his friend from his fifth-floor garret, Miller wrote that he 'rescued me from starvation in Paris and set my feet in the right direction'. The right direction was to Osborn's studio at 2 rue Auguste Bartholdi, where he spent a few months recovering, looking at the Eiffel Tower from his window. From there he moved to Montparnasse, into Villa Seurat at 101 rue de la Tombe-Issoire, taking studio no. 18 in this residence for artists in a quiet cul-de-sac, described in the opening paragraph of *Tropic of Cancer*. 'I am living at the Villa Borghese. There is not a crumb of dirt anywhere, nor a chair misplaced. We are all alone here and we are dead. Last night Boris [his fictional flatmate] discovered that he was lousy. I had to shave his armpits and even then, the itching did not stop. How can one get lousy in a beautiful place like this? But no matter. We might never have known each other so intimately, Boris and I, had it not been for the lice.'

Villa Seurat was conveniently near Le Sphinx at 31 boulevard Edgar Quinet, the notorious Montparnasse brothel which had just opened. Miller became a regular and would get special treatment and occasionally a commission for bringing in clients. He was to return to Villa Seurat from 1934 to 1939, before leaving Paris for good at the outbreak of World War II.

For Miller, who had grown up in a German-American quarter of Brooklyn and spent his formative years in a range of occupations, including handyman, piano teacher and employee of Western Union, Paris was a welcome change, as he was escaping a difficult period in a complicated personal life. He was also desperately hoping to become a writer. 'I refuse to live this way forever. There must be a way out.' It was a good move; he spent the next ten years in Paris, writing the books which made his name. He made a meagre living working as a proofreader for the Paris edition of the *Chicago Tribune* at 5 rue Lamartine, and started submitting his own work to the newspaper under his friend the writer Alfred Perlès's name, as only editorial staff were allowed to publish. He was influenced by the Surrealists with whom he mixed, as well as by nomadic bohemian artists like the photographer Brassaï, who became a close friend.

The tormented Swedish writer August Strindberg, who had found inspiration in Paris when he stayed in 1885, fascinated Miller: 'It was no mystery to me any longer why he and others (Dante, Rabelais, Van Gogh etc, etc) had made their pilgrimage to Paris. I understood then why it is that Paris attracts the tortured, the hallucinated, the great maniacs of love.'

Paris was Miller's inspiration too, and four years after his arrival, in 1934, *Tropic of Cancer* shook the literary world. Originally called *Crazy Cock*, it was accepted by the Obelisk Press, which took on works too explicit to be published by the mainstream press. The 'Paris book', as Miller called his first novel, was a semi-autobiographical account of his experiences in Paris. It is not surprising that with its overt sexual language the book would remain banned for a generation in the US and in the UK. The first edition bore the warning: 'Not to be imported into the United States or Great Britain.' It was a triumph for Miller, who had once written: 'Why does nobody want what I write?'

In *Tropic of Cancer* Miller explains his literary approach: 'Up to the present, my idea in collaborating with myself has been to get off the gold standard of literature. My idea briefly has been to present a resurrection of the emotions, to depict the conduct of a human being in the stratosphere of ideas, that is, in the grip of delirium.' A kind of narrative brings together his friends, colleagues and workplaces. Some chapters are written in a stream-of-consciousness style. The general mood is bleak, with a pessimistic meditation on the human condition. All characters share the narrator's life, dominated by hunger, squalor, loneliness and despair: 'One can live in Paris – I discovered that! – on just grief and anguish. A bitter nourishment – perhaps the best there is for certain people.'

In spite of its controversial approach and brutally explicit language, praise for the novel was almost universal. His friend Anaïs Nin, who had supported it financially, wrote in the preface to the 1934 edition: 'Here is a book which, if such a thing were possible, might restore our appetite for the fundamental realities. The predominant note will seem one of bitterness, and bitterness there is, to the full. But there is also a wild extravagance, a mad gaiety, a verve, a gusto, at times almost a delirium.'

George Orwell was also complimentary: 'I earnestly counsel anyone who has not done so to read at least *Tropic of Cancer*. With a little ingenuity, or by paying a little over the published price, you can get hold of it, and even if parts of it disgust you, it will stick in your memory.'

Samuel Beckett hailed the novel as 'a momentous event in the history of modern writing' and Norman Mailer in *Genius and Lust* (1976) called it 'one of the ten or twenty great novels of our century, a revolution in style and consciousness equal to *The Sun Also Rises*'.

Miller had been an admirer of Rabelais' robust language, of Dostoyevsky's *Notes From Underground* (1864) and of the controversial French writer Louis-Ferdinand Céline. He admired especially the latter's *Voyage au bout de la nuit* (Journey to the End of the Night, 1932). *Tropic of Cancer* had a huge impact on the next generation of anglophone literary figures and influenced younger subversive writers like Genet, Ginsberg, Boris Vian, Lawrence Durrell, Jack Kerouac and William S. Burroughs. It had a liberating effect on the American writer Erica Jong: '... when I was searching for the freedom to write *Fear of Flying*, I picked up *Tropic of Cancer* and the sheer exuberance of the prose unlocked something in me.'

The *flâneur* Miller would write in his essay 'Remember to Remember' that 'There are scarcely any streets in Paris I did not get to know. On every one of them I could erect a tablet commemorating in letters of gold some rich new experience, some deep realization, some moment of illumination.' He was particularly proud to be praised by Blaise Cendrars who wrote that he had 'never read a book by an American, nor by any foreigner for that matter, with descriptions of Paris's streets that could match Henry's'.

Praise poured in after the publication of *Black Spring* in 1936. Anaïs Nin called his writing 'flamboyant, torrential, chaotic, treacherous, and dangerous'. In a 1949 recording Miller commented: 'During the ten years I spent in Paris, I must have written seven or eight books. This one, *Black Spring*, I like the best of all I wrote during that period. It was a wonderful period of my life. The years 1932 and '33, living outside Paris in the town of Clichy, where I wrote the book, I guess were the very best years of my whole life.' At the time he was sharing a flat at 4 avenue Anatole France, beyond the Porte de Clichy, with Alfred Perlès, travelling into the city to spend time at Café Wepler, a favourite haunt in Montmartre which is still there. 'I knew it like a book. The faces of the waiters, the managers, the cashiers, the whores, the clientèle, even the attendants in the lavatory, are engraved in my memory as if they were illustrations in a book which I read every day.'

Quiet Days in Clichy was written in New York in 1940, and gives a nostalgic account of Miller's nocturnal wanderings through the Montmartre streets, cafés and bars and of his sexual encounters and affairs. The first part of the book centres on Joey, an American expatriate who shares a flat with Carl. While searching for food Joey becomes involved with various women, one of them a prostitute he meets at Café Wepler. In the meantime Carl has brought home Colette, a fifteen-year-old runaway. The second part, *Mara-Marignon*, ends with a night of orgy in the flat after Joey had brought back Mara, a prostitute from the Champs-Élysées. It is a strange encounter, beautifully adapted as a thirty-minute short, *Mara*, by Mike Figgis in 1995, starring Scott Glenn as Miller and Juliette Binoche as Mara.

Miller acted as 'technical consultant' for the film *Tropic of Cancer*, directed in 1970 by Joseph Strick. In the same year the film *Quiet Days in Clichy* saw the Miller-based character of Joey played by Paul Valjean. Another adaptation of the same work was made by Claude Chabrol in 1990 with a twenty-six-year-old Andrew McCarthy as Miller (now in his early forties). It was a huge age gap, and Chabrol admitted that the film was not a faithful rendering of the novella.

Angela Anaïs Juana Antolina Rosa Edelmira Nin y Culmell (1903–77), better known as Anaïs Nin, was a Cuban-American novelist and writer born in the Paris suburb of Neuilly. Nin spent her early years in Spain, Cuba and New York and, thanks partly to Miller, became an established author during the sixteen years she spent in Paris from 1924. She first moved with her husband, a banker, to 11 bis rue Schoelcher near the Montparnasse Cemetery, and later from 1929 to 1930 to the more salubrious district of Passy near the Bois de Boulogne. After the stock market crash in 1929 the couple took a lease in the cheaper suburban town of Louveciennes, at 2 bis rue Mont Buisson. Nin claimed to hate Paris and its 'filth', as she wrote in her diary in 1926: 'I shall try to turn my hate of Paris into writing and make it harmless.' A year later she had changed her mind: 'I faced and accepted Paris as a test of my courage.'

She would write extensively in the first volume of her notorious diary, which covered the years 1931–34, about her relationship with Miller and his wife June. She had kept a diary from the age of eleven, originally meant for her absent father, and was still writing it six decades later, continuing until her death. The intellectual and physically intense relationship she had with Henry Miller had a great impact on both her life and her writing. They had met in 1931 through a friend, Richard Osborn (portrayed as Filmore in *Tropic of Cancer*), who had brought Miller to Nin's house in Louveciennes. They started an affair, meeting in room 401 at the Hôtel Central at 1 bis rue du Maine, where Miller occupied a room for which Nin paid. The affair would last for many years, chronicled by countless passionate letters and the *Diary*. 'After our first encounter I breathed some notes, accents of recognition, human admissions. Henry was still stunned, and I was breathing off the unbearable, willing joy. But the second time, there were no words. My joy was impalpable and terrifying. It swelled within me as I walked the streets.'

For her Miller represented complete sexual liberty, inspiration and imagination. They encouraged and helped each other's writing even after the affair was over. Thanks to her financial help the Obelisk Press published *Tropic of Cancer*, which she edited, and which Miller dedicated to her. She also found and paid for his Villa Seurat flat, whose previous occupant was the revolutionary French director and actor Antonin Artaud, whom she greatly admired. She continued to send Miller money after he had become successful, and in return Miller helped her to build a reputation as a writer of fiction. Determined to lead a bohemian life, she exchanged the comforts of a house for a houseboat on the Seine, living in close proximity to the Parisian tramps whom she found 'comical, humorous, their delirious speeches at the corners ironic and witty'.

Their correspondence, published as *A Literate Passion: Letters of Anaïs Nin & Henry Miller, 1932–1953* (1987) and *The Diary of Anaïs Nin, Volume One: 1931–1934* (1966), chronicle those hard but heady days in Paris. In 1990 the director Peter Kaufman shot *Henry & June*, a film based on Nin's diaries and focusing on her relationship with Miller and his wife.

Brassaï (Gyula Halász) (1899–1984) was a Hungarian photographer, sculptor and filmmaker who flourished in Paris between the two world wars, at which time he became an close friend of Henry Miller. 'Then one day I fell in with a photographer; he was making a collection of the slimy joints of Paris for some degenerate in Munich. ... He was a good companion, the photographer. He knew the city inside out, the walls particularly ...'

In his book *Henry Miller, grandeur nature* (1975) Brassaï chronicles Miller's life: 'He cleansed his soul by roaming the streets of Paris without a single sou in his pocket. In later years Henry often recalled the euphoria of his days *en marge*, on the fringes, fraught though they were with uncertainty and even misery. He was happy.' Brassaï describes a love triangle involving Miller, Anaïs Nin and Miller's estranged wife June, as well as Miller's friendship with the novelists Lawrence Durrell, Blaise Cendrars, Raymond Queneau and Alfred Perlès. The book contains sixteen photographs of Paris and of Miller.

Brassaï had arrived in Paris in 1924 from Brassó in Hungary (now Braşov in Romania) to become a painter, but took up photography, and stayed for the rest of his life. He apparently learned French by reading Marcel Proust, and mixed with the young artists in Montparnasse, making friends with Henry Miller and the French writers Léon-Paul Fargue and Jacques Prévert, among others.

Miller's feelings were mixed. 'Fred [Perlès] and I used to steer shy of him – he bored us.' He also had reservations about Brassaï's book, which he thought was 'padded, full of factual errors, full of suppositions, rumours, documents he filched which are largely false or give a false impression'.

Brassaï captured the atmosphere and mood of the city during those special years, however. His first collection of photographs, *Paris de nuit* (Paris by Night), was a great success when it was published in 1933. Henry Miller called Brassaï 'The Eye of Paris'; he portrayed not only scenes from high society, artists and intellectuals, but also the popular and seedier side of the city. The stunning photos of his friends included Salvador Dalí, Pablo Picasso, Henri Matisse, Alberto Giacometti and famous writers of the time such as Jean Genet and Henri Michaux.

Lawrence Durrell (1912–90) claimed that the writers who had the most influence on his writings were his publisher T. S. Eliot, George Seferis (the Greek poet) and Henry Miller.

In 1935 he came across a copy of *Tropic of Cancer* in a public lavatory, and reading it shook him 'from stem to stern'. He wrote to Miller expressing his intense admiration for the novel, and an enduring friendship followed for the next forty-five years. 'And now, illustrious, came the day when *Tropic* opened a pit in my brain. It freed me immediately, I had such a marvellous sense of absolution – freedom from guilt ...' Durrell's next novels, *Panic Spring* (1937) and *The Black Book* (1938) were strongly influenced by Miller.

In August 1937 Lawrence and his wife Nancy travelled to the Villa Seurat in Paris to meet Henry Miller and Anaïs Nin. The four of them, together with Alfred Perlès, 'began a collaboration aimed at founding their own literary movement' with the Obelisk Press as publisher. *The Black Book: An Agon*, was published in the Villa Seurat Series imprint in 1938. Its main character, Lawrence Lucifer, does not escape to Paris but goes to Greece instead, as had Durrell in 1935. In 1939 he was visited by Miller, who stayed at the Durrells' White House in Corfu before he was able to return to the US, where he remained until he died.

When the black American writer **Richard Wright** (1908 –60) arrived in Paris in May 1946, he was already an established name. Born in Mississippi, the descendant of slaves, he had a difficult early life in the US until the publication of his bestselling novel *Black Boy* (1945). American fiction was popular in France, and he was officially invited to Paris. He was welcomed on arrival at Gare St-Lazare by representatives of the French and American governments, and was interviewed on the platform by Albert Camus' left-wing newspaper *Combat*. As the representative of 'Negro writers', literary parties were arranged for him, where he met Camus, André Gide, Jean Cocteau and Jean-Paul Sartre. Wright was an admirer of Camus, and had read his existentialist novel *L'Étranger* (1942), the title of which influenced his own novel of 1953, *The Outsider*. Simone de Beauvoir, Sartre's companion, became a close friend, as Wright's wife Ellen was her literary editor. They all gathered in Left Bank cafés and restaurants to discuss politics, literature and existentialism.

During the following six months Wright stayed at the Trianon Palace Hotel in Saint-Germain-des-Prés, where Gertrude Stein had reserved a room for him. He was deeply impressed by Paris, where he felt 'no race tension or conflict … no social snobbery' and by its iconic buildings like Notre-Dame. In a letter to his publisher, Wright noted that the decision to leave the US had brought him 'a bad press in the United States', but he had had enough of the racial discrimination he had endured there. Moreover his political past was catching up with him, as it had not been forgotten in his country that he was a former member of the Communist Party, although he had left the party in 1942. As he sought to widen his horizons in a more congenial place, where better than Paris? In early 1945 he had written in his journal that Paris was a place ' ... where one could claim one's own soul'.

The return trip to New York confirmed Wright's decision to leave the US permanently, and he was back in Paris with his family in August 1947, becoming a French citizen. They first lived in a flat at 9 rue de Lille, then moved to Neuilly. By 1948 the success of *Native Son* (1940) and *Black Boy* had allowed him to buy a large apartment at 14 rue Monsieur le Prince in the Latin Quarter. His neighbour Sylvia Beach became a friend, and he encouraged her strongly to write her memoirs. She spoke highly of him in a letter sent to her sister: 'Of all the writers I have known, he is the most unselfish and thoughtful. In fact, none of the others – the so-called white ones – were interested in anyone but themselves. Fellas like Hemingway appear uncouth beside Dick Wright.'

Once settled, he published seven books between 1953 and 1958, including two novels, *The Outsider* and the semi-autobiographical novel *The Long Dream* (1958). Both were relatively poorly received, with critics implying that while away he had lost touch with his main subject, the 'Negro problem'. He also wrote non-fiction, based mainly on his travels in the Far East, Spain and Africa. After a trip to the Gold Coast (now Ghana), he coined the term 'Black Power', the title also of the resulting book, published in 1954. He had previously befriended black writers from French-speaking countries in Africa and the French West Indies living and working in Paris, including Léopold Senghor and Aimé Césaire, and in the summer of 1956 he was asked to join the first Conference of Negro-African writers involved in the *négritude* movement, attempting to assert their shared black cultural identity as writers. Wright also worked on a novel set in Paris, *Island of Hallucination*. He had misgivings about it,

PHOTO 12   Richard Wright lived at 14 rue Monsieur le Prince

which he expressed to his agent, Paul Reynolds, when he sent
him a draft in early 1959: 'I can readily think of a hundred
reasons why Americans won't like this book. But the book
is true. Everything in the book happened, but I've twisted
characters so that people won't recognise them.'

Characters were indeed based on himself and people he
met then. Fishbelly, the chief protagonist, who had appeared
in *The Long Dream*, has escaped to Europe to get away from
the racial nightmare in his homeland. Newly arrived in Paris,
he marvels at the relaxed attitude of whites towards him: 'I've
been toting a hundred-pound sack of potatoes on my back
all my life and it's goddamned good to get rid of it.'

Wright was worried that the novel would get the same
treatment as *The Long Dream*, and if it did then: 'I must
seriously think of abandoning writing for a time. One has
to be realistic.' He had moreover become disenchanted with
Paris, once considered 'a city of refuge'. In the Café Monaco
near his home and in Café Tournon he would preside over
a group of young compatriots in exile, but began gradually

to feel under threat from them. He had been deeply hurt by Baldwin's essay 'Everybody's Protest Novel' (collected in *Notes of a Native Son*) which appeared in the spring of 1949 in the first issue of *Zero*, a Left Bank magazine. In the essay Baldwin, his former protégé, argued that Wright's fiction perpetuated the familiar 'lust and fury' situation instead of really helping the black cause. Wright, under surveillance, felt increasingly beleaguered by agents of the CIA and the FBI. According to the English poet Christopher Logue, in Paris at the time, the atmosphere at the Café Tournon was poisonous: 'Everybody thought everybody else was spying on someone or other for somebody.'

It has been claimed that Wright was himself reporting on others. He had visited the American Embassy in September 1954, possibly to provide information on some alleged Communist Party members, in return for a much-needed passport. *Island of Hallucination* describes the unpleasant situation experienced by Fishbelly, who finds himself hounded after the initial excitement of arriving in Paris.

By 1959 a disillusioned Wright was planning to move to London, but after a series of rebuffs when applying for a visa he stayed in Paris, where he died unexpectedly the next year in mysterious circumstances. A few months before his death he had written to his friend, the Dutch translator Margrit de Sablonière: 'You must not worry about my being in danger ... I am not exactly unknown here and I have personal friends in the de Gaulle cabinet itself. Of course, I don't want anything to happen to me, but if it does my friends will know exactly where it comes from ... So far as the Americans are concerned, I'm worse than a Communist, for my work falls like a shadow across their policy in Asia and

Africa … They've asked me time and again to work for them: but I'd rather die first.'

Separated from his family and feeling threatened, he had fallen ill in June 1959 and was diagnosed with amœbic dysentery. Ill again the following November, from the small flat where he was now living in rue Régis near Sèvres-Babylone, he checked into the Eugène Gibez clinic in rue Vaugirard, where he died the same night of a heart attack. It was reported that a mysterious Hungarian woman had visited his bedside an hour before his death.

In his memoir, *My Life of Absurdity* (1976), one of his closest friends, the writer Chester Himes, in Paris at the time, reported that Wright felt he 'was being persecuted'. In October 1990 his daughter Julia Wright suggested in an interview that there might have been 'a CIA plot to isolate him, in order to make him more vulnerable … it was sufficient that a man be sick, isolated and poor to drive him to his death'. It is impossible to ascertain whether foul play was involved, as he was cremated before a post-mortem could be undertaken. His ashes are in the columbarium at Père Lachaise Cemetery (box 848). His biographer Hazel Rowley quotes Ollie Harrington, Wright's friend, who rushed to his bedside after his death: 'I've never met a black person who did *not* believe that Richard Wright was done in. By whom, I don't know … There are so many possibilities.'

In John Alfred Williams's spy novel *The Man Who Cried I Am* (1967) Max Reddick, a black novelist and journalist, has a friend and mentor, Harry Ames, an expatriate and former Communist living in Paris. Harry is killed as he uncovers a sinister plan to eliminate people of African descent, the 'King Alfred Plan'. The book is widely considered a fictionalised account of Richard Wright's life and death.

In 1946 the French jazz musician and writer Boris Vian, who had translated some of Wright's short stories, using the pseudonym of a fictional black American expatriate writer, Vernon Sullivan, decided to write a thriller, claiming to have translated it into French from the American original. He gave it the provocative title, *J'irai cracher sur vos tombes*. With the collaboration of Milton Rosenthal, a colleague at *Temps Modernes*, they translated it into English and published it in 1948 through a fictitious publisher they called The Vendôme Press as *I Shall Spit on Your Graves*. Whereas his novels written in French had not done well, this one in English caused uproar, followed by a court case and a ban, leading to a huge *succès de scandale*. In 1959 Boris Vian also met his death in unusual circumstances, struck down by a heart attack during a screening of the film version in Paris, while shouting his vehement disapproval of the adaptation.

Wright's former protégé **James Baldwin** (1924–87) paid a warm tribute to him after his death in an essay, 'Alas, Poor Richard', stating that 'The man I fought so hard and who meant so much for me is gone.' He admitted how much he owed him: '[He] saw clearly enough, far more clearly than I had dared to allow myself to see, what I had done: I had used his work as a springboard into my own.'

In 1948, an angry and confused Baldwin, desperate to leave the US and its prejudice against colour and homosexuality, had considered going to Israel but had opted for Paris as the journey was more affordable. Once the one-way air ticket had been bought, he was left with just forty dollars. He would explain in an interview for *The Paris Review* in the spring of 1984 how he had come to the painful decision to leave New York and his family: 'It wasn't so much a matter of choosing France – it was a matter of getting out of America. I didn't know what was going to happen to me in France, but I knew what was going to happen to me in New York. If I had stayed there, I would have gone under, like my friend on the George Washington Bridge.' (His friend Eugene Worth had thrown himself from the bridge in New York in 1946.)

On the night of his arrival in November 1948 he was taken to Les Deux Magots, where he was greeted by Richard Wright, whom he had known in New York. Wright had secured him a grant and immediately introduced him to the editor of *Zero*, a new publication, in the first issue of which Baldwin's essay 'Everybody's Protest Novel' duly appeared. It was a good start for an unknown writer, who had just arrived. It was a relief to be in France and to feel accepted as a black man. Now he could develop as a writer. Baldwin felt that his decision to leave the US had been necessary and had saved his life. 'In some deep, black, stony and liberating way, my life, in my own eyes, began during that first year in Paris.'

Life was exciting but tough. Wright found him lodgings in the cheap Hôtel de Rome on the boulevard Saint-Michel, and he would escape from the cold space to work in the Café de Flore, where the upstairs room was a favourite haunt of gay men.

There were compensations, however, and in an article for *Esquire* magazine in May 1961 he told of his joy of feeling liberated in Paris: 'The days when we walked through Les Halles singing, loving every inch of France and loving each other ... the jam sessions in Pigalle, and our stories about the whores there ... the nights spent smoking hashish in the Arab cafés ... the morning which found us telling dirty stories, true stories, sad and earnest stories, in grey workingmen's cafes.'

Always broke, he had problems paying the rent, and left the Hôtel de Rome for another cheap hotel, Hôtel Verneuil

PHOTO 13   Baldwin did much of his writing in Le Flore

at 8 rue de Verneuil in the seventh arrondissement, where
Otto Friedrich, another young writer, was already staying.
In 'Jimmy', an essay collected in *The Grave of Alice B. Toklas
And Other Reports from the Past* (1989) Friedrich described
the grim hotel: 'The room was about four feet wide and ten
feet long, with a window that wouldn't stay shut, and the
September winds blew cold. This grimy little room cost eight
dollars a month ... The rooms above were dark and dingy,
and the whole hotel had only two toilets, of the kind in
which you have to stand or squat over two footrests next to a
hole in the floor ... the Dumonts were paternalistic ... and
they did not mind people cooking in their rooms.'

   Another occupant was Mary Keen, a 'warm-hearted'
English socialist working for the World Federation of Trade
Unions, until her views caused her to be expelled from
France. She could afford to buy food and cooked for the
many that could not. She would sometimes lend her room
to Baldwin when she went away and he could not afford

to pay for his. It was a generous but unwise decision, as he would return it in a pitiful state, having 'borrowed' some of her belongings, her typewriter and her duffel coat (this last was never returned, to her lasting irritation). He was looked after when he caught a bad cold which developed into pneumonia. Madame Dumont, the owner of the hotel, brought him back to health: 'To my surprise I wasn't thrown out of the hotel. This Corsican family, for reasons I'll never understand, took care of me. An old, old lady, a great old matriarch, nursed me back to health after three months; she used old folk remedies. And she had to climb five flights of stairs every morning to make sure I was kept alive.'

Baldwin had become embroiled in a feud with his former mentor Richard Wright over his article for *Zero* in which he attacked the 'protest novel' (such as the ones written by Richard Wright), as being too sentimental. Baldwin wrote again for *Zero* in 1949, producing an article on homosexuality, 'The Preservation of Innocence'. In Paris he was allowed to live more openly and to express himself more freely, and this led to the ground-breaking novels for which he is remembered now. His reading had widened and Otto Friedrich had introduced him to the writing of Henry James. In an interview with his biographer David Leeming he acknowledged that he could have not written without James's influence: 'James became, in a sense, my master. It was something about point of view, something about discipline.' In 1953 his first novel, *Go Tell It on the Mountain*, was published and well received. The book, largely based on his Harlem childhood, brought him a Guggenheim grant which made him marginally better off. Much of his writing was done in the Café de Flore or Brasserie Lipp, but he was also seen at Le Montana on rue Saint-Benoît or Chez Inez on rue Champollion. Unlike Wright he had limited contact with French writers, as initially he spoke little French, and socialised mainly with Americans like Truman Capote, Saul Bellow and Norman Mailer. In more *louche* districts like Les Halles and Pigalle he would mix with American students, mostly former GIs, and in his essay, 'Encounter on the Seine' (in *Notes of a Native Son*, 1955), he looks at their experience (and his own disillusion), once bleak reality has taken over from the romance of being in Paris: 'They are willing, apparently at least for a season, to endure the wretched Parisian plumbing, the public baths, the Paris age, and dirt – to pursue some end, mysterious and largely inarticulate, arbitrarily summed up in the verb *to study*.'

Permanently broke and in debt, he lived hand-to-mouth, and when desperate would hang around the Arab district, where he could eat very cheaply, sometimes ending up singing in a local nightclub. He felt a great affinity with the Arab immigrants, 'my brothers' whom he got to know well: 'I lived mainly among *les misérables* – and in Paris *les misérables* are Algerian …' This emerges in the short story 'This Morning, This Evening, So Soon' (in *Going to Meet the Man*, 1965): 'Most of them had no money. They lived three or four together in rooms with a single skylight, a single hard cot, or in buildings that seemed abandoned, with cardboard in the windows, with erratic plumbing in a wet, cobblestoned yard, in dark, dead-end alleys, or on the outer, chilling heights of Paris.'

When he could not afford to stay at the Hôtel Verneuil he moved to the (not very grand) Grand Hôtel du Bac. The room he occupied there would inspire the novel he was working on, *Giovanni's Room* (1956), the story of a gay love affair set in a tough city for expatriates, condemned to a deep sense of isolation.

The lowest point in Baldwin's time in Paris was in December 1949 when the police turned up at the Hôtel du Bac, accusing him of being in possession of stolen goods. An American acquaintance had given him a sheet which he had stolen from his own hotel. Both were arrested and the Kafkaesque following week spent in prison is beautifully told in his short story 'Equal in Paris' (1955). Baldwin makes the point that during the whole terrible ordeal he was not treated as a black but simply as an American: 'That evening in the commissariat I was not a despised black man. They would simply have laughed at me if I had behaved like one. For them I was an American.'

'Equal in Paris' also gives a lively sense of how he tried to work: 'The moment I began living in French hotels I understood the necessity of French cafés. This made it rather difficult to look me up, for soon as I was out of bed I hopefully took note-book and fountain pen off to the upstairs room of the Flore, where I consumed a lot of coffee and, as evening approached, rather a lot of alcohol, but did not get much writing done.' In a notorious gay bar, La Reine Blanche, Baldwin met a Swiss artist, Lucien Happersberger. Invited by Lucien to spend a few months in his parents' chalet in a remote Swiss village, Baldwin was able to complete *Go Tell It on the Mountain*. He was becoming tired of Paris, where he felt he could no longer work. From 1953 to 1957 he moved between Corsica, Istanbul and New York, and when occasionally back in Paris stayed with the painter Beauford Delaney, who made a stunning portrait of him.

A large part of *Giovanni's Room* was written in Le Select Café in Montparnasse and the novel is set in 1950s Paris. David, the white American narrator, tells the story of his ill-fated love affair with Giovanni, an Italian barman. After

meeting in the bar where Giovanni works they spend the
night in Les Halles market with its 'choked boulevards and
impossible side-streets ... Leeks, onions, cabbages, oranges,
apples, potatoes, cauliflowers, stood gleaming in mounds
all over, in the sidewalks, in the streets, before great metal
sheds.' The book once again portrays the desperate life for
expatriates, spent in sleazy bars and gloomy rooms. Because
of its touchy subject the book did not easily find a publisher,
but it was eventually accepted by Dial Press in 1956.

Paris appears again briefly in Baldwin's third novel *Another
Country* (1962) where Eric, (the alter ego of Baldwin in Paris)
remembers how he found his partner Yves in '... the Rue des
Ss. Pères on a spring evening, and his thoughts had not been
pretty. Paris seemed, and had seemed for a long time, the
loneliest city under heaven. ... Contrary to its legend, Paris
does not offer many distractions ... Then the discontented
wanderer is thrown back on himself – if his life is to become
bearable, only he can make it so.'

Paris plays a part in most of Baldwin's novels, which tend
to be partly autobiographical. In his sixth novel, *Just Above
My Head* (1979), the main protagonist Arthur, a gospel
singer and a homosexual, is involved in a love affair in Paris,
frequenting familiar landmarks, Brasserie Lipp and Café
de Flore. Baldwin wrote several screenplays, but few of his
novels have been made into films. After *Go Tell It on the
Mountain* was adapted for the screen in January 1953 and
for television in 1985, further projects came to nothing. He
had hoped to see a film version of *Giovanni's Room* with
Marlon Brando in the role of Guillaume, the unpleasant
bar owner employing Giovanni, but no producer showed
interest in the project. *If Beale Street Could Talk* (1974)
appeared on the screen in 2018.

Once a recognised author, Baldwin felt an obligation to join the civil rights movement and started spending more time in the US, but he returned to France in 1960, disillusioned. He died of cancer at his French country retreat in Saint-Paul-de-Vence in the South of France in 1987, a year after he was awarded the *Légion d'honneur*.

The year 1931, which saw the huge colonial exhibition in the Bois de Vincennes, was also the year when **Aimé Césaire** (1913–2008), like many young people from French colonies, arrived in Paris to complete his education. Césaire was from a humble background in Martinique (in the Lesser Antilles); however, because of his academic excellence, he was selected to be sent to Paris with a French Government scholarship. He was to spend his first year at the prestigious Lycée Louis-le-Grand at 123 rue Saint-Jacques in the fifth arrondissement, in order to prepare for the competitive entrance exam for admission to the École Normale Supérieure. The eighteen-year-old was in for a shock on arrival: 'My first impression of Paris. It was all the shouting. My God, nothing but Negroes, so many Negroes! Because the Gare St Lazare had been taken over by the Antilles. The whole crowd consisted of my compatriots. All had come to meet the boat train …'

Overcoming his bewilderment, he soon made friends with compatriots and with an African from Senegal, Léopold Senghor. Their meeting, at the Cité internationale universitaire at 55 boulevard Jourdan where they were living, was crucial: 'He taught me the greatness and nobility of Africa.' Through Senghor, Césaire discovered an Africa he knew little about: 'Senghor introduced me to a whole continent. It was a world about which I had the vaguest notion … To understand Martinique, to understand the Antilles, I had to go via Africa.' It was an important discovery for someone who had also just discovered Europe: 'Meeting him was a counterbalance to the influence of European culture. Senghor, with whom I lived for almost ten years before the war in the Quartier Latin, had a considerable impact on my own personal world.' Paris was the place where he was coming to terms with his newly discovered racial identity, which would dominate his writing: 'In Paris just as I was discovering the culture, I better understood the reasons for my own dissatisfaction: I became aware that I belonged to the original condition of the Negro. My poetry was born of this realisation.'

This led him in 1935 to found a review, *L'Étudiant noir* (The Black Student) with Léopold Senghor and Léon Damas from French Guiana. He explained how the concept of '*négritude*' came about as a response to prejudice, and how they turned the negative word *nègre* into a positive notion, a celebration of African culture, values and character: 'One day, I was crossing a road in Paris, not far from the place d'Italie. A character drove by in in a car: "Hey, little nigger!" He was French. So I said, "The little nigger says go to hell!" The next day I suggested to Senghor that we start a review together, *L'Étudiant noir*.' Césaire explained in an interview: 'Our idea was to have the concept of a specific African identity, a specific black identity. But Senghor and I were always careful not to fall into black racism ...'

For them *négritude* was the awareness of the cultural and historical consequence of being African like Senghor or of African descent like Césaire, in a white-dominated world. *Négritude* encouraged black people to take pride in their African roots and to renew their links with tradition. Caribbean people of African descent and Africans had been denied their history, with their cultural heritage assimilated by force into white culture. It was essential to promote

African culture and then to focus on the situation of black Americans and their struggle for equal civil rights.

In 1935 Césaire was admitted to the École Normale Supérieure, where he studied literature and philosophy. In 1937 he married his compatriot Suzanne Roussi in the Mairie du 13ème in Paris, and the couple moved back to Martinique in 1939 with their young son. There in 1941 they founded a literary review, *Tropiques*. The French Surrealist poet André Breton, who was at the time staying in Martinique to keep away from the war, came across the review and championed Césaire's writing. Césaire had been teaching in a lycée in the island's capital, Fort-de-France, and had started on a long poem, *Cahier d'un retour au pays natal* (Notebook of a Return to the Native Land, 1939), based on his personal and powerful perception of the ambiguities of Caribbean life and culture. He had noted in a *cahier* (exercise book) the feelings of anger and frustration he had experienced during his eight years of exile.

Trained in the Classics, Césaire was familiar with Homer's *Odyssey*, which he adapted in his long poem to demonstrate the rift he experienced between assimilation into European culture and the urge to break free from colonialism, racial prejudice and oppression. *Cahier* was eventually published to acclaim in the highest of French literary circles. Jean-Paul Sartre wrote: 'Surrealism, a European poetic movement, is stolen from the Europeans by a black man who turns it against them.' The father of Surrealism, André Breton, particularly appreciated the poem's Surrealist elements and contributed a warm introduction to the 1947 edition: 'the poem is nothing less than the greatest lyrical monument of our times.'

Another Surrealist poet, Benjamin Péret, added further praise: 'I am proud to salute here the first great black poet to cast off and launch himself without any concern for a Pole

Star, for any intellectual Southern Cross, his only guide his own blind desire.'

Césaire and his concept of *négritude* was now showing the way to French-speaking black writers, who were encouraged to demonstrate a new sense of pride and dignity: 'my negritude is not a stone / its deafness hurled against the clamor of the day,' he wrote. 'my negritude is neither tower nor cathedral / it takes root in the red flesh of the soil / it takes root in the ardent flesh of the sky.'

Césaire spent the rest of his life teaching and writing, mainly for the theatre in order to reach a wider audience, rewriting Shakespeare in *Une Tempête* (A Tempest, 1969), or denouncing colonial crimes, as in *Une saison au Congo* (A Season in the Congo, 1967). He served as mayor of Fort-de-France, and from 1946 until 1993 was simultaneously *député* (MP) for Martinique in the French National Assembly, during which time his Paris residence was at 8 rue Albert Bayet in the thirteenth arrondissement. His message that 'no race possesses the monopoly of beauty, intelligence or strength' had a huge impact, and Paris remembers him with a school, a street – quai Aimé Césaire in the first arrondissement (near to quai François Mitterrand) – and a library. A Métro station bearing his name is being constructed in Aubervilliers.

Léopold Sédar Senghor (1906–2001) left Senegal in 1928 for 'sixteen years of wandering' which started with a year at the Lycée Louis-le-Grand to prepare for the competitive entrance exam to the École Normale Supérieure. He lived cheaply at the Cité internationale universitaire but was struggling financially, as his full grant took some time to arrive. Like his compatriots he suffered from loneliness and racial discrimination, evident in the poetry he started to write, encouraged possibly by a fellow student, the future French president Georges Pompidou, who introduced him to the poetry of Baudelaire and became a friend. Pompidou had started to compile *Une anthologie de la poésie française* (An Anthology of French Poetry). Failing at the first attempt to win a place in the ENS entrance examination, Senghor prepared for the *Agrégation*, another competitive exam, which he passed in 1935. It was a great achievement, as he was the first African to do so. This qualified him to teach at the Lycée René-Descartes in Tours and then in Saint-Maur-des-Fossés near Paris, while pursuing his studies in ethnology and linguistics at the École Pratique des Hautes Études, in rue Ferrus in the fourteenth arrondissement.

As with Césaire, the idea of *négritude* was predominant in Senghor's writing and remained a guiding principle when he later started a career in politics. As a reaction against the dominance of French culture in the colonies, and the established idea that Africa did not have a culture developed enough to stand alongside that of Europe, he pointed out that 'the Negro has reactions which are more lived, in the sense that they are more direct and concrete expressions of the sensation, and of the stimulus, and so of the object itself, with all its original qualities and power.' He stressed that Africans can make a positive contribution to Europe and in *Ce que je crois* (What I Believe, 1988) he urged African writers 'to assimilate so as not to be assimilated' and to appropriate European literary innovations while holding fast to their own identities.

At the outbreak of World War II Senghor enlisted in the French army, and was captured by the Germans and imprisoned between 1940 to 1942 before being released on medical grounds. During his internment he started writing poems, and once freed resumed his teaching career, while remaining involved in the Resistance. After the war he was selected as Dean of the Linguistics Department at the École nationale de la France d'Outre-Mer, an institution for the education of colonial administrators. He held the position until Senegal's independence, when he became the first President of the Republic of Senegal on 5 September 1960. From 1946 to 1955 he was married to Ginette, daughter of Felix Éboué, an intellectual and the first black colonial administrator, and from 1956 his second wife was a Frenchwoman, Colette Hubert from Normandy. In 1948, Senghor compiled and edited a volume of francophone poetry, as a kind of *négritude* manifesto, *Anthologie de la nouvelle poésie nègre et malgache de langue française* (Anthology of New Black and Malagasy Poetry in French), for which Jean-Paul Sartre wrote an introduction, entitled '*Orphée Noir*' (Black Orpheus). It included Senghor's work as well as that of Aimé Césaire and the French Guianese poet Léon Damas.

By then *négritude* had in the words of Jacques Chevrier, professor of African literature at the Sorbonne, become 'amazingly fashionable' and the French intelligentsia had embraced it as it 'represented exoticism' and 'questioned Western rationality'. Some of the most illustrious intellectuals in France, Sartre, André Gide and Michel Leiris, were actively involved with the *négritude* review, *Présence Africaine*, launched by Alioune Diop in 1947, and expanded in 1949 to include a publishing house. Africa had started to influence artists in Paris at the beginning of the twentieth century, challenging established European aesthetics and inspiring avant-garde intellectual and artistic movements like Surrealism, Cubism and Primitivism, without forgetting the vogue for jazz. Now, in his introduction to the anthology,

Jean-Paul Sartre predicted that *négritude* would play a vital role in the fight against all forms of oppression.

Senghor became *député* (MP) representing both Senegal and Mauritania, French colonies which had been granted the right of representation by elected individuals. He was an advisory minister in Michel Debré's government from 1959 to 1961, and was the first African to sit in the prestigious *Académie française* when he was elected on 2 June 1983. When he died his seat (no. 16) was taken by the former French president, Valéry Giscard d'Estaing. He was made *Grande-Croix de la légion d'honneur*, *Grande-Croix de l'Ordre national du Mérite*, commander of arts and letters. For his war exploits he was awarded the medal of *Reconnaissance Franco-alliée 1939–45* and the combatant cross 1939–45. Although he died in France, a state funeral was held for him on 29 December 2001 in Dakar, the capital of Senegal. The footbridge *Passerelle Solférino* in Paris, which crosses the Seine near the French Parliament, was renamed after him in 2006, on the centenary of his birth.

Frantz Fanon (1925–61), also from Martinique, had been taught by Césaire in 1941 at the Lycée Schoelcher in Fort-de-France, where Césaire became a kind of mentor and encouraged him to go to France. Once in Paris, Fanon abandoned his plans to study dentistry, and moved to Lyon where he studied psychoanalysis instead. In *Peau noire, masques blancs* (Black Skin, White Masks), published in 1952, he dealt with the effect colonialism had on the individual's racial consciousness. His political and intellectual influence was to reach well into the second half of the twentieth century, supported and admired by left-wing philosophers and writers, especially Jean-Paul Sartre.

In the 1920s and 1930s, Spaniards trying to break free from the restrictive regime in their country moved to Paris, which became a haven for political dissidents during the Spanish Civil War and Franco's dictatorship. Modernism and the Surrealist movement in Paris appealed to writers, and to artists like the Catalan painter **Joan Miró** (1893–1983), hailed by the Surrealist André Breton as 'the most Surrealist of us all'. Miró recalled how inspiration came to him: 'How did I think up my drawings and my ideas for painting? Well I'd come home to my Paris studio in Rue Blomet at night, I'd go to bed, and sometimes I hadn't any supper. I saw things, and I jotted them down in a notebook. I saw shapes on the ceiling …'

In 1899 the poet **Antonio Machado** (1875–1939) visited Paris with his brother, both staying at the Hôtel Médicis, at 56 rue Monsieur le Prince, and working for the publishing house Garnier. Machado was back in 1902 for a few months during which he met other expatriates, including Pío Baroja and Rubén Darío, at the Cabaret des Quat'z'Arts. Despite a good command of French, Machado had relatively few contacts with Parisians and the city is mentioned in his letters only where he refers to meeting Oscar Wilde at the Moulin Rouge and a visit to the Théâtre Antoine. Politically active, he took part in a demonstration in support of Dreyfus. For him Paris was associated with unhappiness; on his third visit in 1911, during which he attended classes with the philosopher Bergson at the Collège de France, his young wife Leonor, with him in an hotel in rue Perronet, was admitted to the Maison de santé, 200 faubourg Saint-Denis, suffering from tuberculosis. Machado just about managed to raise enough money to repatriate her to Spain, but she died the following summer.

His friend, **Pío Baroja** (1872–1956), a writer much admired by Hemingway, took refuge in Paris when the

Spanish Civil War broke out in 1936. He knew the city well as he had been there on many occasions since 1899. He found cheap (if not free) lodgings at Colegio de España at the Cité internationale universitaire. In this student residence the sixty-four-year-old Basque writer felt isolated and out of place. He missed his homeland, and the so-called City of Light seemed a cold and hostile place. Feeling very much a foreigner, he mixed mainly with Spaniards. In his books, his protagonists tend to be thoroughly miserable in their Parisian exile, dominated by loneliness and deep poverty. He moved out of the students' residence when it was to be used as a hospital, and joined his fellow writer Azorín in his flat at 14 rue de Tilsitt near the Arc de Triomphe, the same building into which the Scott Fitzgeralds were to move.

In his autobiographical *Paseos de un solitario* (Solitary Wanderings, 1955), Baroja gives an account of his life as an expatriate, as he does in *Paris no se acaba* (Never Any End to Paris, a phrase used by Hemingway in *A Moveable Feast*), set entirely in Paris. In fact the city appears in more than twenty-five of his novels, but is usually perceived negatively from the exile's point of view. Life there must have had some positive aspects, as in his correspondence he reports visits to the Louvre, where he admired paintings by Botticelli, and an invitation to lecture at the Sorbonne. On one occasion a dinner was organised in his honour at the Closerie des Lilas, a place he particularly favoured. A *flâneur*, he walked endlessly in the Latin Quarter, which he got to know very well. A loner and a misanthropist, he describes the French as '*petulante*' and '*dogmatico*'. He also accuses them of being avaricious, and bitterly resented the fact that they paid little attention to his work. 'My books do not give me the prestige of a gazetteer among writers in Paris,' he wrote in his memoirs. 'Many times I think that it would be more comfortable to die ... so as not to go out at night and spend the minimum. I often keep the breakfast roll and then, at night, it serves as dinner.'

Paris was nevertheless a place where he could write. He had come 'not to get to know the city, for seeing it once was enough ... but to gain a broader and more international viewpoint'. He was an admirer of the great French writers, particularly Verlaine, whom he considered '*el ultimo gran poeta del mundo*', 'the last great world poet'. Baroja, who had written articles against Hitler, had to leave Paris in 1940 when the Nazis occupied the city. He died in Spain, where Hemingway attended his bedside a few days before his death.

The filmmaker **Luis Buñuel** (1900–83) arrived in Paris in 1925. In his memoirs, *My Last Breath* (1983), he describes the following four years he spent on and off in Paris, where he met his Surrealist friends Aragon, Dalí, Masson and Miró, at Café Cyrano, at 3 rue Biot in the seventeenth arrondissement. He also mentions Picasso, whom he found uncongenial. On arrival he headed for 'Hôtel Ronceray in the passage Jouffroy ... where, incidentally I'd been conceived!' He then moved to the Hôtel Saint-Pierre, in rue de l'École-de-Médecine, 'just a moment away from the Boulevard Saint-Michel'. He later found a furnished flat at 3 bis, place de la Sorbonne. He loved the Latin Quarter, where he felt liberated as he marvelled at the 'cultural surprises, like couples kissing in the street and unmarried men and women living together ... At this time Paris was considered the capital of the artistic world.'

Speaking some French, like so many of his compatriots, he secured a job as secretary of the newly founded International Society of Intellectual Cooperation, but he was soon working for the film industry. There he came across Josephine Baker, by whom he was unimpressed: 'the whims of the star appalled and disgusted me. Expected to be ready and on the set at nine in the morning, she'd arrive at five in the afternoon, storm into her dressing room, slam the door, and begin smashing makeup bottles against the wall.'

In 1928 he made his first breakthrough film, *Un Chien Andalou* (An Andalusian Dog). It was co-written with Salvador Dalí and shown in 1929 at the Studio des Ursulines in the fifth arrondissement. The film was deeply influenced by Surrealism and dreams: 'I made *Un Chien Andalou*, which came from an encounter between two dreams.' Buñuel acknowledged his debt to the Marquis de Sade, especially with his next film, *L'Âge d'or* (Age of Gold, 1930): 'His ideas have influenced me in many ways,' but after this film the partnership with Salvador Dalí started to flag. Buñuel resented Dalí's Russian wife Gala and thought she was having a negative effect on his friend. Both films were nevertheless key cultural events in Paris. *Un Chien Andalou*, financed by Buñuel's mother, had been attended by everyone who was anyone in Paris and enjoyed an unexpected success, but things went differently with *L'Âge d'or* in 1930.

Buñuel's generous patron, Vicomte Charles de Noailles, who had found *Un Chien Andalou* 'exquisite and delicious', financed and produced *L'Âge d'or* with his wife, Marie-Laure de Noailles, a decision he perhaps regretted. They were threatened with excommunication by the Catholic Church, which was outraged at the daringly blasphemous content of the film. Battles took place during a showing at Studio 28 at 10 rue Tholozé in the eighteenth arrondissement, and after its launch it remained censored in France for fifty years.

After the election of the Spanish Republican government in 1931, Buñuel worked in an office in rue de la Pépinière cataloguing Spanish Republican propaganda films, but he also spent much time at the cinema or the theatre and directed a short play. By 1938 Buñuel had had enough of Paris, and moved to California and then New York. He did return to Paris however, to shoot films in his favourite Parisian locations, one the Hôtel Aiglon at 232 boulevard Raspail in the fourteenth arrondissement, used for *Belle de jour* (1967) (an adaptation of the scandalous novel by Joseph Kessel, published in 1928), and *The Discreet Charm of the Bourgeoisie* (1972). He used Suite 59, no doubt amused because of its view over Montparnasse Cemetery.

His friend **Salvador Dalí** (1904–89) first visited Paris in 1926, and was back again in 1927. It was then that he met Gala, who was still married to the French Surrealist poet Paul Éluard. After she left Éluard, she moved with Dalí to a flat at 7 rue Becquerel. Reputedly rebellious, Dalí encountered problems with the Surrealist group and particularly with its guru André Breton. The breach was inevitable and he was duly expelled from the group in 1939, moving to the US a year later with Gala. Both Dalí and Buñuel appear in Woody Allen's amusing film *Midnight in Paris*, but without Gala.

Buñuel and many of his compatriots would gather at 2 rue La Pérouse in the small room occupied by the great Spanish philosopher and poet **Miguel de Unamuno** (1864–1936). Unamuno was spending a year of his exile (which lasted from 1924 to 1930) in Paris, arriving on 9 July 1924 from Fuerteventura. In 1925 he published *De Fuerteventura a París: Diario íntimo de confinamiento y destierro vertido en sonetos* (From Fuerteventura to Paris: An Intimate Diary of Confinement and Exile Poured Out in Sonnets):

From the sad banks of the Seine
The first sonnet came to me here in Paris

Here in Paris which has no mountains,
No plains, no sea ...

He also conjures up the presence of Trotsky in the city: 'From
here Trotsky drew faith and hope / dreaming of a paradise to
come.'

At the end of the Spanish Civil War, many more followed
Unamuno into exile, fleeing Francoist Spain, like **Jorge
Semprún** (1923–2011). He had arrived in Paris in 1939 aged
fifteen, and completed his secondary education there, attending
the Lycée Henri IV. Semprún wrote primarily in French. In
an interview discussing his memoir *Adieu, vive clarté* (Farewell,
Vivid Light, 1998), for whose title he uses a line from Baudelaire,
he describes his discovery of adolescence and of exile, of Paris,
the world, women, and importantly, the French language.
There 'a young Spaniard of sixteen, having reached France with
his family after the fall of the Republican government, makes
the double discovery in Paris of humiliation and revelation.'
He recalls a traumatic but critical turn in his life: 'A foul-
mouthed baker on the boulevard Saint-Michel mocks his
accent and throws him out of her shop, calling him "a Spaniard
on the losing side".' After this public humiliation he took the
momentous decision to turn it to his advantage. He proceeded
to eradicate any foreign accent from his French and to seek
solace in literature, starting with a book he particularly admired,
the satire *Paludes* (Morasses, 1895) by the French writer André
Gide: 'The baker's wife of boulevard Saint-Michel excluded
me from the community, but André Gide reintegrated me
surreptitiously. By the light of his prose, I crossed clandestinely
over the border into my probable land of asylum.'

Semprún joined the Resistance in his teens to fight with
the French against Nazi occupation, and was interned in

1943 in Buchenwald. Liberated in 1945, he subsequently spent a great part of his life in Paris living in rue Daubigny and then in rue Félix Ziem in Montmartre. His second wife was the French actress Loleh Bellon, and then from 1958 he was married to the French film editor Colette Leloup, with whom he had five children.

Spanish exiles generally managed to live in relative comfort in Paris, as they often spoke French, which allowed them to find better-paid work. For Latin Americans the language barrier was more of a problem, but for them too Paris remained mandatory for any aspiring writer or artist. The Mexican painter **Diego Rivera** (1886–1957) was aware of this when he decided to spend much of his youth there, a time he recalled in a 1944 interview that later became *My Art, My Life: An Autobiography* (1991).

A steady stream followed, including the Cuban Alejo Carpentier, the Peruvian César Vallejo, the Argentine Julio Cortázar, and Miguel Ángel Asturias from Guatemala. They were seeking the myth of the French city, which in some way served as their cultural capital. 'Paris is everything,' wrote the great Nicaraguan poet **Rubén Darío** (1867–1916), who had first visited the city in 1892 and then spent much time there between 1900 and the outbreak of war in 1914. He had dreamed about Paris since he was a child: 'Paris was for me like a paradise in which you breathed the essence of earthly happiness. It was the city of Art, Beauty and Glory; and, above all, the capital of Love, the land of dreams. And when I arrived at St Lazare station, and stepped onto Parisian soil, I believed I was stepping on hallowed ground.' He stayed first in a simple Spanish hotel, now gone, next to the Bourse, styling itself the Grand Hôtel de la Bourse et des Ambassadeurs. From 1909 to 1912 he was at 4 rue Herschel, where his time in the building is marked with a plaque. He records a brief meeting with Oscar Wilde in 1900 and time spent with his compatriots in Bar Calisayo, as well as with other Surrealist writers and artists at Café Cyrano.

A *flâneur*, he loved walking in the Jardin du Luxembourg and socialised at the Closerie des Lilas nearby. An encounter with the Spanish poet Machado took place in 1902, and his appointment in 1903 as Consul for Nicaragua in Paris allowed him to meet artists and intellectuals from all over the world. He earned his living by reporting for the Argentinian daily *La Nación de Buenos Aires* on the Paris of the Belle Époque, including an article on the 1900 *Exposition universelle*: 'Paris, 20 April 1900. As I write the vast fair has opened. Not all the installations are complete: if you tour the huge array of palaces and pavilions, you are at risk of being covered with dust. But wave upon wave of a human tide has flooded the streets of this fantastic town in which towers, golden domes and spires have sprouted, planting their splendour in this great city.' His detailed chronicles on Paris, written between 1901–02, were also collected in *La caravana pasa* (The Caravan Passes, 1902). Although initially speaking little French, he was well informed on cultural events in the city and from 1911–14 he was in charge of *Mundial Magazine*, a cultural review in which he also published some of his poems. He is generally considered to be in the vanguard of Modernist Spanish poetry, strongly influenced by Hugo and Gautier, and by Verlaine, whom he had met at Café d'Harcourt (which stood on the corner of 47 boulevard Saint-Michel and 8 place de la Sorbonne) on his first visit to Paris. The meeting was disappointing, as he saw 'the Faun, surrounded by dubious acolytes' but was unable to engage with the inebriated French poet, his idol.

Darío loved Paris: '*Mi esposa es de mi tierra, mi querida de Paris*' ('My wife is from my homeland, my beloved from Paris'), but became disillusioned with the city towards the end of his life. He died in Nicaragua and is commemorated in Paris with a statue at 1 square de l'Amérique-Latine in the seventeenth arrondissement.

The Peruvian poet **César Vallejo** (1892–1938) was also in Paris in the early 1920s. Finding it hard to make a living from journalism and teaching, life was tough as he could afford only cheap hotels, occasionally even sleeping rough in the Métro. An innovative poet, Paris appears fleetingly in his poems, most published posthumously. Curiously in his sonnet *Me moriré in Paris*, written probably in 1936, he foresaw his own death:

I will die in Paris in a sudden shower
A day I can already remember
I will die in Paris – and I'm sure of it
Perhaps a Thursday, like today, in autumn.

His death did not happen as predicted on a rainy autumn Thursday in Paris, but rather on a rainy autumn Friday. His funeral eulogy was written by Louis Aragon, and his remains were moved on 3 April 1970 by his widow Georgette Vallejo to Montparnasse Cemetery, where she had inscribed on the tombstone the epitaph: '*J'ai tant neigé pour que tu dormes*' ('I've snowed so much so that you will sleep').

A pioneer of contemporary Latin American fiction, **Miguel Asturias** (1899–1974) had left Guatemala in 1923 to study ethnology, more specifically Mayan myths and religion, at the Sorbonne with Georges Raynaud, who was delighted to have a real Mayan attending his lectures. During the ten happy years he spent in Paris he founded the magazine *Tiempos Nuevos* (New Times) and discovered his vocation as a writer, publishing *Leyendas de Guatemala* (Legends of Guatemala, 1931), based on stories and legends from pre-Columbian times. It impressed Paul Valéry, who wrote the preface. Asturias would tell his friends in exile these stories, 'an entire popular heritage', which had been passed on by his mother and her household in Guatemala. In an interview with his friend and biographer Günter W. Lorenz, Asturias acknowledged how much he owed to Surrealism: 'Between the "real" and the "magic" there is a third sort of reality. It is a melting of the visible and the tangible, the hallucination and the dream. It is similar to what the surrealists around Breton wanted and it is what we could call "magic realism".'

His familiar Parisian surroundings, place de la Sorbonne, the university and the Collège de France, with its bohemians, students, artists and exiles, appeared to him as '*un mundo mágico*: you drank wine, you drank Pernod, we congregated in the café Jockey because we were interested in the debates between supporters of different schools of art, to hear Picasso, for example, often saying "I change the world because it is not the world I want".'

Asturias left Paris in 1933 but was back as Guatemalan ambassador to France from 1966–70. He died in Madrid, but is buried in Père Lachaise Cemetery.

The first language of the Cuban writer and musicologist **Alejo Carpentier** (1904–80), was French, as he was born in Lausanne in Switzerland and attended French-speaking schools. His first stay in Paris was with his parents between 1913 and 1921, after which he returned to Cuba to study architecture and music. There the political situation became

chaotic and Carpentier was arrested in 1927 during a
round-up of dissidents. While in prison he began work on
his first novel, *¡Ecue-Yamba-O!* (Lord, Praised be Thou),
eventually published in 1933. After his release he found that
he was blacklisted and under suspicion. The French poet
Robert Desnos, in Cuba at the time, lent him his press card,
which helped him to escape to France. Carpentier spent the
following eleven years (1928 to 1939) in Paris, during which
time he married. He managed to earn a living by writing
editorials for Cuban publications. He went through a brief
association with the Surrealists thanks to Robert Desnos,
who introduced him to André Breton, Giorgio de Chirico
and others. He broke away from them in order to develop
his own concept of what he called '*lo real maravilloso*', a
precursor of magical realism, which became the hallmark
of Latin American fiction. Carpentier's novel *Homenaje a
nuestros amigos de Paris* (1933) is a grateful tribute to the
city which had welcomed him. A gifted musicologist, he
worked for French radio as a writer, publicist and sound-
effects specialist. He also kept his country informed on the
European cultural mood, maintaining while in exile a strong
sense of Latin American pride.

Like so many others, Carpentier left Paris in 1939, but
returned in 1966 to work for his country as a diplomat, and
remained in Europe for the rest of his life. He died in Paris
but is buried in Havana.

5

Flappers and Amazons

The most capital capital of the world.
(Janet Flanner)

By 1900, the image of the Parisian woman was one of elegance, making her an official symbol for France at the World Fair in Paris. Modern women began to take centre stage. They smoked, and cut their hair '*à la garçonne*'. They travelled alone, played sports, rode bikes and drove cars, and wore 'sportswear', though they were not permitted to wear trousers for some years to come, except from 1909 for cycling or horse-riding, and would be denied entry to a café or other public place without a hat.

Coco Chanel and Poiret started to design looser and more comfortable clothes. Increasing financial independence enabled women like the bookseller Sylvia Beach to publish James Joyce's *Ulysses*.

In 1921 male homosexuality was still proscribed in England, and for both men and women this often meant a marriage of convenience, a 'lavender' marriage, to maintain a respectable front. Paris was more tolerant of women's

PHOTO 14 The modern flapper

emancipation, and had no laws against homosexuality. At the start of the twentieth century many women went to Paris, already a haven for artists and free-thinkers, and now for women who wanted to defy convention and live differently. Independent women could live there alone, or openly with another woman, and discover the city for themselves.

But some restrictions and prejudices remained. Scott Fitzgerald's wife Zelda, an aspiring writer, dancer and gifted painter, remained in the shadow of her more famous husband, and like Lucia Joyce, ended her life in a psychiatric hospital. On the other hand Josephine Baker, who had left the US to get away from racial discrimination, found fame in Paris where she became an icon and a symbol for sexual liberation.

Edith Wharton (1862–1937), the great francophile novelist, was just four years old when she first travelled from the US to France. Edith's parents were great travellers and frequently took the family to Europe, Paris being her father's favourite city. This had a great impact on young Edith, who learned French as a child, despite having received very little formal education. Like many wealthy upper-class Americans, she had a French governess, was instructed in philosophy, history and poetry at home, and became fluent in German and Italian. She was forbidden by her mother to read novels until she was married, as was the norm. Nevertheless she had access to her father's library and read copiously. She started to write poetry at an early age, and produced her own first novel at fifteen. In 1885 she married Edward (Teddy) Robins Wharton, who ought to have been an ideal match, although he was twelve years older than her, and who shared her love for travel (in her lifetime she crossed the Atlantic sixty times). The marriage was not successful, and eventually failed because he used her money to support a mistress. This would be reflected in her novels with recurrent themes of failed or unrequited love and lost chances of happiness. In the US she had become gradually dissatisfied with the rigid role society expected of her as a wife, and she became restless, suffering from bouts of nervous anxiety throughout the 1890s.

In 1906, having just published *The House of Mirth*, which received rave reviews, at the age of forty-four Wharton arrived in Paris with her husband. Staying first at the Hôtel de Crillon at 10 place de la Concorde, they then rented a luxurious residence at 58 rue de Varenne in the seventh arrondissement, owned by the Vanderbilt family; it is now an annexe to the Hôtel Matignon, the French prime minister's office. They lived in style with a staff of six servants, a secretary, a cook, an automobile with chauffeur, and two dogs. In 1910 they moved across the street to a bigger apartment at 53 rue de Varenne, a 'great, good place'.

They returned to New York, but Wharton was nostalgic for Paris. Six months later they were back. She described in her diary her elation: 'the usual demoralising happiness. *Dieu que c'est beau* after six months of eye-starving! The tranquil majesty of the architectural lines, the wonderful blurred winter lights, the long lines of lamps garlanding the avenues & the quays ...!' Gone was her depression, and her spirits soared, but this was not the case for her husband, who had serious bouts of depressive illness, had learnt only the rudiments of the French language, and was now living in her shadow as Wharton immersed herself in French literature, and started to draft her next novel, *Ethan Frome* (1911), in French. Her adaptation to French life was made easier thanks to contact with the novelist Paul Bourget, whom she had met in the US in 1893, when he was commissioned to write a series of articles on American life for *The New York Herald* and *Le Figaro*. She recalled the encounter, when she was 'a young woman impassioned with literature, but not having even a dream of the possibility of herself joining the illustrious brotherhood of writers'. She was now successful, and had dedicated her first novel to the Bourgets. In return he dedicated one of his stories to her and helped the Whartons to settle in Paris. In her autobiography *A Backward Glance* (1933), she found herself:

> ... at once among friends, both old and new. The Bourgets always spent a part of the winter in the quiet and leafy rue Barbet de Jouy, a short walk from our door; and in other houses of the old Faubourg I found three or four of the French girl friends I had known in my youth at Cannes, and who had long since married, and settled in Paris. ...

As a stranger and newcomer, not only outside of all groups and coteries, but hardly aware of their existence, I enjoyed a freedom not possible in those days to the native-born, who were still enclosed in the old social pigeon-holes, which they had begun to laugh at, but to which they still flew back.

Now installed in Paris, the successful author of *The House of Mirth* continued to write novels deeply rooted in the American social scene, where Paris hardly featured, with the exception of the denouement of *The Age of Innocence* (1920). In this frustrating final scene the fifty-seven-year-old American widower Newland Archer, newly arrived in Paris, cannot bring himself to call on his old flame, Countess Ellen Olenska, with whom he had been deeply in love decades earlier when she was living in New York, a passion rendered impossible by social convention. After wandering through Paris, Archer meets his son and they walk together to the place des Invalides. They stop in a square nearby with horse chestnut trees, from where they can still see the gold dome of the Invalides, and where Countess Olenska now lives. Archer sits on a bench and looks up at what could be her apartment, imagining what it might be like inside, thinking that 'it's more real to me here than if I went up'.

In the book the name of the square is unknown, but in his 1993 film version, Martin Scorsese shot the scene in place de Furstenberg in the sixth arrondissement. Daniel Day-Lewis, Michelle Pfeiffer and Winona Ryder were cast for this splendidly sensitive film, ending in a lovely spot on the Left Bank:

Suddenly Dallas stopped short, grasping his father's arm. 'Oh, by Jove,' he exclaimed.

They had come out into the great tree-planted space
before the Invalides. The dome of Mansart floated
ethereally above the budding trees and the long grey
front of the building: drawing up into itself all the rays
of afternoon light, it hung there like the visible symbol of
the race's glory.

Archer knew that Madame Olenska lived in a square
near one of the avenues radiating from the Invalides;
and he had pictured the quarter as quiet and almost
obscure, forgetting the central splendour that lit it up ...
He thought of the theatres she must have been to, the
pictures she must have looked at, the sober and splendid
old houses she must have frequented, the people she must
have talked with, the incessant stir of ideas, curiosities,
images and associations thrown out by an intensely social
race in a setting of immemorial manners ...

The pathos of the scene is sensitively handled by a writer
whose decision to live in Paris had also allowed her to bring
a new dimension to her writing, to tackle sexual love more
knowledgeably and expose the tragedy of lives deprived
of it. Wharton's relationship with her sick husband had
become fraught with tension. In 1907 in a Parisian salon
she met Morton Fullerton, a writer and journalist. He was
an attractive, idealistic, charming bisexual American writing
for the London *Times*. He also happened to be a friend of
her dear fellow writer Henry James. She found him 'very
intelligent, but slightly mysterious', and they embarked
on an affair, meeting secretly and frequently in the Louvre
and at the Jardin des Plantes, and attending plays at the
Comédie Française. They explored the Tuileries Gardens and
Montmartre and ventured out of the city in her car or by

train. The affair was over by 1910 and he disappeared from her life, but she recorded in her diaries all the details of their deeply intellectual and passionate relationship. In 1913 she divorced Teddy after twenty-eight years of marriage and he returned alone to the US, where he died in 1928. Wharton remained in Paris where attitudes towards divorce were more liberated than in the US, and where she could keep her social ordeal private. Furthermore she was accepted in France as a professional '*femme de lettres*', whereas in America her status as a writer 'puzzled and embarrassed [her] old friends far more than it impressed them'. In France she could escape from this disapproval and social stigma and find sympathy in the salons, where a woman could freely express her ideas and views on current events in a congenial atmosphere. She made many friends among the French writers including André Gide, Jean Cocteau and Anna de Noailles, on the edge of the artistic bohemian crowd.

Wharton's life changed at the outbreak of World War I. She could have left Paris, but she was 'in love with the spirit of France' and stayed in rue de Varenne. She became a fearless and intrepid supporter of the French war effort, and dedicated much of her time and money to charities. In August 1914 she created sewing workshops employing more than 800 women, who were fed and paid one franc a day for making clothes for hospitals, and lingerie for a fashionable clientele. She also helped to establish the American Hostels for Refugees, which provided shelter, meals, clothes and work for Belgian refugees who had escaped the Germans. In early 1915 she organised the Children of Flanders Rescue Committee, which gave shelter to nearly 900 Belgian refugees, and she also raised huge sums of money for hostels for tuberculosis sufferers. Her admiring friend Henry James called her the 'great generalissima'. She hosted benefit concerts, and thanks to influential connections in the French government and her long-time friend Walter Berry (then president of the American Chamber of Commerce in Paris), she was allowed to travel to the front line, and to send dispatches from the war front reporting on life in the trenches. She made five trips to the war zone between February and August 1915, submitting articles to *Scribner's Magazine*. They covered life on the Front as well as the appalling reality of the destruction she witnessed in the areas affected by the war. The reports were turned into a book in 1915, *Fighting France: From Dunkerque to Belfort*, which became an American bestseller. It also offered a detailed chronicle of daily life in Paris before and during the war, describing for example a visit to the dressmaker just before the declaration of war: 'At the dressmaker's, the next morning, the tired fitters were preparing to leave for their usual holiday. They looked pale and anxious – decidedly, there was a new air of apprehension in the air.' She described the mood prevailing in the city during what she called the 'mobilization': '… in the rue Royale, at the corner of the Place de la Concorde, a few people had stopped to look at a little white piece of paper against the wall of the Ministère de la Marine. "General mobilization" they read – and an armed nation knows what that means. But the group about the paper was small and quiet. Passers-by read the notice and went on. There were no cheers, no gesticulations: the dramatic sense of the race had already told them that the event was too great to be dramatised.'

On 18 April 1916, the President of France made her *Chevalier de la légion d'honneur*. At the end of the war in 1918 she decided to leave Paris, which appealed less to her now that it was filling with Americans: 'Paris is simply awful – a kind of continuous earth-quake of motor-busses, trams, lorries, taxis & other howling & swooping & colliding engines, with hundreds & thousands of US citizens rushing about in them …,' she complained, and moved twelve miles north of Paris to Le Pavillon Colombe, an eighteenth-century manor house near the village of Saint-Brice-sous-Forêt. She would stay there every summer and autumn for the rest of her life, spending her winters and springs on the French Riviera.

Edith Wharton died of a stroke on 11 August 1937 at Le Pavillon Colombe. She was buried in the American section of the Cimetière des Gonards in Versailles beside her friend Walter Berry. Her love and admiration for France and Paris and the French language are clear in *A Motor Flight Through France* (1908) and *French Ways and Their Meaning* (1919), in which she wrote: 'The French possess the quality and have always claimed the privilege. And from their freedom of view combined with their sensuous sensibility they have extracted the sensation they call "*le plaisir*", which is something so much more definite and more evocative than what we mean when we speak of pleasure. "*Le plaisir*" stands for the frankly permitted, the freely taken, delight of the senses, the direct enjoyment of the fruit of the tree called golden. No suggestions of furtive vice degrade or coarsen it, because it has, like love, its open place in speech and practice.'

Paris also appears in some of her novellas, *Madame de Treymes* (1907), *The Reef* (1912), *A Son at the Front* (1923), which opens at the Hôtel de Crillon, and in a novel published in 1913, *The Custom of the Country*. Wharton is remembered by a plaque erected at her former home at 53 rue de Varenne, inscribed with a quotation from *A Backward Glance*: 'My years of Paris life were spent entirely in rue de Varenne – rich years, crowded and happy years …' *The Age of Desire* (2012) by Jennie Fields is the fictionalised story of Wharton's life and of the period when she found fulfilment for a time with Morton Fullerton in Paris.

So many of the English and American women writers and artists in Paris in the 1920s and 1930s were there because of the restrictions most countries placed on their independence. Many were seeking freedom from convention, both social and sexual. Homosexuality in France had been decriminalised in the 1810 Napoleonic code, whereas as late as 1921 a Tory MP in England proposed 'Acts of Gross Indecency by Females', an amendment to the Criminal Law Amendment Act of 1885, which already proscribed male homosexuality: lesbianism threatened the birth rate, debauched young girls, and induced neurasthenia and insanity.

Seven years later, in 1928, the English writer Radclyffe Hall published *The Well of Loneliness*, a novel which created uproar when the editor of the *Sunday Express* declared: 'I would rather give a healthy boy or a healthy girl a phial of prussic acid than this novel.' It was clear that London was no place for lesbians. Many, including Vita Sackville-West and Winnaretta Singer, made a marriage of convenience to keep up appearances. Others bravely lived out their difference openly and became notorious, like Radclyffe Hall. For them Paris was not only a haven for artists but also for free-thinkers and these so-called 'deviants'. At the end of the Belle Époque the city was known for having a relatively large and visible gay community. Writers like Marcel Proust, who depicted a gay subculture in his novels, had a great influence on 1920s Parisian society. Many women who wanted to live and love differently moved to Paris, particularly those affluent enough, like Eva Palmer, heiress to the biscuit fortune; 'Jo' Carstairs, who inherited millions from Standard

Oil; Winnaretta Singer, who was the daughter of the sewing machine magnate; Gertrude Stein and her lifelong lover Alice B. Toklas; the painters Romaine Brooks and Tamara de Lempicka and the American heiress Natalie Clifford Barney. For fifty years the latter was at the centre of gay Paris, as noted by Sylvia Beach who herself shared her life with Adrienne Monnier and who attended Natalie's Friday salons: 'At Miss Barney's one met lesbians; ladies with high collars and monocles, though Miss Barney herself was so feminine.' Truman Capote, a guest in the late 1940s, described her salon as 'a cross between a chapel and a bordello'. Alongside the financially independent women, there were also those who had to make a living, including Djuna Barnes, author of *Nightwood* (1936, a novel much praised by T. S. Eliot); the *New Yorker* correspondent Janet Flanner; the poet Dolly Wilde (niece of Oscar) and the notorious English poet Renée Vivien. Many French writers also attended the Friday salon, like Lucie Delarue-Mardrus and Colette, who became close friends. Colette wrote to Natalie: 'My door and my arms are always open to you.' They did indeed have a brief affair.

The poet and novelist **Natalie Clifford Barney** (1876–1972) was born into a wealthy family in Ohio but frequently visited Europe for her education. During one short trip to Paris in 1899, while staying in a pension in avenue de la Grande Armée, she saw the famous French courtesan, dancer and poet Liane de Pougy perform at the Bal Bullier (a famous dance hall memorably painted by Sonia Delaunay in 1913), and was enthralled by her beauty. To woo her, dressed in a bellboy's uniform she boldly knocked at her door to offer her a poem, but was denied entry. Back in Paris later with her mother, a painter who was taking lessons from Whistler, she stayed in a pension in Villa des Dames on avenue Victor Hugo, determined to explore the City of Light and to meet Liane again. Liane told the story of their subsequent brief affair in her novel *L'Idylle saphique* (Sapphic Idyll, 1901). Barney's father was not pleased, and arranged for her to be engaged to Lord Alfred Douglas, Oscar Wilde's former friend 'Bosie'. But marriage was not on the cards for her, even for convenience; she started to mix with a bohemian crowd of artists and writers, and never attempted to hide her sexuality: 'My queerness is not a vice, is not deliberate, and harms no one.' Another passionate affair followed with Pauline Tarn, better remembered as **Renée Vivien** (1877–1909), an English poet who like Natalie wrote in French, and who dedicated to her a collection of poems *Études et Préludes* (Studies and Preludes, 1904). By the age of twenty-six, the beautiful, rich and fascinating Barney, known to her friends as Natty, or *rayon de lune* (moonbeam) because of the colour of her hair, had become the toast of the town, a muse who reappeared as Dame Evangeline Musset in Djuna Barnes's *roman à clef Ladies Almanack* (1928), and as Valérie Seymour in Radclyffe Hall's notorious *Well of Loneliness* (1928).

After her father's death in 1902 Barney became financially independent and moved to a large house in Neuilly, hosting lavish dinners, wild parties, concerts of Modernist music and poetry readings. On one occasion the spy and dancer Mata Hari appeared in the garden (the same garden in which the French writer Colette started her acting career) nude, riding a white horse. Neighbours were not amused to see a constant stream of scantily clad women costumed as wood nymphs, and pressure was put on her to move out of the genteel neighbourhood. In 1909, greatly affected by Renée Vivien's early death, she moved to the Left Bank to 20

PHOTO 15   Natalie Barney's salon was at 20 rue Jacob

rue Jacob in the sixth arrondissement, where she stayed for the next fifty years.

Her first collection of poems, *Éparpillements* (Scatterings), was published in 1910. A copy was sent to Remy de Gourmont (1858–1915) who at the time was leading a lonely life and became besotted with her. His *Lettres intimes à l'Amazone* (Letters to the Amazon, 1912) was dedicated to her:

For you are the Amazon
You will remain the Amazon
So long as it does not bore you
And perhaps beyond that
In the embers of my heart

A keen rider in the Bois de Boulogne, Natalie Barney was widely considered an emancipated, intrepid and free spirit, an Amazon in a more general sense, which impressed the Italian poet Gabriele d'Annunzio:

Nothing will tame, neither sword nor flame,
The secret diamond of your youthful heart

The new house had a glorious but slightly unkempt garden which boasted a three-columned Doric temple, called by Barney the 'Temple of Friendship'. This unusual establishment was a magnet for French writers like André Gide, Paul Valéry, Paul Claudel and Max Jacob, as well as for foreign exiles like the Polish poet Milosz, and naturally for Gertrude Stein and Colette. The American expatriates Ezra Pound, William Carlos Williams, Mina Loy and Djuna Barnes were visitors, as recorded in Gertrude Stein's *The Autobiography of Alice B. Toklas* (1933). There was the inevitable meeting with Hemingway, brought to the Friday salon by Ezra Pound, but Barney was not impressed: '*Comme Hemingway était mal élevé!*' 'What terrible manners Hemingway had!' Marcel Proust did not attend her salon, but did pay her a visit when, in the process of writing *À la recherche du temps perdu* he came to quiz her on lesbian culture. She was the perfect choice, since her guest list read like an inventory of lesbian literary Paris. A dedicated feminist, she supported women's writing and founded in 1927 the 'Academy of Women', a response to the conservative, all-male *Académie française*. One guest was the biographer Marguerite Yourcenar, who later became the first woman to be elected to the *Académie*.

'If I had one ambition it was to make my life itself into a poem,' asserted Barney, as her larger-than-life personality overshadowed her writing, which was prolific but rather careless. *Pensées d'une amazone* (Thoughts of an Amazon, 1920) was written as a response to Pascal's *Pensées* (1670). In her novel *The One Who is Legion* (1930), partly autobiographical, the poet A.D. who commits suicide has much in common with Renée Vivien, one of her greatest loves, whose self-destructive behaviour, anorexia, drug and alcohol abuse caused her early death in 1909, aged only thirty-two. Barney was very proud of the contemporary writers in her circle, and described them in further books with wit and irony. In *Aventures de l'esprit* (Adventures of the Mind, 1929) she explores her family tree, enumerates her friendships and associations, uses letters and recreates conversations to evoke the golden age of her cherished salon in a series of literary portraits. *Souvenirs indiscrets* (Indiscreet Memories, 1960) and *Traits et portraits* (1963) offer an extraordinary testimony to the Parisian literary world she knew so well.

Barney also mixed with artists, one of whom remained with her for more than fifty years. She met the American painter Romaine Brooks in 1915 in Paris, where Brooks had gone to escape a miserable childhood: 'My mother stands between me and life.' After a succession of lovers, Ida Rubinstein, Renée Vivien, Winnaretta Singer and possibly d'Annunzio (of whom she made a stunning portrait), Brooks saw in Barney the right partner, although the two women did not live under the same roof (save for six shared years in Italy when Barney fled Nazi occupation in World War II). The relationship was not easy. Romaine was solitary, often depressed and possessive, whereas Barney, promiscuous and unfaithful, could and would have multiple simultaneous affairs. Barney was also extremely generous, and would rather help her friends in need than spend money on possessions

or her house, described as rather untidy in Radclyffe Hall's
The Well of Loneliness. She nevertheless remained devoted
to Romaine Brooks, and her novel *The One Who is Legion*
was dedicated 'To my angel Romaine'. Her poem 'A Parisian
Roof Garden' (1918) celebrates their everyday life in Paris:

> As I must mount to feed those doves of ours,
> Perhaps you too will spend nocturnal hours
> > Upon your roof
> > So high aloof
> That from its terraced bowers
> We catch at clouds and draw a bath from showers.
> Before the moon has made all pale the night,
> Let's meet with flute and viol, and supper light:
> A yew lamb, minted sauce, a raisined bun,
> A melon riper than the melting sun –
> A flask of Xeres, that we've scarce begun –
> We'll try the 'lunar waltz' while floats afar
> Upon the liquid night – night's nenuphar.
> Or else, with senses tuned alike perchance,
> Reclining love will make the heavens dance;
> And if the enemy from aerial cars
> Drops death, we'll share it vibrant with the stars!

The two last lines are a reference to German bombing of Paris
at the end of World War I. Barney was a fervent pacifist, and
her house was a haven for those opposed to the war, and one
of the few places where it could be discussed openly. For her
it was an 'involuntary and collective suicide ordered by men'.
The Pacifist writer Henri Barbusse gave a reading there of his
anti-war novel *Under Fire* (1916), and the house hosted a
Women's Congress for Peace. The salon survived World War

II and Barney relaunched it in 1949, when Truman Capote visited, but Paris had changed. The golden years were gone, and it was a time of post-war austerity.

In 1951 Barney published *In Memory of Dorothy Ierne Wilde*, a tribute to her former lover Dolly Wilde (1895–1941) which included a photo of Dolly dressed as her uncle Oscar. The women had led an intermittent love affair between 1927 and 1939. Nicknamed Oscaria, Dolly Wilde was another vulnerable fragile woman attracted by Natalie's confidence, charisma and money. She aspired to write and live her life as a work of art, but never wrote anything memorable. She appears as the lesbian Vivien Taube in one version of Scott Fitzgerald's *Tender is the Night* (1934). Like Renée Vivien she was self-destructive, and died young and lonely, drugs and alcohol taking their toll. Natalie Barney herself lived to the great age of ninety-six, and was buried in the cemetery in Passy, where her tombstone bears the inscription: Natalie Barney 'The Amazon of Remy de Gourmont'.

'Perverse ... dissolute, self-centred, unfair, stubborn, sometimes miserly ... a genuine rebel, ever ready to incite others to rebellion ... capable of loving someone just as they are, even a thief,' is how Barney was described by Lucie Delarue-Mardrus, the French writer and her friend.

In 1932 a reading of Radclyffe Hall's *The Well of Loneliness* had taken place in Barney's salon. Its publication in England in 1928 had brought about one of the most famous legal trials in British history, and it was banned on publication in 1928 as 'obscene libel'. Unsurprisingly it became a bestseller, selling millions of copies. Radclyffe Hall, or John as she called herself, had been subjected to a vicious campaign of attacks led by the *Sunday Express* for her depiction of lesbian relationships. Hall tells the story of the female 'invert' Stephen

Gordon, who realises at a young age that she prefers to dress in masculine clothes, loves hunting and horse riding and falls in love with women. A lesbian herself, Hall wrote it to 'put my pen at the service of some of the most misunderstood people in the world'. The novel was viciously slated for its treatment of lesbian relationships. To the modern reader this seems unfair, as there is no more than 'she kissed her full on the lips, as a lover' and a night of passion is summarised as nothing more explicit than 'that night they were not divided'.

In this autobiographical novel Stephen moves to London and writes a well-received first novel. Her second novel is less successful, and her friend, the playwright Jonathan Brockett, urges her to travel to Paris to improve her writing and acquire a fuller experience of life. It has been suggested that Jonathan Brockett might be based on Noël Coward. During a visit to Versailles, where he acts as her guide, Brockett hints at a secret history of 'inversion' or opting for the life of the opposite sex, referring to Marie Antoinette's rumoured relationship with her favourite, the Princesse de Lamballe. He next introduces Stephen to Valérie Seymour, who like her prototype Natalie Clifford Barney is the hostess of a literary salon, many of whose guests are lesbians and gay men. Immediately after this meeting Stephen announces she has decided to settle in the vicinity, as she finds Valérie an 'indestructible creature' capable of bestowing a sense of self-respect on 'inverts': 'For Valérie, placid and self-assured, created an atmosphere of courage; everyone felt very normal and brave when they gathered together at Valérie Seymour's. There she was, this charming and cultured woman, a kind of lighthouse in a storm-swept ocean. The waves had lashed round her feet in vain; winds had howled; clouds had spewed forth their hail and their lightning; torrents had deluged but had not destroyed her.

The storms, gathering force, broke and drifted away, leaving behind them the shipwrecked, the drowning.'

In contrast, Stephen's first contact with the gay world happens at Alec's Bar, a depressing Parisian nightspot where she encounters 'the battered remnants of men ... who, despised of the world, must despise themselves beyond all hope, it seemed, of salvation'.

She meets Jamie, a composer, and Wanda, a painter, who have chosen life in exile to dedicate themselves to their art. Jamie is 'a trifle unhinged because of the music that besieged her soul and fought for expression through her stiff and scholarly compositions,' and Wanda is 'struggling to lose herself in her picture, struggling to ease the ache of her passion by smearing the placid white face of the canvas with ungainly yet strange forms ...'

Preceding this stay in Paris, Stephen had joined the war effort during World War I and, like so many men and women, had driven in an ambulance unit and had fought at the Front, earning the *Croix de guerre*. She had fallen in love with a younger driver, Mary Llewellyn, and they live together in Paris when the war ends. They are happy at first, but Mary becomes lonely when Stephen returns to writing, and she throws herself into the depressing Parisian nightlife. Stephen acknowledges that she cannot give Mary happiness, and pretends to have an affair with Valérie Seymour to drive Mary into their friend Martin Hallam's arms, thus sacrificing her own happiness. The outcome of the novel is depressing because of Stephen's lack of courage and vision and her inability to face a lifestyle which could have connected the dual aspects of her personality. She inevitably falls into the Well of Loneliness, doomed to a life of solitude and misery and its 'ceaseless persecution' from 'the so-called just and righteous'.

The book ends with Stephen's urgent plea to 'Give us also the right to our existence!' As she spells out, 'bombs do not trouble the nerves of the invert, but rather that terrible silent bombardment from the batteries of God's good people'.

Djuna Barnes (1892–1982), another American writer and artist who spent the 1920s in Paris, is best remembered for her Modernist novel *Nightwood* (1936), considered a classic of lesbian fiction. Having started her career as a journalist and illustrator in New York, Barnes published *The Book of Repulsive Women*, an illustrated volume of poetry, in 1915. Even as a child she had to look after her siblings, and work to maintain her family, within which she experienced abuse and violence. In 1921 she accepted a lucrative commission allowing her to escape to Paris, where she lived for the next ten years, working for *McCall's Magazine*. There in 1923 she published a collection of poetry, plays, and short stories, *A Book*. In 1928 she published *Ladies Almanack* and an autobiographical novel, *Ryder*.

Barnes felt at home in 1920s Paris, a magnet for those interested in Modernism. With stunning good looks, always elegant in her legendary black cloak, she became a well-known figure and her acerbic wit is remembered in many contemporary memoirs.

'A Night Among the Horses' (1919), a short story first published in *The Little Review*, had been well received and Barnes was soon accepted into the salon of Natalie Barney, who became a lifelong friend and patron. Barney, with whom she also had a brief affair, described her in *Adventures of the Mind*: 'Her appearance is most singular: she has a nose as sharply-angled as an Eversharp pencil; her mouth has an irresistible laugh, and she squeezes her auburn hair tightly under her hat in the manner of Manet ... She is capable of great friendships and limits them to two or three people in whose company she is endlessly.'

In Barney's salon Barnes was introduced by Bernice Abbott to the American sculptor and silverpoint artist Thelma Wood, a statuesque figure six feet tall, boyish and athletic, who exuded sexual magnetism. They embarked on a long-term relationship and in 1923 Wood was living in Barnes's apartment at 173 boulevard Saint-Germain. The relationship was stormy, Barnes was jealous and Wood promiscuous, and their public fights were legendary. Unlike Natalie Barney, Barnes did not consider herself a 'woman born with a difference' and had a series of lovers of both sexes. She was quoted as saying: 'I'm not a lesbian. I just loved Thelma.'

She had arrived in Paris with a letter of introduction to James Joyce, whom she interviewed in 1922 for *Vanity Fair* and who became a friend. She was one of very few writers with whom he discussed his work. He treated her with great respect and allowed her to call him Jim. The headline of her *Vanity Fair* piece referred to him as '*A Portrait of the Man Who Is, at Present, One of the More Significant Figures in Literature.*'

The interview was illustrated with her beautiful drawing of James Joyce. It is assumed that he had a great impact on her writing, although they disagreed on the subject of literature; Joyce focused on commonplace subjects and made them extraordinary, but Barnes was drawn by the unusual, even the grotesque.

In September 1927 the advance she received for her novel *Ryder* allowed her to take an apartment at 9 rue St-Romain, which she shared with Thelma Wood. Their neighbour was Mina Loy, met previously in New York and who was characterised as Patience Scalpel, the sole heterosexual character in Barnes's short novel *Ladies Almanack*. Owing to its sensitive subject matter, *Ladies Almanack* was published in a small privately printed edition under the title 'A Lady of Fashion'. Barnes and her friends sold copies on the streets, and a few were smuggled into the US. It was dedicated to Thelma Wood, as was *Ryder*. Barnes's desire for a monogamous relationship was not shared by Wood, who had become increasingly difficult to live with, drinking heavily and being unfaithful. The last straw was Wood's affair with the heiress Henriette McCrea Metcalf, portrayed rather cruelly in *Nightwood* as Jenny Petherbridge. Barnes and Wood broke up, and this signalled the end of Barnes's golden days in Paris. After returning to the US in 1939, she wrote little apart from some poetry and *The Antiphon* (1958), a long verse play which mentions Paris only briefly.

The French city is most present in *Ladies Almanack*, which was illustrated with Barnes's own drawings. Witty and satirical, it was not taken seriously by the author and was reportedly written to amuse Thelma while she was ill. It describes a predominantly lesbian circle presided over by Dame Evangeline Musset (based on Natalie Barney) at her Friday salon. Dame Evangeline, 'A Pioneer and a Menace' in her youth, has reached 'a witty and learned Fifty', rescues women in distress, dispenses wisdom, and upon her death is elevated to sainthood. Barney's lovers and friends Élisabeth de Gramont, Romaine Brooks, Dolly Wilde, Radclyffe Hall and Una Troubridge all appear in the novel, as do Janet Flanner, her partner Solita Solano, and Mina Loy.

Barnes's reputation as a writer, however, is based on *Nightwood*, a novel written in France but published in England in 1936 by Faber & Faber, and in America in 1937 by

Harcourt, Brace, with an introduction by T. S. Eliot, whom
she called 'Uncle Tom'. It was written under the patronage
of Peggy Guggenheim, to whom the book was dedicated,
and who had become a close friend and patron. It is about
the doomed relationship between Nora (Barnes's alter ego)
and Robin (Thelma Wood) and is set in the underworld of
1920s Paris, where Nora spends whole nights looking for the
elusive and self-destructive Robin.

It received glowing reviews in England, where *The Spectator*
compared Barnes to Virginia Woolf: 'It is clear that a writer of
genuine importance has made herself known to us.' One of
its most fervent admirers was Eliot: 'Miss Barnes's prose has
the prose rhythm ... and the musical pattern which is not that
of verse ... it is so good a novel that only sensibilities trained
on poetry can wholly appreciate it.' To avoid censorship
Eliot had carefully edited *Nightwood*, which was nevertheless
soon labelled 'a lesbian novel'. It is really an essentially urban
novel, as the characters, all exiles in some ways, are observed
alone in a seedy dark city. One of them, Dr O'Connor, a
character in the second chapter, entitled '*La Somnambule*',
hangs around near the church of St Sulpice, and the Café
de la Mairie du VIe, his favourite café. 'To the proprietor
of the Café de la Mairie du VIe he was almost a son. This
relatively small square, through which tram lines ran into
several directions, bounded on the other side by the church
and on the other by the court, was the doctor's "city".'

In the third chapter, 'Night Watch', Nora and Robin are
settling nearby: 'Nora bought an apartment in the rue du
Cherche-Midi. Robin had chosen it. Looking from the long
windows one saw a fountain figure, a tall granite woman
bending forward with lifted head, one hand was held over
the pelvic round as if to warn a child who goes incautiously.'

PHOTO 16 Café de la Mairie appears in Djuna Barnes's *Nightwood*

In the fifth chapter, 'Watchman, What of the Night?', Nora is seen looking for comfort from her 'misery' after Robin's disappearance. She pays a visit to the doctor whom she finds in bed: 'Hearing his "come in" she opened the door and for one second hesitated, so incredible was the disorder that met her eyes. The room was so small that it was just possible to walk sideways up to the bed, it was as if being condemned to the grave, the doctor had decided to occupy it with the utmost abandon ... A swill-pail stood at the head of the bed, brimming with abominations. There was something appallingly degraded about the room ... In the narrow iron bed, with its heavy and dirty linen sheets, lay the doctor in a woman's flannel night gown.'

Some aspects of the disturbing 'lesbian' novel, perceived by some critics as gothic or baroque, might explain why Djuna Barnes has been neglected, despite having many admirers, including Truman Capote, Anaïs Nin, Lawrence Durrell, Graham Greene, Samuel Beckett, Janet Flanner, Sir Herbert Read and also Dylan Thomas, who had warm praise for *Nightwood*: 'It isn't a lah-de-dah prose poem, because it's about what some very real human people feel, think, and do. It's "*Nightwood*" by Djuna Barnes, and one of the three great prose books ever written by a woman.' William Burroughs called it 'one of the great books of the twentieth century'. In a 2007 edition Jeanette Winterson wrote in the introduction: 'It is its own created world, exotic and strange, and reading it is like drinking wine with a pearl dissolving in the glass. You have taken in more than you know, and it will go on doing its work. From now on, a part of you is pearl-lined.' Barnes's rejection of requests to reprint some of her work in her lifetime may have contributed to her present obscurity.

A flapper and muse, the 'queen of the jazz age', **Nancy Cunard** (1896–1965) was an exceptional woman who left a memorable mark on the Paris scene of the swinging 1920s. At once poet, editor, journalist and political activist, she also became a fashion icon when she moved to Paris and adopted her androgynous look, wearing men's clothes, striking make-up, and with her hair bobbed. A celebrated muse to writers and artists in London and Paris she was 'surely one of the major phenomena of that world' according to her friend, the poet William Carlos Williams.

The only child of the heir to the Cunard shipping line, her mother a fashionable American beauty, Nancy Cunard determinedly turned her back on her privileged background and dedicated a great part of her life to fighting for important

causes. Much of her childhood had been spent in the company
of her mother's long-term admirer, the Irish writer **George
Moore** (1852–1933), himself a Francophile, who had decided
that Paris was his 'Oxford and Cambridge' when at the age of
eighteen he opted to spend seven years there, from 1873 to
1880, intending to become a painter. Attracted by the avant-
garde, Moore abandoned the stuffy Académie des Beaux-Arts
to join the Impressionist movement. Rumoured to have been
Nancy's father, he played an important role in her education
and might have influenced her decision to go to France in
1920 at the age of twenty-four. She and her husband Sydney
Fairbairn (a cricketer and army officer, whom she had married
quite probably for convenience in 1916) had separated in
1918 (and were to divorce in 1925), while her lover, Peter
Broughton-Adderley, had been killed in action in France just
a month before Armistice Day. It was said that she never fully
recovered from the loss, and it was perhaps as a reaction that
she moved to Paris. A poet since 1911, and first published
in 1915, she had associated in London with the fashionable
society intellectuals, the 'Corrupt Coterie', and once in Paris
quickly became involved with the latest literary movements
of the time, Modernism, Dada and Surrealism. From 1924
Man Ray, William Carlos Williams, Edith Wharton, Léon-
Paul Fargue, and '*la bande à Cocteau et celle de Breton*' (the
Cocteau and Breton cliques) gathered in her flat on Île Saint-
Louis, at 2 rue Le Regrattier. The independent intelligent
femme fatale attracted great writers and artists, with whom
she also had affairs; Ezra Pound, T. S. Eliot, Aldous Huxley,
Pablo Neruda, Samuel Beckett and Ernest Hemingway,
among many others. The French writer Marcel Jouhandeau
remembered '*une ogresse maigre, d'une beauté farouche*' ('a
thin ogress, with a wild beauty'), and she defiantly described

herself as an anarchist, an outsider and an outlaw, which was also the title of one of her early poems, 'Outlaws' (1921).

The photographs of Cunard taken by Man Ray in 1926 emphasise her unconventional and provocative looks: short hair, kohl-rimmed eyes, and arms heavy with African bracelets, all suggesting glamour, provocation and deep fascination for exotic culture. She had by now become famous for her style and acquired the accolade the 'Gioconda of the Age'. Her poem 'In the Studio' (1923) recreates long sittings for Man Ray and other photographers, as well as for painters of the time; Wyndham Lewis, John Banting, Oskar Kokoschka and the Romanian sculptor Brancusi, who represented her as *Nancy Cunard* (*Sophisticated Young Lady*) in a stunning bronze of 1932:

> Is it March, spring, winter, autumn, twilight, noon
> Told in this distant sound of cuckoo clocks?
> Sunday it is – five lilies in a swoon
> Decay against your wall, aggressive flocks
> Of alley-starlings aggravate a mood.
> The rain drops pensively. 'If one could paint,
> Combine the abstract with a certain rude
> Individual form, knot passion with restraint ...
> If one could use the murk that fills a brain,
> Undo old symbols and beget again
> Fresh meaning on dead emblem ...' so one lies
> Here timeless, while the lilies' withering skin
> Attests the hours, and rain sweeps from the skies;
> The bird sits on the chimney, looking in.

During the 1920s, after several romantic involvements, she started a more serious affair with **Tristan Tzara** (1896–1963),

generally considered to be the founder of the anarchist
Dada movement. Born Samuel Rosenstock in Romania,
he had changed his name to Tzara (Romanian for 'land').
He quickly became a colourful fixture on the Left Bank and
appears in Hemingway's nostalgic short story 'The Snows of
Kilimanjaro' (1936): 'Later he had seen the things he could
never think of and later still he had seen much worse. So
when he got back to Paris that time he could not talk about
it or stand to have it mentioned. And there in the café as he
passed was that American poet with a pile of saucers in front
of him and a stupid look on his potato face talking about
the Dada movement with a Romanian who said his name
was Tristan Tzara, who always wore a monocle and had a
headache …'

Tzara had moved to Paris via Zurich in 1919, where he
joined the Surrealists after meeting André Breton and his
circle. His play *Handkerchief of Clouds* (1924) was dedicated
to Nancy Cunard. Gertrude Stein, who mentions him in *The
Autobiography of Alice B. Toklas*, was at first a friend, but he
later joined with others to accuse her of megalomania in a
1935 critical pamphlet, *Testimony Against Gertrude Stein*.

In one of the most striking Man Ray photographs, taken
at the 1921 ball given by Étienne de Beaumont, Cunard
is seen wearing a top hat, a mask and silk pyjamas as she
stands before Tzara, who is kneeling to kiss her hand. A
walk through literary Paris should include the house Tzara
commissioned the Viennese Bauhaus architect Adolf Loos
to build for him in Montmartre, at 15 avenue Junot in the
eighteenth arrondissement.

As part of her collection of writers and artists as lovers
Cunard had started a tormented affair in February 1926
with the Surrealist poet **Louis Aragon** (1897–1982), a major

figure in the avant-garde movement, who succeeded Tristan
Tzara as her lover. This stunning French writer had had a
most unconventional and entangled upbringing. Provocative,
precocious and prolific, he completed his first novel while
still a pupil at the Lycée Carnot in Paris. After graduating in
Latin and philosophy, he enrolled in 1917 at the Faculté de
Médecine de Paris, where André Breton was a fellow medical
student. A committed pacifist, Aragon was nevertheless
drafted in 1918 and fought in World War I, gaining a medal
for bravery, and beginning to write poems, many based on
his war experience. In 1919, Breton and Aragon edited the
first issue of an avant-garde magazine, *Littérature*, with fellow
poet Philippe Soupault. Aragon also staged Dada events, and
published collections of poetry such as *Feu de joie* (Joyful
Fire, 1920), reflecting the Dadaesque interest in the absurd,
and lambasting the war. It was at this time that he first met
Nancy Cunard. In 1927 he joined the Communist Party
and the next year, after a painful separation from Cunard in
Venice, he met Elsa Triolet, the Russian-born sister-in-law
(and one-time lover) of the poet Vladimir Mayakovsky. They
were to remain committed to each other and to Communism
for the rest of their lives; they married in 1939. Aragon was
to be drafted again during World War II and would again
win commendation for his bravery. Demobilised by 1940,
Aragon and Triolet went on to work for the Resistance,
writing and distributing pamphlets, editorials and poetry,
sometimes in very dangerous circumstances.

His two-year relationship with Cunard in the 1920s was
complicated. The spoiled heiress was dominant. As he wrote
to a friend in April 1926: '*Je suis le prisonnier de l'amour*' ('I
am love's prisoner'). Her political awakening as well as her
Modernist and Surrealist approach to poetry nevertheless

certainly owed much to Aragon. She acknowledged that her poems *Parallax* (1925) and 'Simultaneous' and 'In Provins' (published as *Poems (Two)*, 1925) were influenced by Aragon's technique of allusiveness. The frontispiece to *Parallax*, published by the Hogarth Press, also indicates Cunard's artistic interest in perspective and Cubism, prevailing in Paris at the time. The beginning of 'Simultaneous' is set in Paris:

> At one time, Montparnasse,
> And all night's gloss
> Splendour of shadow on shadow,
> With the exact flower
> Of the liqueur glass in its glass.
>   Time runs,
>   But thought (or what?) comes
> Seated between these damaged table-tops,
> Sense of what zones, what simultaneous time-sense?

In 1928, immersed more than ever in the Parisian literary avant-garde scene, with the help of Aragon she founded the Hours Press, first located in a farmhouse at La Chapelle-Réanville, north of Paris. It was meant primarily to support experimental poetry and provide an opportunity for promising writers like Ezra Pound. Her immense inherited wealth allowed her to take financial risks that other publishers could not. The press later moved to a small shop in Paris at 15 rue Guénégaud and was praised for beautiful book designs and high-quality production, in which Cunard took great pride. It produced Samuel Beckett's first published work, *Whoroscope*, in 1930, and one volume of Pound's *Cantos* in the same year, as well as Bob Brown's *Words* (1931) and writings by George Moore, Norman Douglas,

Richard Aldington and Arthur Symons. Her friend Harold
Acton wrote that 'she inspired half the poets and novelists
of the twenties' and also described her as a dedicated and
overworked publisher: 'The clock did not exist for her: in
town she dashed in and out of taxis, clutching an attaché-
case crammed with letters, manifestoes, estimates, circulars
and her latest African bangle ... she looked famished and
quenched her hunger with harsh white wine and gutsy talk.'

She may have been the model for the impressive Brett
Ashley in Hemingway's *The Sun Also Rises* (1926). Aragon's
autobiographical piece, *Le roman inachevé* (The Unfinished
Novel, 1956) recalls their earlier affair:

Trunks
Hotel rooms
That's how it goes, how it goes, goes, goes
In silent corridors grey runners with red borders
And shoes put outside to see better on the ceiling
The shadowy couple moving
She loved only what passes and I was the colour of the
    weather
And everything, even the Île
Saint-Louis was just a journey to her ...
In Paris we changed districts as one might change a shirt

Light comes from the woman
And at evening and in the morning
Everything finds its place round her ...

Much of Aragon's writing, including his novel *Le con
d'Irène* (1928), acknowledged only late in his life, relives the
passionate affair and Cunard/Irène's callous manner with her

lovers: 'She considers plainly that love is no different from its object, that there is nothing to seek elsewhere. If need be, she says it in a disagreeable way, directly.'

Elsa Triolet, Aragon's wife, would write later: 'They always talk about the poems Louis wrote for me. But the loveliest were for Nancy.'

Nancy Cunard left Aragon for a black American jazz musician, Henry Crowder, with whom she dedicated a great part of the 1930s to active campaigns against racial prejudice and injustice, something no white European woman had done. From 1932 she worked on *Negro: An Anthology of African Culture*, published in 1934, which was an attempt to rehabilitate black culture and black rights. Cunard also used her wealth to support many artists and writers including Duchamp, Pound, Joyce and T. S. Eliot. In 1936 she helped to screen and distribute the surrealist film *L'Âge d'or* by Luis Buñuel and Salvador Dalí in London, as it was then banned in France.

Her work on black civil rights caused her mother to disown her, and created a permanent rift with her family. She now lost the financial security she had enjoyed from family money and, following in the footsteps of her friend Janet Flanner, she started earning a living as a journalist writing for the *Manchester Guardian* and other publications, covering particularly the Spanish Civil War, and actively raising support and funds for war victims and refugees. The Hours Press was requisitioned to print poems and pamphlets. In her articles she exposed much of what she personally witnessed, such as the barbarity of the French 'holding centres' which had been summarily set up in the South of France for Spanish refugees and Republican soldiers.

Her political activism continued during World War II in London, where she worked as a translator for the French

Resistance. At the end of the war, her turbulent life and scant regard for her health had taken their toll: having become increasingly dependent on alcohol and drugs she drank heavily, ate little and smoked. Suffering from 'persecution mania', and plagued by insecurities, she suffered a series of breakdowns. In 1946 she reported in an angry letter to Ezra Pound that on her return to France after the war she had found her French home destroyed by Nazi soldiers and their sympathisers. Gone was her collection of African art; her beloved printing press had been smashed, and many of her books and personal belongings had been damaged or destroyed.

Having lost practically everything, her last years were spent in poverty with bouts of physical and mental illness leading frequently to hospitalisation. Reduced in Paris to a cheap third-floor flat, she was determined to climb the stairs unaided, a process which would take her more than an hour, aged sixty-nine and weighing only sixty pounds. Confused, she would go out and ask passers-by if they knew Pablo Neruda, or she would summon Samuel Beckett to come and see her. Finally on her way one day to visit Janet Flanner she collapsed in the street, was picked up by the police and taken to a public ward in Cochin Hospital at 27 rue du Faubourg Saint-Jacques, where she asked for red wine and material to write 'a long poem against all wars', before dying alone.

Thus ended the life of this extraordinary woman, liberated before her time, obsessed by Africa and civil rights and all types of injustice, who fervently preached sexual, class and racial equality. Her reputation has recently been enjoying a gradual revival. The past two decades have seen the republication of some of her writings, journalism and poetry, and a short story, 'A Lost Night' (c.1920–21), her only work of fiction, has recently been discovered. The female narrator shares Cunard's freedom of spirit and hedonism in the city which she loves: 'My God, how lovely Paris was, making everything else seem futile by its beauty!' But it is also a dangerous place where her lover Leo has been drugged, robbed and nearly killed following '… a chance conversation with two men in some bar …'

In *These Were the Hours: Memories of My Hours Press, Réanville and Paris, 1928–1931*, she describes her work with the printing press: 'The smell of printer's ink pleased me greatly, as did the beautiful freshness of the glistening pigment. There is no other black or red like it. After a rinse in petrol and a good scrub with soap and hot water, my fingers again became perfectly presentable; the right thumb, however, began to acquire a slight ingrain of grey, due to the leaden composition. I soon learned that greasy black hands do not matter when one is at the proofing stage, but an immaculate touch is most important in handling the fair sheet when one has reached the pulling stage. This is part of the craft; to achieve impeccably clean things with fingers grease-laden …'

She is remembered in the testimonies of many former friends including Robert McAlmon and William Carlos Williams, who said 'if there was anything that was not in that courteous, cultured, and fearless mind, I have yet to discover it'. Mina Loy's poem 'Nancy Cunard' (1919–20) evokes all the photographs and paintings she illuminated:

> …
> Your chiffon voice
> tears with soft mystery
> a lily loaded with a sucrose dew
> of vigil carnival,

Your lone fragility
of mythological queens
conjures long-vanished dragons –
– their vast jaws
yawning in disillusion,
...

Her name appears no fewer than six times in Lucky's soliloquy in Samuel Beckett's *Waiting for Godot* (1953), which ends: 'Cunard tennis ... the stones ... so calm ... Cunard ... unfinished ...'

In the spring of 1919 **Hope Mirrlees** (1887–1978), one of the 'Forgotten Female Modernists', (or 'FFM', an acronym first used in the *Times Literary Supplement*), wrote *Paris: A Poem* which, according to the critic Julia Briggs, is the ultimate 'lost masterpiece of Modernism'. Not enough people have heard of this outstanding experimental work, which shares extraordinary similarities with T. S. Eliot's *The Waste Land*, published two years later. A lifelong friend

PHOTO 17   15 rue Guénégaud, one of Nancy Cunard's homes

of Eliot, Mirrlees was born in 1887 in Kent and raised in Scotland and South Africa. She attended the Royal Academy of Dramatic Art before studying at Newnham College, Cambridge, where she met the distinguished classicist Jane Ellen Harrison, who became a close friend and collaborator, and with whom she lived in the UK and in France from 1913 until Harrison's death in 1928. Together they made repeat visits to Paris between 1913 and 1919. Mirrlees wrote three novels: *Madeleine, One of Love's Jansenists* (1919), *The Counterplot* (1924), *and Lud-in-the-Mist* (1926), all well received by contemporary critics including Virginia Woolf. Woolf had urged Mirrlees to write a play or a poem specifically for the Hogarth Press, and *Paris: A Poem*, was published in 1920. Virginia Woolf was pleased with the work, which she assessed as 'very obscure, indecent and brilliant'.

PHOTO 18   Hope Mirrlees's poem *Paris* is set in the Métro

The poem is a journey through the city in spring 1919, set on a single day like Joyce's *Ulysses* (1922) and Woolf's *Mrs Dalloway* (1925). It begins with a descent into the Paris Métro, emerging at night into the streets. It acts as a commentary and a digest of references noted as the author passes through, and especially under, the city, the dominant imagery being that of a journey through the underworld. It provides a visual and cultural snapshot of the city. The opening line: 'I want a holophrase' sets the tone of the Modernist poem, using an invented word, followed by a series of fragmented messages, pastiche, overheard French dialogue, musical notation and advertising slogans. The narrator is a female wanderer, a *flâneuse* who records her journey as she passes through a succession of Métro stations, bombarded by signs, posters, advice and advertisements:

I want a holophrase
NORD-SUD
ZIG-ZAG
LION NOIR
CACAO BLOOKER
Black-figured vases in Etruscan tombs
RUE DU BAC (DUBONNET)
SOLFERINO (DUBONNET)
CHAMBRE DES DEPUTES
Brekekekek coax coax we are passing under the Seine
DUBONNET
The Scarlet Woman shouting BYRHH and deafening St
    John at Patmos
Vous descendez Madame?
QUI SOUVENT SE PESE BIEN SE CONNAIT
QUI BIEN SE CONNAIT BIEN SE PORTE
CONCORDE

Eliot's *The Waste Land* (1922) and *Paris: A Poem* both focus
on politics and mythology. The narrator in *Paris* shares her
thoughts and visions as she negotiates her way through the
Métro, passing many stations, and returns in the evening
to her room at 'the top floor of an old Hotel' at 3 rue de
Beaune (the address is indicated at the end of the poem). She
visualises paintings in galleries, children playing in public
gardens and workers in cafés. She imagines Roman Legions
and ghosts of the past, including Père Lachaise. She notes the
scent of lilac, vermouth and tobacco and hears the chiming
of church bells ... 'And on and on ...'

The poem daringly crosses the traditional boundaries of
poetic form, and owes much to the French poet Guillaume
Apollinaire's 'concrete poetry' such as 'Zone' (1913) and seen
also in his collection *Calligrammes* (1918), subtitled '*Poems
of Peace and War, 1913–1916*'. The poems were experimental
with typeface and the spatial arrangement of words on
the page, and Mirrlees plays similarly with typography,
reproducing adverts, tombstones and memorial plaques, and
even a musical score to mark church bells. The arrangement
of lines on the page contributes, as in Apollinaire's poems,
to creating a world without borders or divisions. Cocteau
might also have been an influence, as cinematic elements
are brought into the journey, which concludes at night with
the constellation of the Great Bear (apparently a coded
dedication to Harrison) and her arrival at her hotel, where
from the window of her room she looks down 'tranced' to
the street below:

> From the top floor of an old Hotel,
> Tranced,
> I gaze down at the narrow rue de Beaune.

Eliot added extensive notes at the end of *The Waste Land* to guide the reader, as did Mirrlees, but her notes give few clues to her journey. She indicates that 'NORD-SUD' is the Métro line between Montmartre and Montparnasse which opened in Paris in 1910, although it was not fully functional until 1916. It was also the name of a Dadaist journal. 'Rue du Bac etc are names of stations' encountered on the journey underground. Dubonnet, Zig-Zag, Lion Noir and Cacao Blooker refer to advertising posters. Literary allusions are made to Shakespeare and, as she passes 'under the Seine' also to Aristophanes, as the narrator is reminded of the chant of the frogs '*Brekekekek coax coax*' living in the river Acheron, which must be crossed on the passage to Hades. '*Vous descendez Madame?*' is a query to a female passenger leaving the train, but it could equally be linked to the metaphor of Hades.

QUI SOUVENT SE PESE BIEN SE CONNAIT
QUI BIEN SE CONNAIT BIEN SE PORTE

(translation: 'Those who weigh themselves often, know themselves well. Those who know themselves well, stay well') was the motto inscribed on the public scales in Métro stations. The poem is packed with such word associations. Concorde is the name of the Métro station where the narrator alights, but is probably also a reminder that the place de la Concorde, where the guillotine stood in the French Revolution, now suggests the notion of peace. The poem is set on 1 May 1919, when a memorable workers' strike took place in Paris. The date had been considered traditionally the workers' day but it is also the day at the start of spring when buying lily-of-the-valley brings luck. Owing to the strike the flowers were not available in May 1919: 'Thereisnolilyofthevalley' is set out in the poem as an image of a lily, with its stem spelling out the phrase in single letters, printed vertically. The following lines refer to the famous paintings in the Louvre Museum:

The Pietà of Avignon,
L'Olympe,
Giles,
Mantegna's Seven Deadly Sins,
The Chardins

The Louvre collection had just been dug up from its temporary grave, or 'subterranean sleep of five long years' after having been stored underground for the duration of World War I, and was rehung in 1919. This recalled too France's war dead, those who would not rise from their eternal 'slumber'. 'Black figured vases in Etruscan tombs' are probably a reference to the Louvre collections, as well as to death and the underworld. The 'blackness' of the figures is doubtless connected to the Métro posters for Zig-Zag cigarette paper, Lion Noir shoe polish and Cacao Blooker drinking chocolate, all of which feature black imagery. The poet's notes explain that Byrrh and Dubonnet were popular apéritifs, widely advertised in France in 1919; Byrrh featured a woman dressed in scarlet and playing a drum. War and death are recurring themes, although the poem's overall mood seems optimistic, as Paris has now entered the post-war reconstruction stage and 'the ruined province of Picardie' will recover. CONCORDE is the last station on her journey, marking the end of the darkness below ground, and alluding to the peace process taking place in Paris at the time, concluded by the Treaty of Versailles: 'Whatever happens, some day it will look beautiful.'

For the *flâneuse* it is now time for consumerism, and she can move freely in the city, attracted by 'the windows of Le Bon Marché, la Samaritaine and the Galéries [*sic*] Lafayette'. Mirrlees has been unfairly neglected. The few references to her include those found in Virginia Woolf's diaries, where she is described in the March 1919 entry (around the time of the composition of *Paris*) as 'a very self-conscious, wilful, prickly & perverse young woman', and in a letter of 1 September 1925 thus: 'She's the daughter of a very rich sugar merchant. ... She is her own heroine – capricious, exacting, exquisite, very learned, and beautifully dressed. She has a passion for Jane Harrison, the scholar: indeed they practically live together and go to Paris to learn Russian ...'

T. S. Eliot's letters confirm that she later gave him refuge at her family house during World War II, and she is mentioned briefly in Anthony Powell's memoirs, as well as in the correspondence of Lady Ottoline Morrell. Records of her Paris years occur in Gertrude Stein's *The Autobiography of Alice B. Toklas*. Mirrlees's circle included André Gide, who was impressed by her erudition and wit and thought that her *Paris* poem was the only good Dada poem written in English. Her literary references include the Surrealists and Charles Baudelaire, one of the fathers of Modernism, who is not named, but appears in *Paris* through a reference to his poem '*Le Voyage à Cythère*' (1857). Characters from Molière's plays (Harpagon and Monsieur Jourdain) appear in Mirrlees's poem, alongside the writers Bossuet and Chateaubriand, and painters including Poussin and Rousseau.

Virginia Woolf (1882–1941) herself never stayed in Paris for long periods like Mirrlees, but was there on occasional short visits, the first to break the journey home from Venice in May 1904 with her siblings after their father's death. They were there again on 28 March 1907, and on 24 September 1908 Woolf accompanied her sister Vanessa and Clive Bell, who had just married.

She returned again in 1923, writing in a letter to Roger Fry on 16 April: 'we are now about to enter Paris, in the dark. There I shall stay a few days and meet Jane Harrison and Hope Mirrlees.' She wished her French had been better: 'I've been reading the life of Cezanne (and Rimbaud and lots of the French whom Gerald has recommended, being disgusted with my own language and in love with theirs) ... We get to Hotel de Londres on the 22nd, and I shall stay on alone till 28th ... what a bore! I look forward to Paris with the excitement of a girl of 16, and intend to talk French like a native by the light of nature. I know the words, but can never think how to make them into sentences.'

Left alone in the French city she writes to her husband Leonard on 25 April 1923: 'lunched at a new place; good; 3 courses; bought china and went to the Louvre; took bus to Notre Dame ... rung up by Hope [Mirrlees], who wants to treat me to ices at Rumpelmayers tomorrow, and asks me to dine on Thursday; says I shall easily get tickets for the Misanthrope. Now I've dined at our usual place – omelette, ham and pots, and spinach; suisse, coffee and cream, then chocolate, very good, at the orchestra café.' The following day she seems less happy: 'I must go first and get money changed: then to the [galeries] Lafayette, and then home to meet Hope and have tea. I'm already rather lonely, and home sick.'

A few days later on 28 April she describes to her sister Vanessa her 'amusing time in Paris', mentioning a visit to the

Louvre and she declares: 'I saw the Poussins at the Louvre – the only pictures I liked.'

On 8 April 1925 in a letter to the artist Gwen Raverat she writes that 'Paris is a hostile, brilliant, alien city', and reflects on those who have settled and worked there: 'Nancy Cunard and Hope Mirrlees and myriads of the ineffective English live there, or rather hop from rock to rock.'

In September 1928 she spent in France a week alone with Vita Sackville-West which started with one day in Paris, recorded by Vita: 'Monday Sept 24. 1928. ... We arrived at Dieppe at 3. and took the train to Paris. In Paris we went to the Hotel de Londres, rue Bonaparte. We left our luggage & walked out to have dinner in a small restaurant on Bd. Raspail. Walking out we got into a bookshop where V. bought *J'adore* by Jean Desbordes, & I bought *L'Immoraliste*. There was an old man sitting in the bookshop, & he & the proprietor (a woman) fired off a rhapsody about Proust. We observed how this could never happen in England, – it was about 8 o'clock, yet there was the old customer sitting & discussing Proust, also Desbordes of whose literary success he said Cocteau would soon be jealous, "even if he had no other causes for jealousy".'

Woolf's early short stays provided possible material for chapter eleven of her 1922 novel, *Jacob's Room*. Young Jacob Flanders, who has been left a hundred pounds, uses the money for travel, starting in Paris before heading for Greece. His friends Cruttenden and Mallinson are hoping to become painters. The characters are partly based on Clive Bell, Duncan Grant and Roger Fry, who studied in Paris, and whom Woolf knew well. They were her sister Vanessa's husband and lovers and became painters and art critics. In the novel the young men discuss painting and literature but also refer to the French, 'the damned frogs':

'Don't listen to a man who don't like Velasquez,' said Mallinson.

'Adolphe, don't give Mr. Mallinson any more wine,' said Cruttenden.

'Fair play, fair play,' said Jacob judicially. 'Let a man get drunk if he likes. That's Shakespeare, Cruttenden. I'm with you there. Shakespeare had more guts than all these damned frogs put together. ...'

...

Well, not a word of this was ever told to Mrs. Flanders; nor what happened when they paid the bill and left the restaurant, and walked along the Boulevard Raspaille [*sic*].

Later on a visit to Versailles: 'Edward Cruttenden, Jinny Carslake, and Jacob Flanders walked in a row along the yellow gravel path; got on to the grass; so passed under the trees; and came out at the summer-house where Marie Antoinette used to drink chocolate.' Jacob's Parisian stay is summarised succinctly by his mother: '"Indeed he seems to be having ..."' said Mrs. Flanders, and paused, for she was cutting out a dress and had to straighten the pattern, " ... a very gay time." Mrs. Jarvis thought of Paris.'

Jacob's Room was a new departure in Virginia Woolf's writing and it has been suggested that Mirrlees's poem, published a few years earlier, had an impact on her narrative approach. Events are seen for example through the perspective of the various women in Jacob's life. Woolf was familiar with avant-garde writing, including Eliot's *The Waste Land* and Nancy Cunard's *Parallax*, as well as James Joyce's *Ulysses*, although she was rather disparaging about the latter, which had been recommended by T. S. Eliot: 'Never did any book so bore me!'

She was also critical of some of Mirrlees's novels, writing in a letter in February 1925, 'Do you admire her novels? – I can't get an ounce of joy from them.' This caused some tension between them, and a few months later she refers to Mirrlees's recently published novel *Madeleine*: '... when my review came out, Hope was very much disappointed: however, we've made it up now. I like her very much, but also find her as indeed I find her writing so full of affectations and precocities, that I lose my temper.'

Janet Flanner (1892–1978) spent her early years in Indianapolis. Having married young she discovered that she was more attracted by women when she fell in love with Solita Solano, an artist and writer whom she met in New York, while working there as a journalist. Solano encouraged her to leave her husband (they divorced in 1926) and start a freer life together, away from families and convention: 'I was looking for beauty with a capital B. And I couldn't find it in Indiana,' and Paris seemed the best destination. 'Each of us aspired to become a famous writer as soon as possible.'

By early autumn 1922 they had reached Paris, where they stayed in a cheap pension in rue de Quatrefages on the Left Bank, and then settled for the next seventeen years in the Hôtel Saint-Germain-des-Prés at 36 rue Bonaparte, where they occupied rooms 15 and 16; from 1932, when they became better off, they also took room 13. It was in this hotel that the French writer Jean Cocteau would come to smoke opium with his friends, in room 6, so perhaps they passed him on the stairs. They would eat in a neighbouring restaurant, La

Quatrième République, which she places in rue Jacob: 'Up to the 1930s I mostly lunched in my rue Jacob restaurant in the company of some minor Surrealists, Surrealism having become the latest Paris intellectual revolutionary aesthetic movement.' It was probably at 42 rue Bonaparte. She may have been recalling Michaud's, which (now Le Comptoir des Saints-Pères) is at 29 rue des Saints-Pères.

The Surrealists also frequented Flanner's favourite café, Les Deux Magots at 6 place Saint-Germain-des-Prés. They 'had their own club table facing the door of the Deux Magots, from which vantage point a seated Surrealist could conveniently insult any newcomer', she remarked in her letters from Paris. In 1925 she had become Paris correspondent for the recently founded *New Yorker* magazine. Her fortnightly *Letter from Paris*, written under the name of 'Genêt', described political, cultural and social life in the city, then in 'its golden hour'.

Paris was Yesterday, 1925–1939 (1972) is a collection of the pieces she wrote during those years. The *Paris Journal, 1944–65* (1965) contains her pieces written after the war. A further volume covered the years 1965–70. Flanner's witty and personal descriptions of the immense variety of the gifted people she met in Paris are a great testimony to her fifty years in Paris. She covered political and cultural figures, outstanding women like the dancers Isadora Duncan, 'a nomad de luxe', who got a lengthy piece in 1927, and Josephine Baker; Nancy Cunard, Coco Chanel (whose clothes she wore); the French writer Colette; and above all Sylvia Beach, whom she helped when her bookshop encountered financial difficulties.

Flanner enjoyed a long-lasting relationship with Hemingway, and in 1934 he invited her and Solita Solano to lunch at Michaud's with James Joyce. Solano remembered that Hemingway spent the whole lunch looking at the Irish

writer 'in a stupor of silent worship'. Flanner enjoyed the
meeting as she thought *Ulysses* 'the most exciting, important,
historic single literary event of the early Paris expatriate
literary colony'.

Flanner joined the group of women around Natalie
Clifford Barney and Djuna Barnes, whose circle also
included Gertrude Stein (it was Flanner who looked after the
ageing Alice B. Toklas, who spent her last years in poverty
after Gertrude Stein's death), Sylvia Beach and Adrienne
Monnier, 'these two extraordinary women – Melle Monnier,
buxom as an abbess, placidly picturesque in the costume
she had permanently adopted, consisting of a long, full
gray skirt, a bright velveteen waistcoat, and a white blouse,
and slim, jacketed Sylvia, with her schoolgirl white collar
and big colored bowknot, in the style of *Claudine à l'école*'.
Colette, the French author of *Claudine à l'école* (1900),
was mentioned in letters of June 1935 and October 1949.
Flanner's excellent French enabled her to translate Colette's
works, *Chéri* in 1929 and *Claudine at School* in 1930, and
she wrote introductions for the *The Pure and the Impure* in
1932 and for *7*, a collection of seven novellas in 1955.

Harold Ross, editor of the *New Yorker*, had chosen for her
the pen name Genêt, mistakenly taking it to be the French
version of Janet. He instructed her on what he wanted: 'I
am not paying you to tell what you think. I want to know
what the French are thinking.' He expected 'anecdotal and
incidental stuff familiar to Americans'. That did not prevent
her expressing her own feelings on the writers and artists she
met in her favourite cafés Les Deux Magots and de Flore: 'I
liked neither Pound's arbitrary historicity, nor his condensed
violence, nor his floating Chinese quotations, nor all his
weighty, ancient, mixed linguistics ...'

She rated Scott Fitzgerald's talent: 'Only Scott had realized that the bootlegger Gatsby represented the perfect picaresque American figure in that extraordinary alcoholic era. In his writing, Scott had the true tragic sense. To my mind, he alone created the pure and perfect anti-hero, the criminal lover defrauded of his love.'

Covering the vibrant Parisian cultural scene, she reported on the Ballets Russes, and George Antheil's *Ballet mécanique*, the preview of which she attended at Salle Pleyel at 22 rue de Rochechouart in the distinguished company of James Joyce, Natalie Barney and the Hemingways. 'It is really wonderful ... It's good but awful,' she wrote in the *New Yorker* on 24 October 1925. Her taste was for less avant-garde music, and she dedicated many admiring pages to composers like Ravel, Bizet, Gounod and Delius. But she also took great pleasure reporting on popular entertainment like the Medrano circus, then at 63 boulevard de Rochechouart. She also excelled in her inimitable prose on subjects like obituaries, *faits divers*, crimes, gruesome murders (the Papin sisters), and the Paris executioner, mentioned in 1932: 'As a matter of fact, the present Monsieur de Paris wears not a blossom, but a derby hat; is middle-aged, taciturn and married; limps; and is morbidly jealous of his position as fourth generation in a Breton family of what amounts to hereditary high executioner, which post he, lacking a son, has fought to have passed on to his daughter's husband. (The job pays three thousand francs a head).' Many pages were dedicated to the Stavisky scandal (1934–35) and to other prominent criminal cases.

In the 1930s her letters became more political, and dealt with more serious European events, the exodus caused by the Spanish Civil War, the wave of antisemitism and the approach of war. On 4 October 1939 she fled Paris for New York, returning promptly after the liberation, and resuming her letters, which appeared less regularly as she travelled in post-war, shell-shocked Europe, covering major events including the Nuremberg trials. The letters, now written under her own name, were more sombre, covering the devastation caused by the war. Her last letter was written in September 1975. By that time, after a brief spell at the Ritz, she had settled in the Hôtel Continental in rue Castiglione, in room 481 on the top floor, with a balcony from which she would survey Paris.

The French appreciated her literary journalism, and she was made *Chevalier de la légion d'honneur* in 1972. Her personal correspondence is also testimony to her fifty-two years in the French capital. She wrote regularly to various friends, including Solita Solano, with whom she stayed in touch to the end of her life, as well as to the Italian publisher and editor Natalia Danesi Murray, her lover in later life.

Sidonie-Gabrielle Colette (1873–1954), generally known as Colette, left provincial Burgundy to go to Paris after her marriage in 1893 to Henry Gauthier-Villars ('Willy'). Willy was much older and was a successful but rather unsavoury literary editor, who encouraged her to write a series of short, partly autobiographical and sexually titillating novels. *Claudine à Paris* (Claudine in Paris, 1901) relates how the very young, newly married Claudine discovers *fin-de-siècle* Paris. The four Claudine novels were produced under duress, as Colette was occasionally locked in a room by her husband until she had written enough pages; he then published them under his own name. After thirteen years she rebelled and they were divorced. Colette now became involved with Mathilde de Morny, also called Missy, an aristocrat with whom she embarked on a scandalous affair. Paris tolerated lesbian relationships only up to a point, and the pantomime *Rêve d'Égypte* at the Moulin Rouge in 1907 provoked a public outcry when Colette and Missy were seen kissing openly on stage.

In 1932 Colette published *Le pur et l'impur* (The Pure and the Impure), a series of reflections on love, desire and relationships, with an introduction by Janet Flanner. During the Occupation in 1944 Colette wrote *Gigi*, a light-hearted novel set in Paris. Its escapism appealed, and a musical adaptation by Anita Loos followed, starring Audrey Hepburn (whom Colette had personally picked), opening on Broadway in 1951. The novel, published in English in 1953, portrays a fifteen-year-old Parisian girl groomed by her grandmother to become a high-class courtesan, but who has her own agenda and marries a wealthy older man for love. The film version, shot in 1958 by Vincente Minnelli, starred Leslie Caron, Louis Jourdan and Maurice Chevalier, and was a great success. The recent film *Colette* (2018), directed by Wash Westmoreland and starring Keira Knightley as Colette, covers this formative period of the French writer's life in Paris, as she learns to become free and independent.

6

The Lost Generation

*'That's what you are. That's what you all are,' Miss Stein
said. 'All of you young people who served in the war. You
are all a lost generation.'*

(Ernest Hemingway)

Eliot's poem *The Waste Land* (1922) is a breakthrough in
Modernist literature, expressing the futility and despair felt
after 1918. For the generation of American and English
writers like Hemingway, Ford Madox Ford and Dos Passos,
who came of age during World War I, Paris represented
everything their homeland was not. Those post-war years
have been dubbed *les années folles*, the Jazz Age, the Roaring
Twenties, but that apparent gaiety masked the continuing
suffering of the so-called 'lost generation'. These writers
settled in Montparnasse on the Left Bank. They wrote
in cafés by day, frequented clubs at night, drank without
restriction, and enjoyed the city's liberated way of life. They
were preparing their own reaction to the war; it had made
traditional writing styles inadequate, and a literary revolution
was under way. Somerset Maugham puts into prose the

lasting effect of wartime: '… you don't know what experience
he had in the war that so profoundly moved him. … I suggest
to you that whatever it was that happened to Larry filled him
with a sense of the transiency of life, and an anguish to be
sure that there was a compensation for the sin and sorrow of
the world.' These young writers owed much to Sylvia Beach
and her bookshop, Shakespeare and Company.

'My loves were Adrienne Monnier and James Joyce and
Shakespeare and Company.' **Sylvia Beach** (1887–1962)
was fourteen when she arrived in Paris in 1901 with her
father, a Presbyterian clergyman from Baltimore who was
called to serve in Paris. The family returned to the US in
1906, but Beach was back in Paris in the spring of 1917
to study, as she had 'a particular interest in contemporary
French writing'. She stayed first at the Hôtel Beaujolais, 15
rue de Beaujolais, and then shared a flat with her sister in
the Palais-Royal. During World War I she volunteered for
relief work and joined the *volontaires agricoles* (agricultural
volunteers), sharing their hard work picking grapes and
grafting trees in Touraine, before working further afield
for the Red Cross in Belgrade. It took her three full years
to decide what to do with her life, but finally in 1919
she decided to settle in Paris permanently and to open
Shakespeare and Company, a bookshop selling mainly
British books at 8 rue Dupuytren in Saint-Germain-des-
Prés. Since interest in American literature was growing
in Paris, she added portraits of Edgar Allan Poe and Walt
Whitman to those of Shakespeare and Oscar Wilde in her
shop, which quickly became too cramped. In July 1921
she moved to larger premises at 12 rue de l'Odéon, which
served as a lending library for the many customers who
could not afford to buy books. For those away from home

it was a godsend, a useful postal address, and somewhere occasionally to borrow money. The subscribers were dubbed 'bunnies', an invented word derived from the French word for subscriber: *abonné*. The bookshop was also an outlet for avant-garde publications like *The Little Review*, *Broom* and the *Transatlantic Review*. Readings, sometimes with music, attracted expatriate writers of the 'lost generation'; Hemingway, Fitzgerald, Eliot, Pound and Ford Madox Ford, as well as many female writers, including Djuna Barnes, Gertrude Stein, Janet Flanner, Kay Boyle and Mina Loy. They were joined by French authors interested in English and American literature including André Gide, Paul Valéry and Jules Romains.

'On a cold windswept street, this was a warm, cheerful place with a big stove in winter, tables and shelves of books, new books in the window, and photographs on the wall of famous writers both dead and living,' wrote Hemingway nostalgically in his memoir *A Moveable Feast* (1964). Sylvia Beach was a good friend to him and lent him money when he went to Toronto with his wife Hadley for the birth of their son. He was grateful for her kindness, 'no one that I ever knew was nicer to me'. She was probably one of the very few people with whom he never fell out. She introduced him to Paris life and French writers, and in exchange he and his wife Hadley took her and Adrienne Monnier to cycle races at the Vélodrome d'hiver at 6 boulevard de Grenelle and to boxing matches in Ménilmontant.

Gertrude Stein also came to the shop, as recalled by Janet Flanner: 'Miss Stein was the first subscriber to Sylvia's lending library, for which she wrote a jocular little advertisement, sent to the rest of us Americans in the quarter, to incite us also to subscribe, which most of us did. It read, "Rich and

Poor in English to Subscribers in French and other Latin Tongues," and concluded with a more cogent statement of Sylvia's book-rental terms ... Gertrude was so outraged when Sylvia began the publication of James Joyce's "*Ulysses*" that she called at Shakespeare and Company to inform Sylvia that thereafter she and Miss Toklas would borrow books only from the eminently respectable official American Library, on the Right Bank.'

Beach had met James Joyce at a party in July 1920. Despite her lack of experience, she had recklessly offered to publish his novel *Ulysses*, banned at the time in Britain and the US for obscenity, and rejected by several established publishers. When *Ulysses* was published by Sylvia Beach in February 1922, according to Janet Flanner it 'burst over the Left Bank like an explosion in print whose words and phrases fell on us like a gift of tongues, like a less than holy Pentecostal experience'. Joyce was delighted, but it was also a breakthrough for the bookshop. It brought a huge reward, even after managing Joyce's extravagant needs and requests, as well as the demanding task of correcting proofs of this complex text and then printing it in English in France. The first thousand copies during the following eleven years were sold exclusively by her shop. Joyce became a regular visitor, as Flanner recalled: 'We also used to see him often in front of Sylvia's shop. He was a frail-looking figure to have caused such an international commotion – with his black hat cocked on the back of his head, twirling his cane and wearing not very clean white sneakers.' As Sylvia herself said, 'There was always something a little shabby about Mr. Joyce.' She thought him handsome, with his deep-blue eyes, one badly damaged by glaucoma, which had half-blinded him. The peak of his prosperity came in 1932, with the news of

PHOTO 19 Sylvia Beach's bookshop Shakespeare and Company was at 12 rue de l'Odéon

the sale of the rights to *Ulysses* to Random House for forty-five thousand dollars. Sylvia maintained that he failed to announce this deal to her, and, as was later known, he never offered her a penny. 'I understood from the first that, working with or for Mr. Joyce, the pleasure was mine – an infinite pleasure: the profits were for him,' she wrote in her memoirs. 'All that was available from his work, and I managed to keep it available, was his.' Sylvia, who lionised him, engineered a brief meeting between Joyce and Gertrude Stein in the 1930s at a party at the studio of the sculptor Jo Davidson in avenue du Maine, where both writers exchanged a few polite words, but never met again.

Sylvia had been encouraged to open her bookshop in 1919 by her French partner **Adrienne Monnier**, who also owned a bookshop, La Maison des amis des livres, which had been running since November 1915 at 7 rue de l'Odéon. It functioned as a cultural meeting point for French writers,

PHOTO 20 Adrienne Monnier's bookshop was at 7 rue de l'Odéon

critics and intellectuals like Gide, Fargue, Valéry, Larbaud and the Surrealists.

Adrienne Monnier knew them all well. She too had a good relationship with Joyce. Monnier had the first French translation of *Ulysses* published, which was launched in her shop. Les amis du dessin; an art shop which was later to occupy the space was named as a tribute to Monnier's bookshop. She published other French translations including Hemingway's short story 'The Undefeated' in 1926 in *Navire d'argent* (The Silver Ship), her influential but short-lived literary monthly which aimed at being 'French in language, but international in spirit'. The name came from the ship in the coat of arms of Paris. Financially unsound, *Navire d'argent* lasted less than a year, but helped to launch the career in France of T. S. Eliot, whose poem 'The Love Song of J. Alfred Prufrock' Monnier published in May 1925. An extract from Joyce's *Finnegans Wake* appeared in October 1925, and a short version of *The Aviator*, a novella by Saint-Exupéry, in April 1926. The March 1926 issue was dedicated to the American writers Walt Whitman, William Carlos Williams and e e cummings, as well as to Hemingway. Financial pressure brought the venture to an end in May 1926, and Monnier had to auction her own collection of books, many with precious dedications, to cover the losses. Literary afternoons took place in the bookshop; these were not always peaceable affairs, and the poet and writer Archibald MacLeish recalled one when he felt the antagonism between André Gide and Hemingway so strongly that he wondered 'whether Hemingway restrained a desire to hit him'.

Adrienne and Sylvia loved entertaining at their apartment at 18 rue de l'Odéon, where writers were treated to memorable dinners. Adrienne's love of cooking was, according to Sylvia, her '… great amusement and indoor sport'. But those were the heydays, and things changed in the early 1930s when many of the Americans suffering from the consequences of the 1929 financial crash returned home, leaving Sylvia Beach's bookshop in a precarious state. Things were not helped after Joyce sold the rights of *Ulysses* to Random House. The bookshop was saved thanks to the active support of reliable friends like André Gide and Paul Valéry, joined by Eliot in 1936, who organised readings to raise money to fend off the closure. He came to read *The Waste Land* in a 'grave, beautifully modulated voice' and Hemingway, who had not completely forgotten Sylvia Beach's former generosity, brought along Stephen Spender, whom he had just met in Spain.

Shakespeare and Company survived until 1941, but things were not easy in occupied France. In December a Nazi officer who professed to be an admirer of Joyce demanded to buy Beach's last copy of *Finnegans Wake*, which he had seen in the window. Beach refused, and the officer threatened to return to confiscate all of her goods and close her bookstore for good. With the help of friends she packed up 5,000 books and files, photographs and furniture in a matter of hours and moved everything to a larger vacant flat further up the building above the shop. She was arrested in 1942 and interned for six months, and after her release she went into hiding for a time in the students' hostel at 93 boulevard Saint-Michel to avoid further arrest. The bookshop never reopened after the liberation of Paris, but Beach wrote articles, and made a start on her memoirs, *Shakespeare and Company*, published in 1959. The book is a delight, as after preliminary chapters on her childhood, she describes the story of her Parisian bookshop with its extraordinary customers and the 'bunnies'. Joyce and his family and circle tend to dominate the narrative, and the last pages give an entertaining description of how she was 'liberated' in August 1944 by a grey-bearded uniformed American arriving in her street with jeeps and men; he turned out to be Hemingway. She still lent books, but to a happy few like André Gide, Simone de Beauvoir and the exiled African-American writer Richard Wright. In 1962 Beach died unexpectedly at 12 rue de l'Odéon. When told she had died alone, Archibald MacLeish pointed out that 'she is not alone, then or ever. She had that company around her'.

'That company' reappeared to general surprise in 1951. In 1947 an eccentric American ex-serviceman, **George Whitman** (1913–2011), came to Paris thanks to a grant through the Servicemen's Readjustment Act of 1944 (or GI Bill), and decided to open a bookshop, Le Mistral, as he needed to find a home for his huge collection of books. He came across a building in the heart of the city by the river at 37 rue de la Bûcherie, next to the iconic building of Notre-Dame. The former monastic building of St Julien had been attached to the cathedral. A great admirer of Sylvia Beach, Whitman managed to salvage material from her legendary bookshop and opened the present-day store in 1951. He lived above the shop, writing two months after the opening: 'In the morning I wake up with the sun in my face and a vision of chimney pots floating above the treetops in the garden of St Julien-le-Pauvre. At night I look out the window at the illuminated spires of Notre-Dame. This is the bookstore I have always dreamed of.'

'Be not inhospitable to strangers, lest they be angels in disguise,' was one of Whitman's sayings to welcome visitors. He wished to keep the tradition of hospitality, started in 'Odéonia' (as the 'bunnies' referred to the bookshops in rue de l'Odéon) by Sylvia Beach and Adrienne Monnier. Beach herself came to speak at the bookshop in 1958. A bed for a night was offered to aspiring writers in exchange for a few hours of work and a commitment to read one book a day. In 1964, to mark the 400th anniversary of Shakespeare's birth, Le Mistral was renamed as Shakespeare and Company, in honour of Sylvia Beach's shop. It attracted writers including Henry Miller (who allegedly arranged midnight rendezvous there), Richard Wright, Langston Hughes, Lawrence Durrell, Anaïs Nin (who left her will under Whitman's bed), Ray Bradbury, Julio Cortázar, James Baldwin and the writers of the Beat Generation, Jack Kerouac and Allen Ginsberg. Nowadays the shop is still packed with signed photos and testimonies, and of course, makeshift beds.

Like its predecessor the bookshop organises public readings, sometimes with music, and book presentations. Whitman's daughter, named Sylvia after Sylvia Beach, began co-managing Shakespeare and Company with her father in 2003, and since 2006 has run the shop with her partner, David Delannet. George Whitman had founded a literary festival in 2003 which hosted writers such as Paul Auster, Siri Hustvedt and Jeanette Winterson, and a year before he died The Paris Literary Prize for unpublished novellas was launched there. Sylvia Whitman and David Delannet opened a café in 2015 next door in a former garage and there is talk of opening a cinema. The history of the bookshop was published in 2016 as *Shakespeare and Company, Paris: A History of the Rag & Bone Shop of the Heart* which includes an epilogue by Sylvia Whitman and a foreword by Jeanette Winterson.

A regular visitor at Beach's Shakespeare and Company was the enormously gifted American poet, musicologist and art critic **Ezra Pound** (1885–1972). Pound studied Romance Languages at the University of Pennsylvania, where his fellow student the poet William Carlos Williams described him as 'the livest, most intelligent and unexplainable thing'. He left the US in 1908 for Europe with very little money. He came to London via Venice, and remained based there until 1921. In Paris from February to August 1911, to work on a volume of poetry, he had an intense poetical experience while leaving the Métro at the place de la Concorde. The result, after many months of editing, was a short poem, written in English, 'In a Station of the Metro' (1913). The original thirty lines were drastically reduced to just fourteen words: 'The apparition of these faces in the crowd / Petals on a wet, black bough.' It is an pioneering experimental example of language in its most lapidary form, doing away altogether with verbs. Considered a leading poem of the Imagist tradition, it is essentially a set of unexpected images conveying the fleeting intense emotion experienced by the poet, who explained that 'In a poem of this sort one is trying to record the precise instant when a thing outward and objective transforms itself, or darts into a thing inward and subjective.'

Pound was one of the first Modernist poets to reduce a poem to one concise image, combined with a kind of musical rhythm suggesting a brief 'instant of time', the ultimate purpose being to trigger the reader's subconscious to create a flash of understanding. He had become acquainted with many of the writers and artists connected with the Imagist and Vorticist movements, in vogue at the time. He also admired James Joyce, to whom he started writing in 1913. Joyce was then based in Trieste, and Pound became one of his most active supporters and unpaid literary agent, and in July 1920, after seven years of correspondence, he finally met him in Italy and subsequently travelled to Paris to be there to help him to settle there with his family, and to arrange a meeting with Sylvia Beach, which led to the publication of *Ulysses*.

Pound followed Joyce to Paris, living there from 1921 to 1924 and becoming one of the most generous and indefatigable supporters of the expatriate intellectual community. He befriended a wide range of fellow artists and writers including Braque, Brancusi, Cocteau and Tzara. In rue Notre-Dame-des-Champs, the street where Whistler (an artist he loved) had lived, he found accommodation at no.70 bis, and a painter's studio for his wife, the artist Dorothy Shakespear, in which Pound also made some sculptures, described later by Ernest Hemingway in *A Moveable Feast*. It was far from luxurious accommodation, but it was comfortable with a stove, good light, and furniture he made himself.

In 1921 T. S. Eliot gave Pound the manuscript of *The Waste Land* to read. Pound was deeply impressed and possibly envious, but started working on it to produce a reduced final version which Eliot must have liked, since he dedicated the poem to him, calling him '*Il miglior fabbro*' (the finer craftsman). They got on well, although many found Pound arrogant, resenting his dandyish figure in bohemian Montparnasse: 'His costume – the velvet jacket and open-road shirt – was that of the English aesthete of the period. There was a touch of Whistler about him; his language, on the other hand, was Huckleberry Finn's,' wrote Sylvia Beach.

In late 1921 Pound met Hemingway, who initially disapproved of the bohemian *poseur* look, but subsequently warmed to him. The older Pound took the younger writer, who had just arrived in Paris, under his wing, to give him advice on his writing in exchange for boxing lessons: 'I have been teaching Pound to box with little success. He habitually leads wit[h] his chin and has the general grace of the crayfish or crawfish. He's willing but short-winded,' reported Hemingway in a letter to Sherwood Anderson. They also often played tennis together. Generous with his time, and eager to share his connections, Hemingway introduced Pound to other writers and to Natalie Barney, who received every Friday afternoon in her salon at 20 rue Jacob. Pound's visit to Gertrude Stein's Saturday afternoon salon had been a disaster, as he had broken one of her nice chairs and was never invited again. He called her 'an old tub of guts' while she referred to him disparagingly as 'the village explainer'.

His clumsiness and style of conversation had been described by Stella Bowen, Ford's partner: 'His movements, though not uncontrolled, were sudden and angular, and his droning American voice, breaking into bomb-shells of emphasis, was rather incomprehensible as he enlightened on the Way, the Truth, and the Light, in Art.'

In 1923 Pound published *Indiscretions*, a short autobiography, and was invited to join the *Transatlantic Review* as assistant editor by Ford Madox Ford, whom he had met in 1909 in London.

Busy also on the avant-garde music scene, Pound had composed an opera, *Le Testament de Villon*, in 1919, and promoted the American composer George Antheil, for whom he wrote *Antheil and the Treatise on Harmony* (1924). With his mistress, the violinist Olga Rudge, whom he had met at a musical afternoon in Natalie Barney's salon, Pound performed his own compositions and eighteenth-century airs which he had discovered. Any possible spare time he had was spent writing his *Cantos*, a collection of poems on which he worked until the end of his life, as well as working on essays and anthologies on the French poets.

In 1924, growing tired of Paris, which was, according to him, too full of Americans, he left for Italy with his wife. As he put it: 'We came to find something, to learn, possibly to conserve, but this lot came in disgust.' He could not keep away for good, however, and Pound and his wife were staying at the Hôtel Foyot in rue de Tournon in 1926.

The move to Italy with Dorothy and Olga Rudge, who had followed them, proved ultimately to be disastrous. Pound's open support for Fascist ideology, as well as his antisemitic broadcasts on Roman radio, led to his arrest for treason in May 1945. After suffering from a breakdown

caused by his incarceration, he escaped the death penalty.
He was repatriated to the US a year later and placed in St
Elizabeth's, a mental hospital outside Washington, where
he remained for twelve long years. His liberation in 1958
was assisted by many artists and writers he had known
in London and Paris, including Hemingway, Eliot and
MacLeish. Now a broken man, who had 'missed out twenty
years of life', according to his daughter by Olga Rudge,
Mary de Rachewiltz, he spent the rest of his life with Olga in
Italy, but he celebrated his eightieth birthday in Paris on 30
October 1965, when Dominique de Roux organised a party
for him, to which Natalie Barney was invited. Friends took
him to see Samuel Beckett's *Endgame* and the two writers
met, although only a few words were exchanged. There was
one last visit to Paris in September 1968, before he died. His
obscure tomb is in San Michele cemetery in Venice, the city
where he had started his European journey more than sixty
years earlier.

Ernest Hemingway (1899–1961), born in Illinois in the
US, first experienced Paris in 1918 on his way to serve as
a Red Cross ambulance driver in Italy when he was not yet
twenty, but it was in 1921 that, armed with a commission
to write on France for the *Toronto Star*, he returned with his
new wife Hadley.

He had planned a move to Rome, but changed his mind
when the author Sherwood Anderson advised him to go to
Paris instead, partly because of the favourable exchange rate,
which would allow funds to stretch further, but above all
because Paris was 'where the most interesting people in the
world lived'. After a brief stay in the Hôtel Jacob et d'Angleterre
at 44 rue Jacob, the couple could afford only a small flat at

PHOTO 21   Hemingway's studio at 39 rue Descartes

74 rue Cardinal Lemoine, situated above a *bal musette* (dance hall). The writer, determined to succeed, rented a small attic studio nearby at 39 rue Descartes where he started on some short stories, inspired perhaps by being in the building where the French poet Paul Verlaine had died in 1896.

Much of what he wrote was lost when Hadley mislaid a suitcase full of his early writing at the Gare de Lyon. The Hemingways left Paris in 1923, and returned in 1924 with their baby son Jack (nicknamed Bumby), who had been born in Canada. Hemingway had stopped working for the *Toronto Star*, and they were worse off, as he recalled in *A Moveable Feast*: 'But when you are poor, and we were truly poor when I had given up all journalism when we came back from Canada, and could sell no stories at all, it was too rough with

a baby in Paris in the winter.' They settled in a modest flat
at 113 rue Notre-Dame-des-Champs, above a sawmill. Fame
came quickly however, as a collection of very short stories,
Three Stories and Ten Poems, was published in 1923, followed
by *In Our Time* in 1924.

Sherwood Andersen introduced him to Gertrude Stein,
who took immediately to him: 'I remember very well the
impression I had of Hemingway that first afternoon. He was an
extraordinarily good-looking young man, twenty-three years
old ... rather foreign-looking, with passionately interested,
rather than interesting eyes.' She included him in her circle
of friends, which included Picasso and Ezra Pound, and in
April 1925 he met Scott Fitzgerald at the Dingo, a popular
bar at 10 rue Delambre. Hemingway enjoyed this stimulating
and varied crowd, and encouraged and guided by Ezra Pound
and Gertrude Stein, started to experiment with a new style
of writing, a factual, straightforward journalistic approach
combined with the innovative use of short sentences, which
he himself described succinctly: 'My aim is to put down on

PHOTO 22 The Dingo Bar (now Auberge de Venise), where
Hemingway and Fitzgerald met

paper what I see and what I feel in the best and simplest way.'
This innovative approach brought him fame when his novel
The Sun Also Rises came out in 1926.

All had changed by this stage in his domestic life, as he had
fallen in love with the fashion journalist Pauline Pfeiffer and
separated from Hadley. He married Pauline on 10 May 1927
in the Église de Saint-Honoré d'Eylau. She was well-off, and
they were able to move to an elegant flat at 6 rue Férou,
near the church of Saint-Sulpice. It was there that in March
1928 the accident-prone Hemingway pulled the bathroom
skylight chain mistaking it for the WC chain. The skylight
crashed down onto his head and he had to be rushed to the
American Hospital at 63 boulevard Victor Hugo. The injury
left him scarred for life, and the incident provoked one of
Gertrude Stein's malicious comments: 'Ernest is very fragile,
whenever he does anything sporting something breaks, his
arm, his leg, or his head.'

During the first years in Paris, keen to improve his literary
knowledge, Hemingway joined the regular meetings at La
Maison des amis des livres, Adrienne Monnier's bookshop,
where he also borrowed books, as he did from Sylvia Beach's
Shakespeare and Company. 'In those days there was no
money to buy books. Books you borrowed from the rental
library of Shakespeare and Company, which was the library
and bookstore of Sylvia Beach at 12 rue de l'Odéon.' At
Shakespeare and Company one evening he attended a
lecture on Joyce's *Ulysses* and was introduced to the author,
who became a drinking companion. The Irish writer would
drop in regularly to read reviews and inquire about sales.
Hemingway also befriended the journalist Janet Flanner
and the composer Virgil Thomson, who were long-term
residents in Paris. For relaxation the active and sporty

'champ' (as he was dubbed), went to box at the *Montmartre sportif*, followed by a stop at Harry's New York Bar at 5 rue Daunou. When they were married, he and Hadley attended horse racing at Enghien and Auteuil. John Dos Passos described also his passion for cycling around the city 'in a striped jumper like a contestant on the Tour de France'. He attended races at the Vélodrome d'hiver and would insist on dragging his friends along. In his novel *Islands in the Stream* (published posthumously in 1970) the older writer revisits the good old times, possibly 'the happiest times? ... A bicycle was more fun than a motorcar. You saw things better and it kept you in good shape and coming home after you had ridden in the Bois you could coast down the Champs Elysées well past the Rond-Point ...' The novel which brought him instant fame in 1926, *The Sun Also Rises*, was a *roman à clef* portraying disillusioned English and American expatriates, drawn from his circle of friends and acquaintances in Paris. The main protagonist, Jake Barnes, a kind of alter ego, is doomed, as his war injuries have made him impotent. Afraid of being corrupted by his wealthy compatriots, he leaves Paris with a group of friends, hoping to find a more authentic way of life in Spain. The book captured the mood of the time and sold well, but Hemingway's mother hated it and decided that it was: 'one of the filthiest books of the year'. She obviously disliked her son's plain language: 'surely you have other words in your vocabulary than "damn" and "bitch"? Every page fills me with a sick loathing.' Others found the novel misogynistic, homophobic and antisemitic. But his publisher, Scribner, praised its innovative qualities: '[Hemingway] was inventing a whole new idiom and tonality ... and he was completely 20th century.' Hemingway had learned a great deal from his

Paris friends, including Gertrude Stein, Pound and Joyce. A keen visitor to the Musée du Luxembourg, he also claimed to have learned from Cézanne's paintings. A critic noted at the time that he succeeded in doing for writing what Picasso and the Cubists had been doing for painting. A film version of *The Sun Also Rises* was directed by Henry King in 1957 with Tyrone Power and Ava Gardner. The French singer and actress Juliette Gréco plays Georgette, the prostitute whom Jack meets in the opening chapter. After the novel's successful publication and his divorce from Hadley, who was granted the proceeds in settlement, Hemingway left Paris in March 1928 with Pauline, planning to return to the US and settle at Key West. But Paris was not forgotten, and the city appeared in later writing, in short stories like 'The Snows of Kilimanjaro' (1936), but above all in *A Moveable Feast*, which describes how he became a writer in those first hopeful youthful years of apprenticeship, which had so much to do with Paris. Hemingway started *A Moveable Feast* in 1956 after having rediscovered some trunks stored in the basement of the Ritz before his departure in March 1928, as recalled by his biographer A. E. Hotchner:

> Ernest did not remember storing the trunk, but he did recall that in the 1920s Louis Vuitton had made a special trunk for him. Ernest had wondered what had become of it. ... It was filled with a ragtag collection of clothes, menus, receipts, memos, hunting and fishing paraphernalia, skiing equipment, racing forms, correspondence and, on the bottom, something that elicited a joyful reaction from Ernest: "The notebooks! So that's where they were! *Enfin!*" There were two stacks of lined notebooks like the ones used by schoolchildren in Paris when he lived there in the '20s. Ernest had filled them with his careful handwriting

while sitting in his favorite café, nursing a *café crème*. The
notebooks described the places, the people, the events of
his penurious life.

The notebooks were transcribed, and in Cuba in 1957, almost
thirty years after the events, he began putting together the
memoirs which would eventually become *A Moveable Feast*.
After his suicide in 1961, his fourth wife and widow Mary,
who was acting as his literary executor, allegedly deleted some
of the section devoted to his first wife Hadley. *A Moveable
Feast* was published posthumously in 1964, too late for
Ford Madox Ford, Scott and Zelda Fitzgerald and Gertrude
Stein to read his often unkind descriptions of them. His
relationship with Stein had started well. Thanks to her he
had been introduced to a new world in her weekly salon:
'The pictures were wonderful and the talk was very good.
She talked, mostly, and she told me about modern pictures
and about painters … and she talked about her work.' She
and her partner Alice B. Toklas were the godmothers of
his young son. He helped her out by having her very long
novel *The Making of Americans* (1902–1911) published in
Ford's *Transatlantic Review*. As he reflected in *A Moveable
Feast*: 'By that time we liked each other very much and I had
already learned some time before that everything I did not
understand probably had something to it. Miss Stein thought
that I was too uneducated about sex and I must admit that I
had certain prejudices against homosexuality since I knew its
more primitive aspects.' But the friendship was not to last.
'She quarrelled with nearly all of us that were fond of her
except Juan Gris and she couldn't quarrel with him because
he was dead. … Finally she even quarrelled with the new
friends but none of us followed it any more. She got to look
like a Roman emperor and that was fine if you liked your

women to look like Roman emperors.' Hemingway claimed
that Stein quarrelled with everyone, but he himself fell out
with most of those who helped him. His comments on Ford
Madox Ford are vicious: 'I had always avoided looking at
Ford when I could and I always held my breath when I was
near him in a closed room …' A few friends like Ezra Pound
are spared: 'Ezra Pound was always a good friend and he was
always doing things for people. The studio where he lived
with his wife Dorothy on the rue Notre-Dame-des-Champs
was as poor as Gertrude's studio was rich.' The final section is
a nostalgic tribute to Paris: 'There is never any ending to Paris
and the memory of each person who has lived in it differs
from that of any other. … [Paris] was always worth it and we
received a return for whatever we brought to it. … But this is
how Paris was in the early days when we were poor and very
happy.' He also expresses his deep regret for having separated
from his wife Hadley: 'I wished I had died before I loved
anyone but her.' Many of his books are regretful reflections
on the years spent in Paris between 1922 and 1926, for
example the novel *Islands in the Stream* and the short story
'The Snows of Kilimanjaro'. In the latter, the protagonist,
Harry, has gone to Africa to get away from Paris and his rich
and pretentious friends. He recalls his past life, in which he
experienced, like the author, years of poverty in Paris, bearable
then, since life was full of hope and true love. This section
of the book surely inspired Woody Allen's *Midnight in Paris*.
One of Hemingway's most memorable returns to Paris was at
the end of World War II in July 1944. He was reporting for
the magazine *Collier's* but arrived as 'an irregular combatant'
in full military gear, joining the Allies (who had landed in
Normandy the previous month) in their march to liberate
Paris. Hemingway, who had claimed that he would be the first

American 'to liberate the Ritz', his favourite bar, descended on the hotel in the place Vendôme in a jeep, brandishing an illicit machine gun. The Ritz, however, was deserted and the Germans long gone. He nevertheless checked into the hotel, allegedly ordered sixty dry martinis for his troop of irregular soldiers and proceeded to clear the cellars. He called on a few old friends like Sylvia Beach, who was delighted to see him, but Picasso was not at home. Later he reported to Hadley on 24 April 1945 that he had 'liberated' more of his favourite watering-holes: 'We liberated Lipp (old man gave me a bottle of Martell) and then liberated the Nègre de Toulouse. It was the wildest, most beautiful wonderful time ever.' One of five new stories completed in 1956, but published only recently by *Strand Magazine* in 2018, 'A Room on the Garden Side', is a fictionalised account of the episode in the Ritz Hotel. It portrays Robert, the inevitable alter ego character, also dubbed 'Papa', which was Hemingway's own well-known nickname. It is a reflection on whether Paris can recover from the war, and on the dangers of corruption brought by fame. Hemingway was back in Paris with his fourth wife Mary in 1953. It was in 1956 that he was again staying at the Ritz and miraculously found the trunk with the famous notebooks which he used to write *A Moveable Feast*. After his suicide in America in 1961 Hemingway became largely forgotten in France, but the legend lived on, and when Paris suffered terrorist attacks on 13 November 2015, in which 130 people were killed, *A Moveable Feast* (*Paris est une fête*) became a symbol of celebration, of defiance in the face of terrorism. There has been much recent writing on Hemingway and on those memorable years in Paris, including a fictionalised account of his life with Hadley, in Paula McLain's *The Paris Wife* (2011).

De janvier 1922 à août 1923 a vécu, au troisième étage de cet immeuble, avec Hadley, son épouse, l'écrivain américain

Ernest HEMINGWAY
1899 - 1961

Le quartier, qu'il aimait par-dessus tout, fut le véritable lieu de naissance de son œuvre et du style dépouillé qui la caractérise. Cet Américain à Paris entretenait des relations familières avec ses voisins, notamment le patron du bal-musette attenant.

« Tel était le Paris de notre jeunesse. au temps où nous étions très pauvres et très heureux »
Ernest Hemingway (Paris est une fête)

Association la Mémoire des Lieux

PHOTO 23   Hemingway is commemorated at 74 rue du Cardinal Lemoine

Francis Scott Fitzgerald (1896–1940) and **Zelda Sayre Fitzgerald** (1900–48) arrived in Paris on their way to the Riviera in May 1924 with high expectations: 'We were going to the Old World to find a new rhythm for our lives with a true conviction that we had left our old selves behind forever – and with a capital of just over seven thousand dollars.' This move turned out to be disastrous, as Scott, who had started to drink heavily before leaving for Europe, continued to do so in France, eventually becoming an alcoholic, and Zelda succumbed gradually to depression and mental illness.

Scott Fitzgerald had met Zelda Sayre in her birthplace, Montgomery, Alabama, where he had been drafted to train for the war in Europe. Unlike his hero Gatsby he never saw action, as the Armistice was signed before he was due to leave. He had fallen in love with Zelda, attracted by her wild and uninhibited lifestyle. The success of Fitzgerald's novel *This Side of Paradise*, published in 1920, enabled them to marry, and following the birth of their daughter Scottie in 1921 they moved to New York, where their hedonistic lifestyle became legendary over the next four years. Another novel followed in 1922 with the somewhat prophetic title, *The Beautiful and Damned*, and the beautiful (but not yet damned) 'golden couple' became the toast of the town. Scott loved New York (where he had coined the expression 'The Jazz Age') and was not particularly attracted by Paris, but his writing was not progressing. He did not speak much French, and nor did Zelda, and his priority was to get his writing going again and complete his third novel, *The Great Gatsby* (1925). The couple had been spending wildly and had run out of funds. The idea of going to France, with its relatively inexpensive cost of living, was meant to be a new start for both of them. Zelda recognised herself in the character of Gloria Gilbert in *The Beautiful and Damned* and had become increasingly unhappy at the fact that her husband was using her letters, diaries and conversations in his novels and short stories, sometimes verbatim.

On arrival in Paris they checked in at the Hôtel des Deux Mondes at 22 avenue de l'Opéra, but left almost immediately and headed for the South of France. The idea had come from Sara and Gerald Murphy, a wealthy American couple who lived partly in the elegant sixteenth arrondissement at 2 rue Greuze, but also spent much time on the Riviera. They were patrons of the arts and supporters of the Ballets Russes. In Paris Gerald had studied painting with Fernand Léger, and Sara, also an aspiring painter, kept a salon and looked after their three small children. They enjoyed an enviable lavish lifestyle and were credited to have 'discovered' summering on the Riviera, where their villa at Antibes was now under construction. Once settled in the Villa Marie in St Raphael, Fitzgerald finally got back to work on *The Great Gatsby* and Zelda, left very much to her own devices, spent most days on the beach, falling in love with a young French pilot. The damage caused by this affair was never repaired and became a theme in Scott's further writings, as did so much of what Zelda said or wrote.

They returned to Paris in spring 1925, staying briefly at the Hôtel Florida in boulevard Malesherbes, until they moved to an apartment at 14 rue de Tilsitt near the Arc de Triomphe. They made a conscious choice to stay on the more elegant, fashionable and expensive Right Bank. The flat did not impress their new friend Hemingway, however: 'I cannot remember much about the flat except that it was gloomy and airless …'

In the area of the Champs-Élysées the couple had little contact with the Left Bank bohemian community. In the

PHOTO 24 14 rue de Tilsitt, occupied by Scott and Zelda Fitzgerald

City of Light with all its temptations Fitzgerald found it difficult to work in a disciplined way, rising at 11 a.m., not to begin work until 5 p.m. Although he claimed in his letters that he wrote most days until 3 a.m., he and Zelda would be seen regularly around the fashionable cabarets and clubs where they drank and flirted and where Zelda danced into the small hours.

Through the Murphys they met a brilliant crowd, including Cole Porter, Jean Cocteau, Picasso, Mirò, Sherwood Anderson, Dos Passos and Ezra Pound. Eventually in April 1925 Scott was introduced to Hemingway at the Dingo Bar. Hemingway took immediately to him, and gave an admiring description in *A Moveable Feast*: 'His chin was well built and he had good ears and a handsome, almost beautiful, unmarked nose. This should not have added up to a pretty face, but that came from the coloring, the very fair hair and the mouth. The mouth worried you until you knew him and then it worried you more.'

Hemingway brought the Fitzgeralds to Gertrude Stein's Saturday salon, and she too was impressed by Scott, later professing openly her admiration for *The Great Gatsby*: 'Fitzgerald will be read when many of his well-known contemporaries are forgotten.' No comment was made on Zelda, who did not enjoy the occasion as, following the usual routine reserved for the wives of guests, she had been sent to join Stein's partner Alice B. Toklas to drink tea in another room, treatment she was unused to.

Fitzgerald liked Hemingway's simple, economical writing style and envied the discipline which he himself lacked. He was also attracted by Hemingway's good looks and the macho persona of a 'real man', but these feelings were not shared by Zelda, and a mutual antipathy developed between her and Hemingway. This became a cause of friction, expressed openly in *A Moveable Feast*. Hemingway considered that she had a malign effect on Fitzgerald's writings, implying that she was jealous of her husband's fame, enticing him to stay out all night so that he would be incapable of writing on the following day: 'I was sure he could write a better one [wrote Hemingway, referring to *The Great Gatsby*] [but] I did not know Zelda yet, and so I did not know the terrible odds that were against him.'

Zelda felt excluded from the relationship between the two writers, and referred to Hemingway as 'phony', going so far as to call him a 'pansy with hair on his chest'. He in turn thought she was dangerous and crazy, willingly wrecking Scott's talents. The friendship between the two writers ended ultimately in 1929. Hemingway avoided them when they moved near to the flat he occupied with his second wife Pauline, who disliked the 'golden couple'.

The Fitzgeralds were often seen at Harry's New York Bar at 5 rue Daunou, but they also patronised the Ritz, which they preferred to the bohemian cafés in Montparnasse. Fitzgerald was drinking so much that he usually had to be helped into a cab to get home. The Ritz is described in his fourth novel *Tender is the Night* (which would eventually be published in 1934) as well as in the short story, 'Babylon Revisited' (1930). The couple would nevertheless condescend to visit the Left Bank for a drink at the Dingo Bar or for a show at Les Folies Bobino in Montparnasse. Sometimes Scott's drunken state would last for days or weeks. He is reported to have turned up drunk in the middle of the day at the office of the *Chicago Tribune* and in other public places. His behaviour alienated many people. He could also be rude and violent towards friends and staff.

In spite of everything the Murphys remained steady friends: 'What we loved about Scott,' Gerald wrote, 'was the region in him where his gift came from, and which was never completely buried. There were moments when he wasn't harassed or trying to shock you, moments when he'd be gentle and quiet, and he'd tell you his real thoughts about people, and lose himself in defining what he felt about them. Those were the moments when you saw the beauty of his mind and nature, and they compelled you to love and value him.'

Their chaotic lifestyle in Paris and on the Riviera, as well as Zelda's erratic behaviour, provided Scott with the inspiration for his fourth novel, *Tender is the Night*. It is dedicated 'To Gerald and Sara. Many fêtes', which suggested that its protagonists Dick and Nicole Diver were based on the Murphys. Nicole Diver is first described on the beach wearing a long string of pearls like Sara's, and close friends recognised their house at Antibes, Villa America, as the Divers' house and garden, but their destructive behaviour had more to do with Scott and Zelda, whose medical reports were extensively included in the novel. Zelda's mental state had become very worrying. She wanted to become more than her husband's muse; she wanted to write, and did produce articles and short stories, but always published with her husband's name attached to 'help sales'. She could never compete, and he did not particularly encourage her, so she took up painting during their short stays in Paris and even had an exhibition. Finally she discovered ballet, which then became an overwhelming passion, but at twenty-seven it was unfortunately far too late for her to have a successful classical dancing career. In Paris she attended Madame Egorova's school at the Olympian Music Hall at 18 rue Caumartin.

The dream of becoming a ballet dancer became an obsession which took over her life.

The couple finally opted for the Left Bank, and rented an apartment at 58 rue de Vaugirard, overlooking the Jardin du Luxembourg. The flat appears as the Divers' apartment in *Tender is the Night*. Scott was drinking more than ever and their life was so dominated by arguing, shouting and fights that occasionally he even ended up in jail. All this surfaces in *Tender is the Night*, but its completion had to wait as, short of money, Fitzgerald needed to write more financially rewarding short stories.

There were some good moments. On 27 June 1928 they were invited to the apartment of Adrienne Monnier and Sylvia Beach at rue de l'Odéon to have dinner with James Joyce. A delighted Fitzgerald drew a picture of the occasion in Beach's copy of *The Great Gatsby*. Among the other guests was André Chamson, who became a friend, and was later to write the introduction to the French translation of *The Great Gatsby*. Chamson was charmed by Fitzgerald: 'He came into my life with that smile and, probably because of the sunlight coming through the stairway window ... as though in a halo of light.'

In the meantime Zelda pursued more obsessively than ever her arduous schedule of dancing lessons, for up to eight hours a day. As a result she no longer wanted to drink or party every night. Bitter quarrels followed, as their marriage had turned into deep resentment, and he blamed her for his drinking. After a short break in the US in September, they were back in Paris. There was little change, until it became clear that Zelda was increasingly ill. In March 1929 they moved to their last apartment at 3–5 rue Palatine, next to the church of Saint-Sulpice, where their daughter Scottie attended Sunday mass.

It was very close to Hemingway's flat at 6 rue Férou, but he now avoided the doomed couple. Zelda in her confused state had become convinced that her husband and Hemingway were having a homosexual affair. Deeply hurt, Fitzgerald said to her in a letter that: 'The nearest I ever came to leaving you was when you told me thot [*sic*] I was a fairy in the rue Palatine ...'

Zelda was having some of her short stories published, which Scott may have resented, as he had problems with his own writing. Her behaviour became increasingly unpredictable and self-destructive. The 1929 financial crash was a turning point; they were badly affected financially, and in April 1930 Zelda was admitted to the Malmaison psychiatric hospital outside Paris. She discharged herself after two weeks, desperate to return to the solace of Madame Egorova's ballet routine, but soon afterwards she became incoherent, started to suffer from hallucinations, talked of suicide and took an overdose of pills. There was no choice but a clinic, and she was admitted to Les Rives de Prangins in Switzerland.

Fitzgerald was also fighting depression, his drinking now out of control. His writing had lost its appeal, and he was earning just enough to pay for Zelda's medical care and their daughter's education. Looking for a reliable source of much-needed income he went to Hollywood to write a film script, but the work was gruelling and his novel remained unfinished. He and Zelda were never in Paris together again, but he provided the money for her medical care and remained in touch with her until his early death in 1940. She died tragically on 10 March 1948 in a fire in the Highland Hospital in the Blue Ridge Mountains to which she had been transferred. She was buried next to Scott in Maryland.

The tormented love story of Zelda and Scott provided the inspiration for the majority of Fitzgerald's novels, some of them based in Paris, such as *Tender is the Night*. He had spent nine years writing it, rewriting it, rearranging it, drawing heavily on their lifestyle, sexual jealousy and the mental illness which they lived through in Paris, the Riviera and Switzerland. He had great hopes for it, but by 1934 when it was finally published in the midst of the Depression, stories about spoilt expatriates, out of control, had lost their glamorous appeal, and sales were disappointing.

Paris is the setting for one of his most striking and moving stories, 'Babylon Revisited', written in December 1930, just eight months after Zelda's final breakdown. The story deals with the theme of redemption and the high price to be paid for a past extravagant lifestyle, when chances and abilities have been squandered; the fate of the Fitzgeralds. Their last flat in rue Palatine is used in the story to create the home of the protagonist Charlie Wales. An American expatriate who had lived a profligate life in Paris during the 1920s and who lost everything, Charlie returns to Paris to redeem himself and reclaim his daughter (named after the Murphys' daughter Honoria). He recalls the evening when he storms home alone after a quarrel with his wife, Helen, who retaliates by kissing another man. Later Helen, too drunk and disoriented to find a taxi, wanders around in the cold and dies. Charlie has a breakdown and is institutionalised, before losing all his money in the financial crash. In the meantime Honoria has been looked after by Helen's sister Marion. As the story opens in Paris three years after these dramatic events, Charlie has returned sober, financially successful again, and determined to pull his life together.

The story was written when Zelda had just been admitted to the first clinic and Fitzgerald must have been reflecting on his own past life during *les années folles*. Charlie's story was wishful thinking, as by that stage Fitzgerald's health was seriously damaged by his constant drinking, and his fortune almost gone. Charlie revisits old haunts on the Left Bank and admits regretfully: 'I spoiled this city for myself. I didn't realize it, but the days came along one after another, and then two years were gone, and everything was gone, and I was gone.'

He realises painfully the extent of his squandering: 'All the catering to vice and waste was on an utterly childish scale, and he suddenly realised the meaning of the word "dissipate" – to dissipate into thin air; to make nothing out of something. … He remembered thousand-franc notes given to an orchestra for playing a single number, hundred-franc notes tossed to a doorman for calling a cab. But it hadn't been given for nothing.' Nine years after the publication of 'Babylon Revisited' and less than a year before his own death at forty-four, Fitzgerald wrote his daughter a letter telling her how much the story was drawn from private life: 'You have earned some money for me this week because I sold "Babylon Revisited", in which you are a character, to the pictures (the sum received wasn't worthy of the magnificent story – neither of you nor of me – however, I am accepting it).'

It was adapted into a rather disappointing film, *The Last Time I Saw Paris*, directed in 1954 by Richard Brooks and starring Elizabeth Taylor as Helen. The theme song was composed in 1940 by Jerome Kern with lyrics by Oscar Hammerstein. A film adaptation of *Tender is the Night* was directed by Henry King in 1962, starring Jennifer Jones and

Jason Roberts. Fitzgerald wrote other short stories set in Paris, 'The Bridal Party' (1930) and 'News of Paris, (Fifteen Years Ago)' (1947).

In her novel *Save Me the Waltz* (1932) and other thinly disguised autobiographical short stories, Zelda also drew heavily on their personal lives and their time together in Paris. Away from Scott she was more her own person, trying to build her confidence in the Parisian context. The visit to Gertrude Stein had not been a great experience but she found Natalie Barney's salon more to her taste. She was writing her usual articles about flappers and the Jazz Age and short stories for the *Saturday Post*, but always under Scott's better-known name.

For the remaining eighteen years of her life, from the time she started to move in and out of hospitals, she wrote articles, short stories and two novels, and painted when she was better. *Save Me the Waltz* was written in six weeks in 1932 while she was being treated in a clinic in Baltimore. The heroine Alabama, whose past greatly resembles Zelda's, accepts what Zelda had turned down, an offer to dance solo for the San Carlo ballet, but an injury ultimately puts an end to her dancing career, and she returns to her family. Fitzgerald, who took almost ten years to complete *Tender is the Night*, which drew on the same autobiographical material, was unhappy about Zelda's novel, although he did help to edit it.

Zelda's life in the shadow of her famous husband has recently inspired many works, including Gilles Leroy's novel *Alabama Song* (2007). The actress Scarlett Johansson has been chosen to play Zelda for a projected film, *The Beautiful and the Damned*, while the director Ron Howard has cast Jennifer Lawrence as Zelda in a biopic of her life, *Zelda*. Finally, Christina Ricci played Zelda in *Z: The Beginning of*

Everything, an American television series broadcast in 2017. Woody Allen's *Midnight in Paris* offers a delightful light-hearted view of the unforgettable 'golden couple'.

Ford Madox Ford (1873–1939) changed his name from Ford Hermann Hueffer in 1919.

A novelist, essayist, critic and founder of both the *English Review* and the *Transatlantic Review*, he was the grandson of the Pre-Raphaelite painter Ford Madox Brown, and a prolific writer, remembered mainly for his 1915 novel *The Good Soldier* (originally titled *The Saddest Story*).

Already forty-three when he enlisted in the army in 1916, Ford was severely wounded at the battle of the Somme. His tetralogy *Parade's End*, written between 1924 and 1928, relates the profound impact the war had on him personally. In *It Was the Nightingale* (1933), a collection of memoirs, Ford describes himself as 'a broken officer'. Somewhat older than most of this so-called 'lost generation', he left his wife Elsie Martindale and moved to Paris in 1923 with Stella Bowen, an Australian painter. His Parisian literary connections were good, and it was while waiting for James Joyce in a restaurant that he made the decision to live in Paris. He was no stranger to the city, since he had visited it several times in his youth owing to his family connections, and he spoke fluent French and German. He may even have planned his novels in French.

In his preface to Jean Rhys's *Rive Gauche and Other Short Stories* he describes his mixed feelings towards Paris: 'In my hot youth I disliked Paris … stony and infested with winds … stony, windy, expensive, solitary – and contemptuous; that was Paris. And I hated her.' But now it was the perfect place for him as 'Paris gyrated, seethed, clamoured, roared with the

PHOTO 25   Ford Madox Ford lived at Cité fleurie in boulevard Arago

Arts.' The couple settled in an artists' colony, the Cité fleurie
at 65 boulevard Arago.

In Paris Ford presided over a community of younger
writers, and mixed with the cultural elite. He was preceded
by his formidable reputation in the Anglophone community
as former editor of the *English Review* and by his friendship
with writers like Conrad. With the encouragement of the
indefatigable Ezra Pound, he founded the *Transatlantic
Review*. It focused on young writers like James Joyce
(publishing extracts from *Finnegans Wake*), Djuna Barnes,
Hemingway, Pound, Jean Rhys, Gertrude Stein and others
who had yet to make their mark in the literary world. In
Memories and Impressions (1907) Ford recalls those exciting
days when 'the *Transatlantic Review* was born amidst turmoil

and had a tumultuous if sometimes gay career'. Ezra Pound brought Hemingway along, and Ford invited him to be guest editor for the August 1924 issue, a decision he would come to regret, as his relationship with the ambitious but as yet unknown American soon soured. 'Naturally the idea of editing a new review in Paris which was crammed with young writers from all over the world was just jam for Ford,' wrote Stella Bowen. The *Transatlantic Review*, based at 29 quai d'Anjou, was to be published monthly, but only twelve issues appeared, as it quickly ran into financial difficulties.

In *It Was the Nightingale* (1933) Ford described Nancy Cunard 'like a jewelled tropical bird', Ezra Pound playing the bassoon, and seeing Gertrude Stein from the top of a bus in her Ford, driving through Paris with solemn 'snail-like precision', as if she were a Pope or a Pharaoh borne aloft. Apart from being a protagonist in Rhys's *Quartet* he was described unfavourably by his former protégé Hemingway: 'It was Ford Madox Ford, as he called himself then, and he was breathing heavily through a heavy, stained mustache and holding himself as upright as an ambulatory, well-clothed, up-ended hogshead.' Ford also appears briefly as Henry Braddocks in Hemingway's *The Sun Also Rises*.

His relationship with Joyce was more serene: 'For Mr Joyce's work I had the greatest admiration and for his person the greatest esteem. I also like his private society very much. He made thin little jokes, told rather simple stories and talked about his work very enlighteningly.' His closest friend in Paris was undoubtedly Ezra Pound, 'his oldest accomplice'. Ford also enthusiastically supported the self-proclaimed 'bad boy of music', the American composer George Antheil. Ezra 'had persuaded Mr Antheil to practise his latest symphony for piano and orchestra in Mr Pound's studio'.

In *Drawn from Life* Ford's partner Stella Bowen draws an affectionate portrait of him: 'Ford was considerably older than the rest of our friends and much more impressive. He was very large, with a pink face, yellow hair and drooping, bright blue eyes. His movements were gentle and deliberate and his quiet and mellow voice spoke, to an Australian ear, with ineffable authority.' She also gave a detailed account of the life they both enjoyed in Paris in the 1920s with their friends, the Thursday teas and the Friday dances at the *bal musette* in rue du Cardinal Lemoine, which she used to organise to promote the *Transatlantic Review*. As Ford wrote to Ezra Pound, 'We dine practically every evening at Le nègre de Toulouse, next to the Closerie des Lilas and almost as invariably go to drink coffee at the Closerie des Lilas itself.'

Bowen admired Ford's ability to spot undiscovered talent, but noted his failings as an organiser, particularly when it came to financial management of the review. She provided much help, financial and otherwise, and was prepared to put her career as a painter to one side to dedicate herself to Ford, having also their small child to look after: 'Ford would put it to me that he could not finish his book if his mind was upset, and that I must manage to keep all worries from him, which was difficult.' 'His book' was *Parade's End*, but he also wrote essays, reviews and literary criticism. All this came to an end with the arrival of Jean Rhys on their domestic scene, as Bowen records: 'When we met her she possessed nothing but a cardboard suit-case and the astonishing manuscript. She was down to her last three francs and she was sick. She lived with us for many weeks whilst we tried to set her on her feet ... I was singularly slow in discovering that she and Ford were in love. ... She had a needle-quick intelligence and a good sort of emotional honesty, but she was a doomed soul, violent and demoralised ... She nearly sank our ship!' She did sink their ship, as in 1928 Ford and Bowen separated and he took a flat at 32 rue de Vaugirard. Two years later he met the artist Janice Biala, who was to be his partner until his death, and both left Paris in 1932. After spending a few years in New York, in 1937 he took a post as a visiting lecturer in Michigan, but at the age of sixty-five he died in France on a visit with Janice to Deauville, where he is buried. It seems that the drunken gravedigger buried him in the wrong place. Janice's comment was 'that was Ford all over'.

The American poet **Archibald MacLeish** (1892–1982) was also attracted by the City of Light in the early 1930s to pursue his vocation. MacLeish, from Illinois, interrupted his studies to enlist as an ambulance driver and then as an artillery officer when the US joined World War I in 1917. He fought in the second battle of the Marne, and after the Armistice he returned home to train as a lawyer. Like Dos Passos he condemned the war, writing in *Reflections*, reminiscences published posthumously in 1986, that it was 'nothing but a commercial war. There was no reason for it except reasons of commercial competition. There were no moral reasons, no humanitarian reasons, no humane reasons. Nothing. It killed millions of men. It slaughtered an entire generation. It's the most disgusting thing that happened really in the history of this planet.'

Back home in the US, and working as a lawyer, he felt restless, and decided in 1923 to leave for Paris with his wife and two children. He considered his real vocation to be poetry. Moreover his wife Ada wanted to further her musical career in France. Their four years in Paris started in a second-floor flat at 85 boulevard Saint-Michel on the Left Bank, where they met Sylvia Beach, who introduced them to other

Americans. MacLeish wanted also to spend time with French writers and to familiarise himself with the French poets Baudelaire, Rimbaud and Laforgue.

Among the Americans they met were Sara and Gerald Murphy, to whom MacLeish dedicated a poem while they were spending time together on the Riviera. The Murphys introduced them to their impressive circle: Fernand Léger, Picasso, Stravinsky, the Fitzgeralds and Dos Passos. When they returned to Paris, they found a house in Saint-Cloud, keen to remain near the Murphys, as: 'there was a shine to life wherever they were'. Many years later in 1948 MacLeish wrote of his enjoyment of Paris in a nostalgic poem, 'Years of the Dog' (1948):

> Before, though, Paris was wonderful. Wanderers.
> Talking in all tongues from every country.
> Fame was what they wanted in that town ....

Fame was found by a compatriot who also became a close friend, Ernest Hemingway. Having picked up a copy of his recently published *In Our Time* at Sylvia Beach's bookshop, MacLeish wished to meet him. This happened in the summer of 1924. MacLeish was impressed by his innovative style, which he valued as 'one intrinsic style of our language ... produced in this century'. A strong friendship ensued as they cycled, boxed, drank and met at the Closerie des Lilas, and he remembered a visit to his home above the sawmill in the same poem:

> ... the lad in the Rue Notre Dame des Champs
> At the carpenter's loft on the left-hand side going down –
> The lad with the supple look like a sleepy panther –

And what became of him? Fame became of him.
Veteran out of the wars before he was twenty:
Famous at twenty-five: thirty a master –
Whittled a style for his time from a walnut stick
In a carpenter's loft in a street of that April city.

Their friendship survived those four years in Paris, and it is to
the MacLeishs that Hemingway turned when he left his wife
Hadley in 1926. By the end of the 1930s they had however
quarrelled bitterly, and Hemingway belittled MacLeish's
poetry in his correspondence. MacLeish's relationship with
T. S. Eliot and Ezra Pound was also complicated, as he greatly
admired them, but felt somewhat inferior. Pound accused
MacLeish of imitating him, and rejected his poems for
publication in the *Exile* in 1926. As for T. S. Eliot, MacLeish
was disappointed when he turned up at Eliot's bank in
London, to find that Eliot 'was not available' to see him.
However Eliot did subsequently publish some of MacLeish's
poems in the *New Criterion*. MacLeish's poem 'Land's End, for
Adrienne Monnier' (1927), despite its title suggesting a link
to T. S. Eliot, had no connection with him, but was a poem
dedicated to Sylvia Beach's companion (the owner of the
bookshop La Maison des amis des livres in rue de l'Odéon).

Ada, a gifted musician, sang in concerts in Paris as well
as with James Joyce, also a good singer, and who would
become a friend: 'They would invite us and we would invite
them, and we always gave Joyce a case of a new kind of white
Alsatian wine every Christmas.'

In 1926, after a short trip to the US, they were back in
Paris where MacLeish took a small studio at 44 rue du Bac, to
work quietly. Those years in Paris were very productive, and
he published two collections of poetry. He obviously relished

and benefited from the Left Bank cultural ambiance, as he recalled after the death of Sylvia Beach: 'Turning up from St Germain to go home past the bottom of the gardens to the boulevard St Michel one kept Shakespeare and Company to starboard and Adrienne Monnier's Amis des Livres to port, and felt, as one rose with the tide towards the theatre, that one had passed the gates of dream – though which was horn and which was ivory … It was enough for a confused lawyer in a grand and vivid time to look from one side to the other and say to himself, as the cold came up from the river, Gide was here on Thursday and on Monday Joyce was there.'

Back in the US he remained a part-time poet for the rest of his life, and became politically active, as well as having a prestigious public career. This served him well when he later worked hard to have Ezra Pound released from St Elizabeth's Hospital. He bore the poet no grudge, although he had not been supportive in the Paris years. In 1957 he asked Hemingway to write a letter to support Pound's release. Hemingway agreed, and even provided some financial help. MacLeish also hired a prestigious lawyer, and together they finally enabled Pound to regain his freedom in 1958.

Chicago-born **John Dos Passos** (1896–1970) had known France since early in his life. He had been born illegitimately, and at his father's suggestion, his mother took him to Europe when he was less than a year old, where they spent time in Brussels and Paris. After school in Connecticut, his father, who had by now married his mother, suggested he undertake a Grand Tour in 1911 to include Paris, where he spent some time learning French. This might have encouraged him to study French writers during his subsequent time at Harvard, where he considered joining the World War I 'gentleman's

ambulance corps', 'to see what the war was like'. Although a
committed pacifist, he did volunteer as an ambulance driver
in France in 1917. What he saw of the war reinforced his
pacifist views. His first novel, *One Man's Initiation: 1917*
(1920), was written in the trenches, where the naïve young
hero Martin Howe reacts to war with a mixture of anger,
fear and disillusionment and a sense of shame for still being
alive. These are feelings no doubt experienced by the author,
who was stationed in the French village of Érize-la-Petite on
the road to Verdun. A reprieve from the horror of war came
when he returned for three months to Paris. He then joined
the Red Cross, and was sent to the Italian Front, where in
May 1918 he briefly encountered Ernest Hemingway. On
his return to Paris a month later, he took a room at Madame
Lecomte's hotel, Au rendez-vous des mariniers, at 33 quai
d'Anjou, where he put the finishing touches to his novel,
not published until 1920. It sold only sixty-three copies in
the first six months, considered too candid and graphic in its
description of the horrors Dos Passos had witnessed in the
trenches.

Life in Paris, where his landlady Madame Lecomte darned
his socks and cooked delicious meals, was very different. He
enjoyed living on Île Saint-Louis, drinking hot chocolate in
a local patisserie and indulging in his passion for painting: 'I
live on the Ile St Louis, in the Seine, a beautifully old seedy
part of Paris that I love – I spend my spare time writing and
sketching up and down the river.'

Keen to remain in Paris after being discharged from the
American Ambulance Corps at demobilisation in 1919, Dos
Passos took advantage of a soldiers' educational programme
to enrol in anthropology classes at the Sorbonne. He then
registered as a doctoral student at Paris University, moving

to a convenient room near Montagne Sainte-Geneviève at 45 quai de la Tournelle. He painted and wrote intensively. On 1 October 1919 he sent the last part of a further novel, *Seven Times Round the Walls of Jericho* (unpublished), to his agent. He was also working on *Three Soldiers*, another anti-war book, to be published in 1921 to reviews which this time hailed him as a leading novelist. He recalls seeing Ernest Hemingway, now a journalist, in 1922: 'I believe I'd run into Ernest the year *Ulysses* came out while he was in Paris working for *The Toronto Star*. There's a dim recollection of eating a meal with him and Hadley at Lipp's before there was any Bumby, and of Ernest's talking beautifully about some international conference he'd recently attended. When he was a young man he had one of the shrewdest heads for unmasking political pretensions I've ever run into.'

They shared left-wing views, but Dos Passos, a committed Communist at the time, was more radical. Apart from meeting at the popular Brasserie Lipp at 151 boulevard Saint-Germain, both spent much time at the Closerie des Lilas at 171 boulevard du Montparnasse, drinking and reading aloud excerpts from the Old Testament and discussing their work. Dos Passos, who spoke excellent French and by now knew Paris well, introduced his new friend to the Shakespeare and Company library and bookshop. In return 'Hem' took him to Gertrude Stein's, where he felt uncomfortable or even intimidated: 'I wasn't quite at home there. A Buddha sitting there, surveying us.' He and Hemingway shared a love of sport, and attended cycle races together at the Vélodrome d'hiver: 'Hem was mad about bicycle racing', not to mention the legendary boxing matches. Both joined the rich expatriate couple Sara and Gerald Murphy to ski in Austria, and followed them to the sunny Riviera.

In 1924 Hemingway recommended him to Ford Madox Ford, who agreed to include an early version of *Manhattan Transfer* (1925), called *July*, for publication in the summer issue of the *Transatlantic Review*. At that stage they enjoyed each other's company, Hemingway's wife Hadley reporting that 'John Dos Passos was one of the few people at certain times whom Ernest could really talk to.' The friendship lasted about twenty years, although things were not always easy between them. When Dos Passos was asked in the *Paris Review* if Hemingway's descriptions of 'those times' in *A Moveable Feast* were accurate, his reply was carefully worded: 'Well it's a little sour, that book. His treatment of people like Scott Fitzgerald – the great man talking down about his contemporaries. He was always competitive and critical, overtly so ...' No comment was made on the fact that Hemingway had maliciously referred to him as an untrustworthy 'pilot fish' and later described him disparagingly as being as 'white as the under half of an unsold flounder'. They fell out over differing political views of the Spanish Civil War.

Dos Passos developed his own style in Paris, influenced by Modernism and the development of mass communication. The war and Paris were the main inspirations for his early writing, as well as for *Nineteen Nineteen* (1932), the middle volume of his *USA Trilogy*, set partly in Paris. It is a novel of stunning scope and stylistic innovation. He had been struck by James Joyce's *Ulysses*, which revolutionised fictional narration. Dos Passos uses many experimental techniques; fictional and non-fictional biographies, a poetic, stream-of-consciousness voice entitled '*The Camera Eye*' and a '*Newsreel*' approach, as well as a cinematic-montage technique (using newspaper headlines, news stories and songs). The novel

sweeps through the decade from 1910 to 1919. It traces
historical events, particularly the devastating results of World
War I, through the lives of those caught up in the gigantic
forces which reshaped the twentieth century. Richard (Dick
Savage) is a pacifist, who in order to avoid being drafted into
the war joins the French ambulance service and arrives at
the Hôtel de Crillon, 'the hub of Paris', to attend a Peace
Conference, where he meets another pacifist newspaperman,
Jerry Burnham. They settle with other young men in Paris:
'Except for the occasional shell from the bertha, Paris was
quiet and pleasant that November. It was too foggy for air
raids. Dick and Steve Warner got a very cheap room back
at the Panthéon; in the daytime they read French and in
the evenings roamed round cafés and drinking places. Fred
Summers got himself a job with the Red Cross at twenty five
dollars a week and a steady girl the second day they hit Paris.'

Dos Passos's excellent French allowed him to mix easily
with French writers and to translate some of their books.
He also illustrated Blaise Cendrars' long poem *Le panama ou
les aventures de mes sept oncles* (Panama, or The Adventures
of My Seven Uncles) in 1931, and was greatly admired by
radical French writers like Jean-Paul Sartre, who hailed him
in 1936 as 'the greatest writer of our time'. Sartre appreciated
his politics as well as his experimental writing, himself
adopting stream-of-consciousness and newsreel cinematic
montage techniques.

From the US, where he wrote *Manhattan Transfer*, Dos
Passos returned to Paris in 1945 as a war correspondent,
staying at the Hôtel Scribe at 1 rue Scribe (a luxury hotel
where Orwell had unsuccessfully tried to get a job in the
early 1930s). There he reports to his wife that Paris 'looks
almost frighteningly unchanged' and notes sadly the overall

poverty in the aftermath of World War II. A street in the Paris suburb of Thiais has been named after him (near another named after Ernest Hemingway), but unlike his former friend he is now practically forgotten, despite Sartre's admiration and the great impact his innovative style had on later writers.

Another American, **William Carlos Williams** (1883–1963), sometimes called 'the godfather of avant-garde poetry', hailed from New Jersey, where he trained as a doctor, specialising in paediatrics, although he wanted above all to be a poet. Ezra Pound, whom he had met at the University of Pennsylvania, encouraged him to take a 'sabbatical' in Europe in 1924 for what turned out to be a 'magnificent year'.

Unlike many other Americans in Paris at the time, he already knew Paris and spoke good French, having been brought up by a half-French mother who had studied for three years in Paris. Between the ages of fourteen and sixteen he found himself staying in Paris with French cousins in rue La Bruyère, and attended the prestigious Lycée Condorcet for a short while. He had been in Paris again in 1909 on his way to study medicine at Leipzig University.

The idea of spending a year in Europe was a gamble, as it meant leaving his New Jersey medical practice as well as his two young sons, but it proved to be worth it. His main contact in the French capital was the writer and publisher Robert McAlmon, with whom he had founded *Contact* in 1920. It was a literary review dedicated to young experimental writers, recently relocated to Paris. During the initial ten days, thanks to McAlmon, who was a key expatriate, Williams met an eclectic group of intellectuals, including James Joyce, Man Ray, Sylvia Beach, Adrienne Monnier and their lodger George Antheil. His excellent French meant that he had no problem mixing with Valéry Larbaud, Jean Cocteau and what remained of the 1919 group of French Surrealists, represented by Louis Aragon and Philippe Soupault.

In February 1924 he wrote home happily that 'all values have grown simpler for me since I have hit Paris'. Williams however felt ill at ease with Ezra Pound and other intellectual expatriates, and was much happier with Philippe Soupault, with whom he walked extensively at night in the city, in proper *flâneur* fashion. His translation of Soupault's *Dernières nuits de Paris* (1928) (Last Nights of Paris) was warmly praised, reading as an original work. Surrealism, which he encountered in Paris, undoubtedly had an impact on his writing, and it influenced his imagist approach to poetry, which focuses on the concrete.

His stay in the capital lasted only a few months, but he contemplated the idea of moving to Paris permanently to work as a paediatrician: 'Paris has gotten violently into our blood in one way or another. I wonder if I could be happy here as a child specialist,' he wrote in his *Autobiography* (1951).

His foremost interest was poetry; working as a doctor was primarily for financial independence. But as a part-time writer, Williams felt snubbed by the intellectual group around Ezra Pound. He had gone directly from high school to medical school and was put at a disadvantage by the spectacular show of erudition by T. S. Eliot in particular. Williams admitted that 'Literary allusions ... were unknown to us. Few had the necessary reading.' Later he confessed in an interview that he was 'insanely jealous' of Eliot, 'who was much more cultured'.

After reading Eliot's *The Waste Land* he felt that 'it wiped out our world as if an atom bomb had been dropped upon it ... Eliot had turned his back on the possibility of reviving my world. And being an accomplished craftsman, better skilled in some ways than I could ever hope to be, I had to watch him carry my world off with him, the fool, to the enemy. If with his skill he could have been kept here to be employed by our slowly shaping drive, what strides might we not have taken!' After a short tour of Europe Williams returned to Paris in April 1924, where he met Hemingway, who invited him to his apartment at 113 rue Notre-Dame-des-Champs. Williams arrived as Hemingway's young son Bumby was being bathed, giving the baby an expert medical examination and the parents some useful advice.

His letters and *Autobiography* give descriptions of simple pleasures like watching children playing in the Jardin du Luxembourg or visiting Notre-Dame. Sharing his mother's interest in art, Williams also met painters and artists, and he gives an idea of what the Romanian sculptor Brancusi's studio looked like: 'a barn-like place filled with blocks of stone, formless wooden hunks and stumps for the most part ... [He] served us cognac, poked up the fire and then began talking of Ezra Pound's recent opera *Villon* ...'

Paris appears in *A Voyage to Pagany* (1928) in which the protagonist Dr 'Dev' Evans travels to Pagany, set in a pagan Europe. The first five chapters cover his journey to France, during which Evans rediscovers Paris, which he had known as a child. Sitting at the Dôme, Evans catches sight of Kiki (de Montparnasse), Fernand Léger and others. For him the whole stay proves stimulating but bruising, just as it was for the author. As Pound (to whom the novel is dedicated) had originally warned Williams when he suggested a 'sabbatical' away from the US: 'I think you are afraid to take it for fear of destroying some illusions which you think necessary to your illusions.'

In the American Grain (1925) includes a conversation with the French poet Valéry Larbaud. There are further references to Paris in the poem 'The Descent in Winter', published in *Exile* in 1928, *Novelette and other Prose* (1932) and in Williams's *Autobiography*.

William Cuthbert Faulkner (1897–1962) spent four months in Paris from August 1925, where he worked on some short stories, one of which, 'Elmer', remained unfinished, and was published only posthumously in 1979. In this partly autobiographical story young Elmer Hodge is seen sitting in a café in Paris, possibly Les Deux Magots on place Saint-Germain-des-Prés, where Faulkner was often to be found. Faulkner wrote of his creation: 'Elmer is quite a boy. He is tall and almost handsome and he wants to paint pictures. He gets everything a man can want – money, a European title, marries the girl he wants – and she gives away his paint box. So Elmer never gets to paint at all.' Would the diminutive Faulkner have liked to be tall like Elmer, a kind of alter ego, who felt that a stay in Paris was essential for any ambitious young man? Faulkner moved to a cheap room at Le Grand Hôtel des Principautés at 26 rue Servandoni (now 42 rue de Vaugirard and bearing a commemorative plaque), a short walk from the Jardin du Luxembourg, where he spent much time watching children play, as he reported in regular letters to his mother. Equipped with introductions to James Joyce, Ezra Pound and T. S. Eliot, he made no effort to meet any of them: 'I knew of Joyce, and I would go to some effort to go the café that he inhabited to look at him.' But they never met, as he preferred to spend his time exploring the city on

foot, occasionally taking boat trips to the suburban towns of
Auteuil, Meudon and Suresnes, and visiting Père Lachaise
Cemetery: 'I particularly went to see Oscar Wilde's tomb,
with a bas-relief by Epstein.' He wondered at Notre-Dame
Cathedral with its 'saints and angels, and beautiful naked
Greek figures that have no religious significance whatever
and gargoyles – creatures with heads of goats and dogs,
and claws and wings on men's bodies, all staring down in a
jeering sardonic mirth'. He attended Mass at Saint-Sulpice,
his local church, and also spent much time in the Louvre.
In his satirical poem – or perhaps self-parody – *Ode to the
Louver* (1925), he pokes fun at uneducated tourists:

> The Louver is on Ravioli street
> You can take the cars or go by feet
> The river is very deep and wide
> It is more than a 100 metters [*sic*] from either side
> The boats on it is called a barge
> They are big but not as large
> As the Louver

After just five months of this, 'restless' Faulkner, unlike
some of his compatriots, decided to return to America, and
drew on his knowledge of Paris only at the end of his novel
Sanctuary (1931), in a scene taking place in his beloved Jardin
du Luxembourg, where the central character Temple Drake
attends a concert with her father: ' ... in the Luxembourg
Gardens as Temple and her father passed the women sat
knitting in shawls and even the men playing croquet played
in coats and capes, and in the sad gloom of the chestnut trees
the dry click of balls, the random shouts of children, had that
quality of autumn, gallant and evanescent and forlorn ...

They went on, passed the pool where the children and an old man in a shabby brown overcoat sailed toy boats, and entered the trees again and found seats ... she seemed to follow with her eyes the waves of music, to dissolve into the dying brasses, across the pool and the opposite semicircle of trees where at sombre intervals the dead tranquil queens in stained marbles mused, and on into the sky lying prone and vanquished in the embrace of the season of rain and death.'

Faulkner, now famous and a Nobel Prize winner (1950), did come back to Paris in 1952 for a short stay, unfortunately marred by illness. He was greatly admired by French writers, and *Requiem for a Nun* (1951), the sequel to *Sanctuary*, was adapted for the stage in 1956 by Albert Camus, who translated it and directed it for the Théâtre des Mathurins in Paris. It continues the dramatic story of Temple Drake who, after her peaceful interlude in the Jardin du Luxembourg, has returned to her fate in Mississippi. Both novels were adapted by Tony Richardson in 1961 for his film *Sanctuary*, which included the Jardin du Luxembourg sequence. Lee Remick played Temple Drake, and Faulkner contributed to the film adaptation.

7

Patrons and Artists

*The whole of Paris is a vast university of Art,
Literature and Music.*

(James Thurber)

Unknown struggling artists eager to be recognised and to
achieve fame had been supported towards the end of the
nineteenth century by art dealers like Durand-Ruel, who had
brought them to the attention of the English-speaking market.
In the early twentieth century Paris began to attract wealthy
people, often from America, who were prepared to finance
the careers of aspiring artists. Revolutionary painters like
Matisse and Picasso were encouraged, thanks to discerning
Americans including the Steins. Winnaretta Singer and the
Murphys followed suit, and patronage increased to include
musicians, dancers and writers. They held well-attended
weekly salons. Wealthy Parisians including Coco Chanel,
her friend Misia Sert and many of their friends were also
patrons of musicians, while Étienne de Beaumont and other
French aristocrats and socialites organised unforgettable
balls and banquets to promote artists, musicians and

writers. Vicomte de Noailles and his wife Marie-Laure also supported surrealist experimental films by Salvador Dalí and Luis Buñuel. Gertrude Stein advised young writers like Ernest Hemingway, and Adrienne Monnier and Sylvia Beach through their bookshops encouraged James Joyce, lent money and invited young writers to use their premises.

Winnaretta Singer, Princesse de Polignac (1865–1943), the Modernist society hostess, was eleven years old when she inherited 900,000 dollars on the death of her father Isaac Singer, the founder of the eponymous sewing machine company. This allowed her to live abroad comfortably until the end of her life. She moved with her French mother and siblings to Paris in 1878, and in 1879 they acquired a grand house at 27 avenue Kléber in the fashionable sixteenth arrondissement. Winnaretta studied painting, but her real passion was music. 'Although I secretly loved music most, painting attracted me almost equally, and I spent all the time possible at the Musée du Louvre, without understanding much of what I saw there ...' That year her mother married Victor Reubsaet, a professional violinist and aspiring socialite, and Winnaretta quickly became knowledgeable about music, encouraged by the composer Gabriel Fauré, from whom she took lessons in 1880. As her relationship with her mother and in particular her stepfather deteriorated, in 1886 she bought her own house as an escape at 43 avenue Henri-Martin (today avenue Georges-Mandel), a short distance from place du Trocadéro. Now independent, she immediately purchased a painting by Manet and another by Monet, painters she greatly admired. The huge house had a pavilion opening onto rue Cortambert which she used as her studio and later for concerts. It was not however socially acceptable for a young woman to live alone, and pressure was building for her to marry. In 1887 she duly accepted Louis-Vilfred de Scey-Montbéliard, an impoverished aristocrat. The story goes that her husband entered the bedroom on her wedding night to find her on top of a wardrobe, brandishing an umbrella, screaming: 'If you touch me I'll kill you!' She had the foresight to have her fortune put in her own name by establishing a trust, not an easy process, but necessary, since according to French law at the time, a married woman's estate became her husband's property. Marriage did open the doors of aristocratic salons, but hers was doomed from the start and led to separation in 1889 after only two years. Her mother later wrote in a letter that Winnaretta's former husband's family 'have bothered her so much for money that she can't stand it any longer'. During that difficult period Winnaretta found increasing solace in music, and started to organise concerts for composers like Fauré, Debussy and Chabrier. She also learned to play the organ, which she continued to do to the end of her life. Her friend Élisabeth, Comtesse Greffulhe, suggested that she should marry again; this time she made a more suitable choice. Prince Edmond de Polignac, whom she married in 1892, was homosexual and a composer. The '*mariage blanc*' or 'lavender marriage' was successful, as they had music in common, and they got on well until his death in 1901.

They launched a salon and became increasingly involved in the Parisian music scene, commissioning work from Maurice Ravel, Reynaldo Hahn, Igor Stravinsky, Manuel de Falla, Erik Satie, Darius Milhaud and Kurt Weill, and supporting Diaghilev's Ballets Russes financially.

Winnaretta also translated one of her favourite books, Thoreau's *Walden, or Life in the Woods* (1854), to the dismay of one young French writer, 'a handsome young man with melting brown eyes'. **Marcel Proust** (1871–1922) had also been planning to translate the work, and some temporary friction ensued, but he was a friend of her husband and was still invited to their salon, often accompanied by the young Venezuelan musician, Reynaldo Hahn. In 1901 Proust invited the Polignacs to dine in his new flat in rue de Courcelles, and when the prince died a few months later, Winnaretta turned to him in her grief. In 1903 Proust wrote an article for *Le Figaro*, 'The Salon of the Princess Edmond de Polignac; Music of Yesterday, Echoes of Today', which praised her salon: 'That is to say that the musical performances in the hall at rue Cortambert, always wonderful from a musical point of view, where one could sometimes hear perfect renditions of early music, such as performances from *Dardanus*, sometimes original and fervent interpretations of the latest melodies by Fauré, Fauré's sonata, dances by Brahms, these performances were also, as they say in the language of society commentators, "of supreme elegance". Often held during the daytime, these entertainments glittered from the thousand lights that bathed the studio with beams of sunlight captured in the prism of the windows …'

She took offence however at some comments he made on her marriage: 'Some ten years ago the prince married Mlle Singer whose annual exhibitions of painting would regularly receive and recompense some remarkable entries. He was a musician, she was a musician, and both of them sensitive to all forms of intelligence. Only she was always too hot, and he was extremely susceptible to the cold. And how was he to know what would become of him in the incessant and deliberate currents of air in the studio at rue Cortambert. He protected himself as best he could, forever wrapping himself up in blankets and travelling rugs.' She was not amused and they did not meet again until 1907. However uneasily, the relationship resumed, and Proust invited her to a grand dinner and recital he had organised at the Ritz.

When in 1919 he asked whether he might dedicate his recently completed novel *À l'ombre des jeunes filles en fleur* (In the Shadow of Young Girls in Flower, 1919), the second volume of *À la recherche du temps perdu*, to the late Prince de Polignac, she refused, fearing that the dedication might suggest a homosexual connection between the Prince and the writer. It was a decision she may have regretted, as the next year the book, without the dedication, was awarded the *Prix Goncourt*. There is no doubt that the salon culture Proust describes in *À la recherche du temps perdu* was much inspired by the concerts he attended in Singer's salon. Proust may well have even put her into his novel in the character of Madame Verdurin.

Rumours circulated about Winnaretta's association with the so-called *Paris-Lesbos*, which included members of the aristocracy, as well as Left Bank artists and writers like Natalie Barney, Colette and Renée Vivien. In 1903 Winnaretta started a brief affair with the British composer, singer and suffragette Ethel Smyth, and this was followed by a more serious affair in 1905 with the American painter Romaine Brooks, who painted her portrait and was a neighbour.

'*La grande mécène*', 'the great patron', as she was called, was generous not only to musicians but also to dancers, and in 1909 she came to the rescue of Isadora Duncan, the American dancer, who was in permanent need of cash. At about that time Isadora had started an intermittent affair with Winnaretta's brother Paris Singer, by whom she had a son. The little boy and his half-sister were tragically drowned in April 1913 with their governess, when the car in which they were travelling plunged into the Seine.

Winnaretta rescued impoverished composers like Erik Satie financially, but also supported them in other ways. In 1917 the French writer Paul Morand found himself in her salon listening to music by Cole Porter, whom he described as 'a young Yankee author on a mission in Paris'. The 'Yankee' had asked Winnaretta to procure an introduction to Stravinsky, as he wanted to take composition lessons with the Russian composer, who however refused to collaborate.

She also helped Christabel Pankhurst to find suitable lodgings in Paris when she fled there in 1912 to avoid arrest during the suffragette movement in England. A bewildered Annie Kerney, Christabel's deputy, recalls finding her at the Polignacs' luxurious household in her *Memories of a Militant* (1924): 'I was shown into the largest room I had ever seen in a private house. I felt so tiny! There were beautiful books everywhere. I picked one up and found it to be a translation of Sappho's poetry. The colour of the leather binding was the shade of a ripe pink cherry.'

As a patron of the Ballets Russes, Winnaretta mixed with many central figures like Jean Cocteau, whom she met in 1908. He refers to her in *Professional Secrets* (1922): 'I love the way she wheedles irrevocable verdicts to destruction with a gossamer smile, swaying her head from side to side like a sly baby elephant. I love her superb profile – a cliff eroded by the sea.' She was guest of honour for the celebration dinner organised by Gerald and Sara Murphy on 17 June 1923 following the premiere of Stravinsky's ballets *Les Noces* (The Wedding) and *Pulcinella*. The memorable event took place on a barge on the river near the Pont de la Concorde and was attended by Picasso, Diaghilev, Cocteau and Tzara.

Stravinsky was placed next to her. The dinner lasted all night and the table was decorated with toys instead of flowers. Cocteau, dressed as a ship's captain, kept whispering to the guests: 'We're sinking!' Another memorable musical event took place in her salon in 1927, at which Stravinsky and Prokofiev, politically and musically incompatible, played a piano duet together.

It had been her father's dream to improve the lives of working people, and her brother Paris Singer suggested in a letter that she should dedicate herself to 'many noble and charitable works to be done in Paris'. In 1911 she began to finance housing projects intended for low-paid workers, including one at 72 rue de la Colonie in the Glacière district of the thirteenth arrondissement, for which she engaged the architect Georges Vaudoyer. In 1926 she became involved with the construction of the annexe of the Salvation Army's Palais du Peuple at 29 rue des Cordelières, followed in 1929 by the Cité de refuge at 12 rue Cantagrel, also in the thirteenth arrondissement, insisting on choosing for both projects an architect she very much admired, Le Corbusier. The huge Cité de refuge was a 500-bed shelter and was completed in 1933. This *machine à vivre* (machine for living) was advanced for the time, as it also offered work training to its residents. Her range of charitable works was wide.

In the meantime concerts continued in avenue Henri-Martin, as recorded by the writer Julien Green in his *Journal* (1961) at a Christmas Day concert in 1930: 'A soirée at Madame de Polignac's. Many elegant society people there … after the second concerto there was a more or less general stampede toward the buffet, and the third was played to barely half the audience. The murmur of the other half carried right up to the music room, and sometimes, in the softest passages, it invaded, battling victoriously with the orchestra. "I detest this contemplative atmosphere," whispered one lady to her neighbour. Finally, no longer able to hang on, they, too, went to the buffet.'

The French government acknowledged Winnaretta's generosity, and in 1931 she was made *Chevalier de la légion d'honneur* for her 'generous and discreet philanthropy, as well as the enlightened and informed support that she has brought to the arts, and, in particular, to music'. She was presented her rosette by her friend the French poet Paul Valéry. One of her closest friends, Anna de Noailles, introduced her to the composer Nadia Boulanger, who in turn became a close friend and musical collaborator. In June 1933 Boulanger helped her to organise an impressive concert with a thirty-voice chorus and twenty-three-piece orchestra. Winnaretta, in full evening dress, had to wear tennis shoes in order to reach the organ pedals. The music chosen was by Bach and Vivaldi, and Colette, amongst the guests, wrote a thank-you note: 'To find Friendship, to give it, means crying out: "shelter, shelter!" My dear Winnie, I only cried out to you before in a whisper, but your ear is so fine. Your Colette. The music of Bach is a sublime sewing machine.'

We probably owe to Winnaretta in part the revival of baroque music, particularly by Vivaldi, as Olga Rudge, a violinist whom she had taken under her wing, was instructed by her at the time to transcribe and edit music by composers waiting to be rediscovered. At the start of World War II Winnaretta moved to London, where she came across writers like Stephen Spender who, impressed that she had known Proust, would find conversing with her 'fascinating!' Rosamond Lehmann remembers her as 'a grand old girl with a rocky, masculine, aquiline profile'. In 1943, in a letter to

Nadia Boulanger, with whom she kept in touch to the end of her life, she recalls nostalgically her days in Paris, so full of music: 'All around us is the sound of Fauré being played, Ravel, Jean Françaix and Francis Poulenc. More and more I live for and in music and I share your view: the soul and the spirit count almost all.'

She is buried in a family vault with Edmond de Polignac in Torquay in Devon, where she spent part of her childhood, and a memorial was organised for her in Paris in 1944. She was the inspiration for a number of writers as well as Proust, and appears as Princesse de Seyriman-Frileuse in Jean Lorrain's *Monsieur de Phocas* (1901).

The Pescara-born writer, poet, military hero and political figure **Gabriele d'Annunzio** (1863–1938) went into self-imposed exile in France from 1910 to 1915, fleeing his extravagant Italian lifestyle and compulsive buying, and the inevitable crippling debt and irate creditors. A well-known Lothario, he was at the time conducting an affair with Countess Nathalie de Goloubeff, a Russian socialite

PHOTO 26 D'Annunzio stayed at the luxurious Hôtel Meurice

and part-time dancer and singer, who enticed him to follow
her to Paris. Despite his disastrous financial situation, he
moved into the elegant Hôtel Meurice in the rue de Rivoli,
where she was also staying. If d'Annunzio was to live in
exile, he certainly intended to make it as pleasant as possible
for himself. He arrived from Genoa with just a couple of
suitcases, his *nécessaire de toilette* and a servant, as he was
planning to stop in Paris for about ten days, but ended up
spending almost six years in France.

Preceded by his reputation as the archetypal 'Italian lover',
the first giddy six months in the City of Light were dedicated
to pure pleasure. He was quickly introduced to writers,
artists, composers and adoring women. Isadora Duncan, one
of the few who may never have succumbed to him, wrote in
her memoirs: 'That was the genius of d'Annunzio. He made
each woman feel she was a goddess in a different domain.'

He did get down to work in late 1910, and asked one of
his favourite composers, Claude Debussy (whom he used to
call Claude de France), to compose the music for his three-
act play *Le Martyre de Saint Sébastien* (The Martyrdom of St
Sebastian, 1911), which he had just completed in French.
His interest in French literature had started early in his life
and he was probably better known in France, his 'second
homeland', than in his own country. He spoke and wrote in
French, adopting the French-sounding pseudonym of Guy
d'Arbres, based on the initials of his name. Two more plays
in French followed, *La Pisanella, la mort parfumée* (Pisanella,
the Scented Death) with music by Pizzetti in 1912 and *Le
chèvrefeuille* (Honeysuckle) in December 1913.

The Italian poet had been struck by the sight in 1909
of the Russian dancer Ida Rubinstein in the title role of
Cleopatra for the Ballets Russes. So captivated was he by her

androgynous beauty and long bare legs that he kissed her feet at the end of the performance. She subsequently agreed to perform in a production of *Le Martyre*, which mixed sacred drama with profane elements, provoking a scandal in Paris, as he insisted that St Sebastian could be played only by Rubinstein, a woman and a Russian Jewess. She was for him the perfect incarnation of the martyred Roman saint, as with her exotic beauty she fitted the traditional representation of the saint as a beautiful youth with homoerotic and violent overtones. He suggested that as men often played female roles in medieval mystery and miracle plays, Rubinstein's portrayal of the saint was 'women's revenge'. Steeped in a decadent atmosphere, the play introduced touches of magic and mysticism, enhanced by the magnificent costumes, sets by Léon Bakst and Fokine's choreography. Even before the premiere at the Théâtre du Châtelet on 22 May 1911, the Vatican had placed all of d'Annunzio's works on the index of forbidden books, and the Archbishop of Paris forbade Catholics to attend. Both playwright and composer, in a letter to the press, claimed that their work was 'deeply religious' and 'the lyrical glorification ... of all Christian heroism'.

This *succès de scandale* established d'Annunzio's reputation in Paris, and less eventful performances of *La Pisanella* followed in 1912 at the Théâtre du Châtelet, the choreography again by Fokine, and scenery by Léon Bakst. With his eclectic tastes, d'Annunzio fully enjoyed Paris. The doors of the fashionable and artistic worlds were opened to him, thanks in great part to the French aesthete and poet Robert de Montesquiou, who introduced him to the rich and famous, and to Marcel Proust and Maurice Barrès. *Le Martyre* was dedicated to the latter, with whom he shared the same deep love for art and a strong patriotic sense. He also met those at the heart of the literary establishment, Romain Rolland, André Gide, André Suarès, Henri de Régnier and his wife, Anna de Noailles, Henry Bordeaux, Anatole France and Paul Valéry.

In constant need of cash, d'Annunzio continued to live beyond his means, moving from place to place, (as did James Joyce) from one unpaid hotel room to the next. After the first few luxurious months at Hôtel Meurice and then the less elegant Hôtel d'Iéna, he lived at 8 rue Bassano and at 47 avenue Kléber in 1913. In 1914 he saw the first bomb fall on Paris from the windows of his next flat, at 26 rue Geoffrey l'Asnier ('the house of a thousand Buddhas', a reference to his collection). His friend and secretary Tom Antongini, in his *Vita Secreta di Gabriele d'Annunzio* (The Secret Life of Gabriele d'Annunzio, 1938), tells us also that wherever the poet settled, even for a short while, the place had to be remodelled and decorated in an orgy of rich velvets, cushions, carpets, glass objects (usually from Murano), pictures and musical instruments, including a piano displaying Claude Debussy's original scores. When entertaining at home guests would be dazzled by the most exquisite decoration, food and drink.

D'Annunzio did not however spend all his time in Paris, often retiring to Chalet Saint-Dominique near Arcachon to write, where he was known locally as 'Superman'. He also spent much time in a farm outside Paris kept by Nathalie de Goloubeff, La Grange Dame Rose at Villacoublay in the south-western suburbs of Paris. There he could spend time with his beloved greyhounds and would organise races for them and his horses. As for Nathalie, he soon lost interest in her, although she continued to subsidise his expensive lifestyle, and he became entangled in a complicated love triangle with Ida Rubinstein and the American painter, Romaine Brooks. He called the latter 'Cinerina', due partly to her rather melancholic approach to life and also because her paintings tended to use tones of ash-coloured grey, as in the three portraits she made of him. They would remain friends even after she had started an affair with Natalie Barney in 1914, and both visited him in 1931 at Il Vittoriale, the luxurious retreat at Gardone in Italy where he spent the last years of his life.

He dedicated a sonnet to Brooks, praising her strength of character: 'No fate can tame, not sword nor flame / the secret diamond of your untouched heart.'

D'Annunzio's literary reputation was such that in 1911 he was approached by a film company keen to adapt some of his earlier works. Professing no interest whatsoever in this very new art form, the promised financial remuneration did have some appeal. He signed contracts but never bothered to see the finished product. Antongini recalls how in 1913 the writer received a letter from the Italian director Pastrone, who had just completed his great silent film *Cabiria* (described by d'Annunzio as 'a Graeco-Roman-Punic drama, in the manner of *Quo Vadis?*'), offering him a then huge sum of money (fifty thousand lire) to revise the already written film captions and give his name to the project. According to Antongini, d'Annunzio changed the title from *Trionfo d'Amore* to *Cabiria* in a matter of minutes, but took several weeks to revise the captions, driving Pastrone to distraction. Once the work was completed and the money pocketed, he lost all interest in the film.

The good days were over in Paris at the outbreak of World War I, when, as described dramatically by d'Annunzio: 'The invader's cavalry is riding down the valley of the Oise towards

Paris, entering the very heart of France, crushing the most sensitive part of this afflicted land.' He was invited to return to Italy in May 1915 where he dedicated the rest of his life to the war and to politics. He never returned to Paris.

The Russian dancer **Ida Rubinstein** (1885–1960) came from a wealthy family in Kharkov. She was orphaned at an early age but was looked after by relatives in St Petersburg, where she started to show a keen interest in theatre. In 1908 she made her premiere in Oscar Wilde's *Salome* with music by Glazunov, where her performance in the 'Dance of the Seven Veils' caused it to be banned by censors after the first public performance, and thereafter it could be performed only at private gatherings. Her family was scandalised and had her confined to a mental asylum from which she escaped. In 1909 she left for Paris with the Ballets Russes, starring in their first season there, in *Cléopâtre* in 1909 and *Scheherazade* with Nijinsky in 1910. Although considered a mediocre dancer, she graced the company with her striking beauty and scandalous reputation, inspiring many artists and attracting large audiences. For Cleopatra, choreographed by Fokine, she appeared on stage as a mummy rising from a sarcophagus, revealing her magnificent body wrapped in an equally magnificent Egyptian costume.

Very independent, and having received a substantial family inheritance, she now had sufficient funds to run her own company. She was inspired by Isadora Duncan's new style of dancing and she took lessons from Fokine, as well as studying the French actress Sarah Bernhardt on stage. She met Romaine Brooks in 1911 after the first performance of *The Martyrdom of St Sebastian*. D'Annunzio was besotted by Rubinstein, who had fallen in love with Brooks, and a complicated romantic triangle ensued. When World War

I broke out, Ida volunteered for the war effort and one of Romaine Brooks's portraits depicts her as an heroic nurse, dressed in a specially tailored uniform (designed by her friend Léon Bakst), standing against the background of the city of Ypres in flames.

After the war Rubinstein returned to the stage and played Cleopatra again in 1920, this time in Shakespeare's *Antony and Cleopatra*, in a French translation by André Gide. Her artistic collaboration with d'Annunzio survived for a while. She acted in 1921 in the silent film *La nave* (The Ship) directed by his son, and in his adaptation of *Phaedra* in 1923 with music by Pizzetti, employing some of the greatest artists of the time. Like Diaghilev, she produced ballets conceived by the great Nijinsky, Massine and Fokine. Ravel composed his famous *Boléro* in response to her request for a Spanish dance in which she could perform. She commissioned and performed in *Le baiser de la fée* (The Fairy's Kiss) by Stravinsky in 1928, and many others including Sauguet, Schmidt and Ibert wrote for her, enabling her to continue well into her forties. The company disbanded in 1935, but she carried on performing in works she had herself commissioned. She was last seen on the stage in Paris as Joan of Arc in an oratorio, *Jeanne d'Arc au bûcher* (Joan of Arc at the Stake), commissioned from Paul Claudel and Arthur Honegger.

Rubinstein was made *Chevalier de la légion d'honneur* in the 1930s, but had to leave France on the outbreak of World War II. She eventually found refuge in London until her return to France in 1950, spending her last ten years in seclusion in Vence in the South of France.

Arriving in Paris, Rubinstein greatly admired the American dancer **Isadora Duncan** (1877–1927), remembered today as 'The Mother of Modern Dance'. Born in San Francisco, she and her mother joined her brother Raymond in bohemian Paris in 1900 after a stay in London.

They occupied a cheap studio in rue de la Gaîté in the Latin Quarter, moving later to a bigger place in avenue de Villiers. In her memoir *My Life* (1927) Duncan recalls being taken by a friend to the 1900 *Exposition universelle* in the French capital, where she was struck by the performance of a compatriot in exile, the American dancer Loïe Fuller. A great innovator on the stage and using a mixture of lighting below stage, phosphorescent materials and mirrors, Fuller conjured magical shows which revolutionised contemporary dancing. Her appearance on the stage wearing several metres of light flowing silk was far removed from classical ballet. Its innovation inspired the ambitious avant-garde dancer, who had drawn her inspiration so far from the classical Greek mythology and iconography which she admired in the British Museum in London and in the Louvre in Paris.

A century of ideas and discovery was on display in the 1900 *Exposition*, in countless rooms and pavilions. The biggest attraction was perhaps the Palace of Electricity, a space devoted to the recent invention. There was also an entire stage for dance. Isadora Duncan's biographer Peter Kurth noted that her first Parisian mornings were spent dancing 'through the Luxembourg Gardens on her way to the Louvre'. It was in Paris that she discovered her body as 'something other than an instrument to express the sacred harmony of music'. One day, tipsy before dancing, Duncan could not get her dancing shoes on, so wearing her flimsy flowing Grecian costume, she gave up footwear altogether and danced barefoot for the first time, noticing that it accentuated the freedom of her movement. The audience loved her bare legs and her beautiful

PHOTO 27 Isadora Duncan, photographed by Otto

feet and she never wore shoes on stage again. Her fame grew and she started performing also at the fashionable salons of Comtesse Greffulhe and Anna de Noailles. Once the generous Winnaretta Singer visited her hotel in rue Marguerite and left a large sum of money for her. In those elegant circles, and thanks to Robert de Montesquiou, she met writers and composers like d'Annunzio and Pierre Louÿs, as well as artists including the sculptors Rodin and Bourdelle. Thanks also to the generosity of Winnaretta's brother Paris Singer (whom she met in 1909 and with whom she had a son), she managed to open a dancing school in Paris.

Travelling and adventures, amorous and otherwise, took her away from Paris but she was back in 1927 where she was seen dancing for the last time at the Théâtre Mogador to the music of Schubert's *Ave Maria*. In *My Life* she remembers taking a walk with d'Annunzio in a forest, when he exclaimed: 'Oh, Isadora, it is only possible to be alone with you in Nature. All other women destroy the landscape; you alone become part of it. … You are part of the trees, the sky, you are the dominating goddess of Nature.'

She is much better remembered than Loïe Fuller and Ida Rubinstein, and many books have been dedicated to her, as well as films. A 2016 film *The Dancer* by Stéphanie di Giusto touches on her rivalry with Loïe Fuller. Two other films were made in the 1960s, *Isadora Duncan, the Biggest Dancer in the World*, directed by Ken Russell in 1966, and *Isadora*, directed in 1968 by Karel Reisz, with an impressive Vanessa Redgrave in the title role. On the façade of the Théâtre des Champs-Élysées in avenue Montaigne one of her many admirers, Antoine Bourdelle, has immortalised her in a bas-relief in which she is represented dancing with Nijinsky.

The early years of the twentieth century saw a wave of extraordinary Russian artists and dancers leave their country to seek novelty, artistic freedom and work abroad. Many found the French capital particularly inviting. The Russian impresario **Sergei Diaghilev** (1872–1929) found himself in that situation. Very intelligent and cultured, charismatic but always non-conformist, he spoke fluent French and German. Failing to make a career in the Russian music world (he was a good pianist and singer) he had the idea of bringing a whole ballet company from St Petersburg to Paris in 1909. It consisted of a group of exceptional Russian dancers from the Russian Imperial Ballet including Anna Pavlova and Vaslav Nijinsky, as well as the choreographer Michel Fokine, who was much influenced by Isadora

Duncan's new approach to dancing on stage. Alexandre Benois was Diaghilev's first stage designer, and the gifted Russian composer Igor Stravinsky joined them a year later. Overall 250 dancers and an eighty-piece orchestra settled in the cheap hotels of boulevard Saint-Michel, while Nijinsky, his sister and their mother stayed in Hôtel Daunou at 6 rue Daunou near the Paris Opéra. Diaghilev, who always preferred lavishly luxurious places, stayed in a rather grand hotel near the Paris Opéra, the Hôtel de Hollande in avenue de l'Opéra (now demolished), where his protégé Nijinsky, with whom he was having an affair, ultimately joined him. Alexandre Benois reported in his *Reminiscences* (1941) the amazing impact their first performance had in Paris: 'Those of us who sat watching the work from the stalls were equally happy; here, we felt something was maturing that would amaze the world.' They did indeed together amaze the world for the next twenty years, until Diaghilev's death in 1929.

In the spring of 1909 *le tout Paris*, the whole of Paris society (politicians, aristocrats, writers, painters, couturiers, actors and dancers) attended the first performance of *Le Pavillon d'Armide* at the Théâtre du Châtelet. This ballet was quite traditional in style, but it was followed on the programme by something totally new, a performance of Borodin's *Prince Igor*, which dazzled the audience with its exotic Russian costumes. Nijinsky was the star of the show, and created a real sensation with his new style of movement on the stage. Until now ballet had concentrated on ballerinas, but now the focus was on the male dancers. The plots were also male-centred, like *Petrushka* (1911) and *L'après-midi d'un faune* (The Afternoon of a Faun, 1912), and the performances with their frank eroticism appealed especially to a male audience.

It was indeed a revolutionary approach to ballet, hitherto perceived as lightweight. Ballet now became the art-form of the moment, encompassing painting, design, fashion and literature. In 1910 the famous couturier Paul Poiret was very much inspired by *Scheherazade* for his new creations, and other couturiers followed as well as stage and interior designers. At the notorious premiere of *The Rite of Spring* in 1913 'every woman wore a head-dress: dazzling tiaras, embroidered bandeaux, or turbans with aigrettes and birds-of-paradise plumes'. The French writer Marcel Proust in his novel *Sodom and Gomorrah* (1922) includes a description of a fashionable beauty and patron of the arts of the time, Russian-born Misia Sert, who appeared at a premiere in a Russian-inspired outfit: 'Princess Yourbeletieff, the youthful sponsor of all these new great men, appeared wearing on her head an immense, quivering aigrette that was new to the women of Paris and that they all sought to copy; it was widely supposed that this marvellous creature had been imported in their copious luggage, and as their most priceless treasure, by the Russian dancers ...'

Proust went so far as to compare this new fashionable trend to the furore caused in France by the Dreyfus case, which had dominated the country at the turn of the century: '[This] charming invasion ...', he wrote, 'infected Paris, as we know, with a fever of curiosity less agonising, more purely aesthetic, but quite as intense perhaps as that aroused by the Dreyfus case.'

In 1910 the Ballets Russes appeared in an even more prestigious venue, the Opéra Garnier, with two new pieces composed by Rimsky-Korsakov, *Sadko* and *Scheherazade*. The more traditional *Giselle* was followed by the great innovation of Stravinsky's *L'Oiseau de feu* (The Firebird). Suddenly the

PHOTO 28 The Théâtre du Châtelet saw many Ballets Russes performances

East became fashionable, taking Paris by storm and breaking once and for all with the boundaries of tradition. Bewitched, Marcel Proust declared later in a letter to his friend the composer Reynaldo Hahn that he had never seen 'anything more beautiful'. It is thought that the production of *Giselle* inspired him to choose the name of Gisèle for one of the female characters in the book he was then writing, *À l'ombre des jeunes filles en fleur*.

Diaghilev also commissioned French composers for his productions, Maurice Ravel and Reynaldo Hahn among others, as well as the ubiquitous Jean Cocteau and painters like Pablo Picasso. This is the description Jean Cocteau gave of Nijinsky's performance in *Le Spectre de la rose* (The Spirit of the Rose) in *Comœdia illustré*, the daily newspaper which covered theatrical events in Paris at the time: 'After he has bid a last farewell to his beloved victim, he evaporates through the window in a jump so poignant, so contrary to all the laws of flight and balance, following so high and curved a trajectory, that I shall never again smell a rose without this ineffable phantom appearing before me.'

Many professed however to be shocked when attending the sexually charged performance of *L'après-midi d'un faune* in 1912, with music by Debussy. Among them was Gaston Calmette, the editor of the conservative newspaper *Le Figaro*, who wrote in his review: 'Anyone who mentions the words "art" and "imagination" in the same breath as this production must be laughing at us. This is neither a pretty pastoral nor a work of profound meaning. We are shown a lecherous faun, whose movements are filthy and bestial in their eroticism, and whose gestures are as crude as they are indecent. That is all. And the over-explicit miming of this misshapen beast, loathsome when seen full on, but even more loathsome in profile, was greeted with the booing it deserved. Decent people will never accept such animal realism.'

Nijinsky had indeed appeared to simulate orgasm on stage lying face down on a veil dropped by one of the nymphs. An extraordinary controversy ensued involving even the great sculptor Auguste Rodin, who publicly acknowledged his admiration for the ballet, and who was consequently pilloried by those looking for an excuse to challenge him and his work.

Some productions were less controversial, for example Maurice Ravel's *Daphnis et Chloé*, but there was more to come at Stravinsky's *The Rite of Spring* at the elegant Théâtre des Champs-Élysées in May 1913. The new ballet created such an uproar that the show degenerated into a riot both inside and outside the theatre. A cultural bombshell had exploded on the Parisian cultural scene. While composing

The Firebird in 1910, Stravinsky had already conceived the idea for this innovative ballet, encouraged by the Russian folklorist Nikolai Roerich, who provided drawings from scenes of historical rituals.

In his autobiography Stravinsky wrote: 'One day, when I was finishing the last pages of *The Firebird* in St Petersburg, I had a fleeting vision which came to me as a complete surprise, my mind at the moment being full of other things. I saw in my imagination a solemn pagan rite: sage elders, seated in a circle, watched a young girl dance herself to death. They were sacrificing her to propitiate the god of spring.'

The revolutionary choreography was of course by Nijinsky. Many pointed out that the Parisian public was getting a foretaste of the October Revolution four years later, with the whole production, including the music, choreography, subject matter and stage set creating an artistic revolution, fitting the Modernist movement perfectly and anticipating what was to occur politically and socially. The primitivism portrayed in the ballet with its crude representation of pagan Russia, and the human sacrifice performed daringly on stage, amazed and delighted many, but a great part of the audience was deeply shocked.

Jean Cocteau, who attached himself 'like a leech' to the rich and famous, had met Diaghilev at Misia Sert's house and started to contribute to the productions, as well as chronicling the performances. He reported in his cultural memoir *Cock and Harlequin* (1921):

All the elements of a scandal were present ... Thus we made the acquaintance of this historic work in the midst of such an uproar that the dancers could no longer hear the orchestra and had to keep time to the rhythm which

Nijinsky, stamping and shouting, was beating in the
wings. The audience behaved as it ought to; it revolted
straight away. People laughed, booed, hissed, imitated
animal noises and possibly would have tired themselves
out before long, had not the crowd of aesthetes and a
handful of musicians, carried away by their excessive zeal,
insulted and even roughly handled the public in the *loges*.
The uproar degenerated into a free fight.

Another witness, Valentine Gross, noted in a broadcast: 'The
theatre seemed to be shaken by an earthquake. It seemed
to shudder. People shouted insults, howled and whistled,
drowning the music.'

Nijinsky's marriage in 1914, and the breach which ensued
between him and Diaghilev, was considered by many as the
beginning of the end for the Ballets Russes: 'He alone gave
life to the whole company' wrote Jacques Rivière in *Nouvelle
Revue Française* in July 1914.

Moreover, as World War I broke out, the company was
looking beyond Europe, and went on tour to North and
South America. It returned to the French capital in May 1917
and to the Châtelet with *Les contes russes* (Children's Tales),
The Firebird and the legendary *Parade* based on an idea by
Jean Cocteau, to music by Erik Satie and with the set by
Picasso. Satie had included gunshots and clacking typewriter
keys in his bizarre score, and the ballet dared to make fun
of nationalist propaganda. The poet Guillaume Apollinaire,
who had returned seriously wounded from the Front, also
contributed by writing the programme notes, in which he
first coined the term 'Surrealism'.

The ballet told the story of a travelling troupe presenting
a parade in the Paris streets, in an attempt to recruit an

audience for a show. It included a Chinese magician as well as an American girl, the first of a long list of Americans in Paris on stage as well as in novels. Jean Cocteau gives a lively description: 'The Chinaman pulls out an egg from his pigtail, eats and digests it, finds it again in the toe of his shoe, spits fire, burns himself, stamps to put out the sparks, etc.'

The Ballets Russes were back in 1920, presenting *Le chant du rossignol* (The Song of the Nightingale). The painter Henri Matisse had finally agreed to work for Diaghilev, perhaps wanting to emulate his friend and chief rival, Picasso. For this production Diaghilev, permanently broke, had obtained the financial support of the French couturier Coco Chanel, who also produced the costumes for *Le train bleu* (The Blue Train, 1924). She was also underwriting another impecunious Russian, Stravinsky, with whom she allegedly had an affair at the time, by generously installing his whole family in her house in the Paris suburbs. On 18 May 1922 a legendary party was organised by Violet and Sidney Schiff on the occasion of the first Paris Opéra performance of Stravinsky's *Renard*, choreographed by Bronislava Nijinska, with sets by Larionov. The venue was the Hôtel Majestic, one of the most prestigious Paris hotels in the elegant avenue Kléber. An amazing gathering of Modernist writers and artists was invited, including Picasso, Stravinsky, Proust, Larionov and Joyce. Someone had the idea of bringing together the two literary geniuses of the time, James Joyce and Marcel Proust. According to witnesses the Irishman turned up drunk and the conversation between him and Proust did not match up to everyone's expectations. They reportedly talked about food and truffles and discussed their respective ailments.

A one-act play, *Of Thyme and Rosemary*, was written about this momentous encounter by the American writer Debbie Weiss, performed in New York in 2012.

Having found some degree of financial stability, Stravinsky went on to compose the music for *Les Noces*, produced by Ballets Russes in 1923. It took place at the Gaîté-Lyrique theatre and was choreographed by Nijinsky's sister. More followed with Poulenc's *Les biches* (The Does) in 1924 and finally *Le bal* (The Ball) in 1929, choreographed by Balanchine and designed by Giorgio de Chirico, who also contributed to the final production of *The Prodigal Son*, performed a few months before Diaghilev's death in 1929.

Diaghilev's main designers were Alexandre Benois, Léon Bakst and Natalia Goncharova. As Marina Tsvetaeva wrote, 'Such is Goncharova with her modernity, her innovation, her success, her fame, her glory, her fashion … she did not lead a permanent school, she did not convey a one-time discovery into a method and did not canonise. To sum her up? In short: talent and hard work.'

Before going to Paris, the Russian artists **Natalia Goncharova** (1881–1962) and her partner **Mikhail Larionov** (1881–1964) worked together as avant-garde painters and designers. Goncharova was prolific, and had an exhibition in Moscow in 1913 which included more than 800 of her works, combining Russian tradition and European Modernist trends: 'Modern French painters opened my eyes.' In 1913 Sergei Diaghilev and his designer Alexandre Benois went to Moscow and met Goncharova and Larionov, who had attracted public attention for their green and purple wigs, bright clothes decorated with flowers and birds and outrageous make-up. It was Benois' idea to choose Goncharova to design the sets and costumes for the 1914 Ballets Russes production of Rimsky-Korsakov's *Le Coq d'or* (The Golden Cockerel). Goncharova and Larionov went to Paris on 29 April 1914 but the outbreak of World War I forced them back to Russia. In the summer of 1915 they were on tour in Switzerland, Italy and Spain with the

PHOTO 29 Goncharova and Larionov lived and worked above La Palette

Ballets Russes, never imagining that they would not return to Russia, however, in late 1917 the Revolution broke out. They rented a Paris apartment at 16 rue Jacques Callot in the Latin Quarter, which Goncharova was to occupy until her death, and had their meals below the flat at the café La Palette, still around the corner at 43 rue de Seine in the sixth arrondissement. Paris remained their base, although once the war was over Goncharova and Larionov travelled to Norway, Italy, England, Switzerland and Spain. They applied for and received French citizenship in 1938.

In Paris they met Picasso, Braque, Dadaists and Surrealists. Picasso's friend Apollinaire admired her skills: 'Goncharova's personality is revealed through the entire spectrum of her work.' She became influenced by the artists living in Paris, but a significant part of her painting remained devoted to working life in the Russian countryside, her way of expressing her nostalgia for Mother Russia. She was 'a country girl' according to Tsvetaeva: 'When I call her a country girl, I naturally include the life of the gentry, too – all that boundless outpouring of spring, yearning, ploughed fields, rivers, and working the land.' Between 1922 and 1926 she created textiles, and richly embroidered and appliquéd dress designs for Maison Myrbor on the rue Vincent, strongly influenced by Russian folk art, icons and Byzantine mosaics. Later, with money growing tighter after Diaghilev's death, the immensely resilient and creative artist worked on clothes, posters, book illustrations and apartment interiors. She was the mastermind for artists' balls like the *Grand bal des artistes* in 1923, for which she produced posters, tickets, programmes, masks and puppets.

Goncharova is remembered mainly for her Ballets Russes productions, and especially for Stravinsky's *Les noces*, a ballet featuring a peasant marriage where she could display her knowledge of folklore, rural life, labour, religious festivals and rites. She collaborated with the choreographer Bronislava Nijinska to create outfits that would not inhibit the dancers' movement, replacing colourful but bulky outfits with simple brown pinafores worn over cream blouses. In the mid-1920s Diaghilev planned to revive *The Firebird*, which had been one of the most successful of the early works of the Ballets Russes. The original designs and dancers' costumes by Léon Bakst were tired, and Diaghilev commissioned new sets and costumes from Goncharova, whose style he admired. The bold colours and simplified shapes she used were perfectly suited to the folk-tale elements in the ballet.

Larionov worked with Goncharova for Diaghilev's company on the revival of *Sadko* in 1916. In *Kikimora* (1917) he too resorted to the Russian peasant style boldly mixed with Cubist and constructivist elements. He also worked on *Soleil de nuit* (Midnight Sun, 1915) and on *Renard* in 1922. He chronicled the daily life of the company, sketching caricatures, and was also in charge of supervising new choreographers.

In 1932, to capture her impressions of Goncharova, Marina Tsvetaeva wrote an essay titled 'Natalia Goncharova: Life and Art'. It was 'an attempt at the biography of an artist's soul' and was drawn directly from Tsvetaeva's conversations with her. 'I cherish Goncharova because she does not realise her value – either as a person or as an artist. So for me, she is like nature, and I am the artist painting from nature.'

Although they were in close contact from 1928 to 1932, Tsvetaeva seemed to be unaware that her artist friend wrote poetry. 'Take Goncharova – she's never written poetry, she's never lived poetry, but she understands because she looks and she sees,' she wrote in 1929, describing her friend's perceptive appreciation of her poem 'To the Herald'. But undated poems were found in four of Goncharova's notebooks, some in French, associating images of the sea with their studio at 13 rue Visconti:

Today, Paris is a seaside town.
The breeze carries a salty smell
At the end of the boulevard, perhaps there are masts.
I wish I could go to the shore, look at the seagulls,
Listen to the waves.

For the artist in exile the sea conjures her longing for Russia:

How I wish I could fall asleep peacefully
And wake up in a birch grove.

The 'birch grove' represents Russia. Paris also appears in her poem 'Geography', reminding Larionov of their early happiness together in Paris:

This morning I made the rounds
Of the places we used to go.
Here's the café where we went
To share our modest breakfast.
Here is the bench on the boulevard,
Where I waited for you so often.
Little things, but not forgotten,
Little things, but how it hurts –
My eyes are filled with tears.

Natalia Goncharova is buried in Division 7, Row 1, Lot 14 in Ivry cemetery in the Paris suburb. In a poem she urges her friends to remember her in life:

My friends, do not visit my grave.
You will often encounter my spirit in life,
And my grave is far.
A long way to go, and with sad thoughts …

A solo retrospective of her work was organised at the Tate Modern in London in 2019.

Without the many wealthy women like Coco Chanel, Luisa Casati, Misia Sert, Winnaretta Singer, Comtesse Greffulhe and Marie-Laure de Noailles, who were patrons and financial supporters of Diaghilev, pivotal experimental works would never have been realised. The powerful, music-loving **Élisabeth, Comtesse Greffulhe** (1860–1952) invited Diaghilev to her salon at 8–10 rue d'Astorg in the eighth arrondissement when he arrived in Paris, and introduced him to the financier Gabriel Astruc, who opened the doors of the Théâtre du Châtelet to the first Ballets Russes performance in the French capital. One of her admirers, the French writer Marcel Proust, was inspired by her and other contemporary aristocratic ladies to create the character of the Duchess of Guermantes for his novel *À la recherche du temps perdu*. Everyone recognised her husband as the Duc de Guermantes in the novel. She sponsored many musicians including Gabriel Fauré, who dedicated *Pavane* to her, first performed at a garden party in the Bois de Boulogne.

The fashion designer and icon **Coco Chanel** (1883–1971) met Diaghilev at the end of World War I through her friend **Misia Sert** (née Misia Godebska) (1872–1950). She paid anonymously for the 1920 revival of *The Rite of Spring* and became a close adviser and costume designer for *Le train bleu*, influenced by Suzanne Lenglen, the great tennis player of the time. Chanel and Misia Sert rushed to Diaghilev's deathbed in Venice in 1929 and settled the bills for his funeral and burial, as well as for his hotel room.

Hemingway and Scott Fitzgerald's friends, the wealthy American couple **Gerald Murphy** (1888–1964) and his wife **Sara** (1883–1975) befriended, among others, Picasso. They financed many of the artists and musicians who circled around the Ballets Russes.

The most well-known collector living in Paris in the beginning of the twentieth century was probably **Gertrude Stein** (1874–1946). Although known for some time as a shrewd collector of avant-garde art, she was also keen to be considered a serious writer. Her brother Leo, with whom she lived in Paris for many years, her eldest brother Michael and sister-in-law Sarah may have been more discerning as collectors. What remains undeniable is that she appeared to her contemporaries as the sibling with the strongest personality.

Leo and Gertrude had first gone from America to Paris to join the millions of tourists at the prestigious 1900 *Exposition universelle*. Leo then opted to stay for a while in Florence and London, before deciding eventually to settle in Paris, as he had now decided to become an artist. A certain amount of family money allowed him to find a newly built studio and apartment at 27 rue de Fleurus, near the Jardin du Luxembourg.

Gertrude moved in with him in 1903, and very soon after both started collecting pictures by well-established artists including Cézanne, Degas, Toulouse-Lautrec and Bonnard, but also by bold, promising unknown geniuses like Pablo

PHOTO 30   27 rue de Fleurus, where Gertrude Stein held her salon

Picasso. The younger Steins were joined in January 1904 by Michael and Sarah who followed them to Paris with their son, and took a neighbouring flat at 58 rue Madame.

In her book *Paris France* Gertrude noted: 'So Paris was the place that suited those of us that were to create the twentieth century art and literature, naturally enough.' As an aspiring artist Leo Stein tended to choose the paintings, but Michael and his wife Sarah also collected, and befriended the artists who gathered at their weekly salon. Michael Stein was the businessman of the family and had been managing the family affairs for a while. The Steins were rich enough to act as patrons to unknown artists. They established a strong friendship with the young Henri Matisse and gave him financial support to open his Art Academy.

The Parisian artistic scene is very present in Gertrude's memoirs, in her correspondence and in *The Autobiography of Alice B. Toklas*, her book about herself, but written through the voice of her partner Alice Babette Toklas. She happily shared 27 rue de Fleurus with her brother Leo until the end of 1910, when Alice B. Toklas moved in. This new arrangement gave rise to some tension between the siblings, and in the spring of 1914 Leo Stein left the apartment, taking with him part of their joint collection, mainly works by Matisse and Renoir. Gertrude kept most of her beloved Picassos. For many years the legendary weekly salon held on a Saturday afternoon at 27 rue de Fleurus included painters, their partners and friends. Picasso, Gertrude's favourite from the beginning, brought along his friend, the critic and poet Guillaume Apollinaire. American writers like Ernest Hemingway and Scott Fitzgerald mixed with French and European writers and artists attracted by Leo's 'brilliant conversation on modern French art and the remarkable collection, mostly of contemporary paintings which he made at little cost with the aid of his independent and exacting judgment', recorded by the American journalist and collector Agnes Meyer, visiting in 1909.

Gertrude presided over the proceedings 'in her robe of coarse cotton cord, with her leather-strap sandals', as described by the art dealer Ambroise Vollard in *Souvenirs d'un marchand de tableaux*: '... you might have taken her for a housewife whose horizon was limited to her dealings with the milkman, the grocer and the greengrocer.'

Even for the liberated early 1930s Gertrude's appearance was rather unconventional. She liked unusual bohemian clothes consisting mainly of corduroy suits and bulky velvet robes. The leather sandals she wore on bare feet were hand-made by Raymond Duncan (Isadora Duncan's brother). In fact on many occasions she was refused entry to elegant places because of her unorthodox footwear. In company and in her salon she preferred to talk to men, while Toklas was left with their wives or partners. From 1926 Gertrude cut her hair very short, which emphasised her mannish appearance, and she replaced the corduroy suits with jackets, skirts and waistcoats. She was a striking sight as she steered her open two-seater Ford 'Lady Godiva' through the streets of Paris.

A friend, the American writer Sherwood Anderson, described her thus: 'Imagine a strong woman with legs like stone pillars sitting in a room hung with Picassos ... The woman is a very symbol of health and strength. She laughs. She smokes cigarettes. She tells stories with an American shrewdness in getting the tang and the kick into the telling.'

In her early years in Paris Gertrude, often attracted to young men, developed a special relationship with Picasso, a friendship which survived until her death. In *The Autobiography of Alice B. Toklas* she relates the first time Picasso came to dinner: 'He was thin dark, alive with big pools of eyes and a violent but not rough way. He was sitting next to Gertrude Stein at dinner and she took up a piece of bread. This, said Picasso, snatching it back with violence, this piece of bread is mine. She laughed and he looked sheepish. That was the beginning of their intimacy.' She goes as far as to claim that she and Picasso are 'the two greatest twentieth century geniuses'. The friendship was reinforced when she sat for the legendary portrait of her which he started in 1905. More than twenty-five artists painted her at the time, but she maintained that Picasso's portrait was the most authentic: (*'c*)*'est le seul portrait de moi qui reste toujours moi*' ('It's the only portrait of me where I am still me'). The

astonishing finished product made a great impact on those
who saw it. The English art critic Roger Fry was so filled
with excitement that he wrote an article in *The Burlington
Review* claiming that it was equal in value to a portrait by
Raphael. The painting took a long time to complete, and
during the many hours she sat for it she developed the
urge to write about her personal experience of visual art.
She wrote: 'During these long poses and these long walks
Gertrude Stein meditated and made sentences ... She had
come to like posing, the long still hours followed by a long
dark walk intensified the concentration with which she was
creating her sentences.' In spring 1906 Picasso erased her
face completely, as he was not happy with it. Many months
later after a trip to Spain he began again, and made her face
resemble a mask. She was aware that her special relationship
with Picasso created some rivalry with others like Henri
Matisse, and might even have derived some pleasure from it,
noting mischievously: 'Matisse was irritated by the growing
friendship between Picasso and Gertrude Stein.'

   On the surface she appeared as a kind of maternal figure for
the artists whom she entertained and so generously helped.
She was known as the Mother Goose of Montparnasse. She
also took an especial interest in young writers, many still
unknown, although she did not always condone the excesses
of bohemian life in the cafés. In *Autobiography* she describes
the antics of a particular party where 'all of a sudden André
Salmon ... leaped upon the by no means solid table and
poured out an extemporaneous eulogy and poem. At the
end he seized a big glass and drank what was in it, then
promptly went off his head, being completely drunk, and
began to fight. The men all got hold of him ... The others
with Picasso leading, because Picasso though small is very

strong, dragged Salmon into the front atelier and locked
him in. Everybody came back and sat down.' The friendship
with Picasso did not run smoothly. At one stage they were
estranged for a whole year after a quarrel. Her writing was not
always taken seriously, but she gave the studied impression of
not caring too much. Her literary career was stimulated by
works written by contemporary Modernist writers like Eliot,
Pound and Joyce. Her style, deliberately simple, 'Rose is a
rose is a rose is a rose,' started to be recognised as truly new
and Modernist. She believed that her experimental approach
to writing was similar to Picasso's breakthrough experimental
approach to painting. She compared herself to him and
Matisse in her notebook: 'Pablo and Matisse have a maleness
that belongs to genius. *Moi aussi*, perhaps.'

In many ways she was indeed a pioneer, as Adam Gopnik
notes in his introduction to Stein's book *Paris France*, published
in 1940: 'Hemingway was in many ways the populariser of a
style she had invented. One could even say, to borrow Picasso's
famous disparaging remark about his imitators, that Stein did
it first and he, Hemingway, did it pretty.'

In 1921 Sherwood Anderson, who knew Gertrude Stein
well, had convinced Ernest Hemingway and his wife, newly
married, to spend her family inheritance not in Italy, as
they had planned, but rather in Paris. Initially Gertrude
and Hemingway had got on, as he reported in a letter
home: 'Stein and me are just like brothers, and we see a
lot of her.' They shared an interest in Spain and bullfights.
In 1924 Hemingway proofread *The Making of Americans*
which she had written in 1903, and arranged for publication
of extracts in the *Transatlantic Review*. However the 'good
pupil' infuriated her when his *Torrents of Spring* published
in 1926 satirised her friend Anderson's latest novel *Dark*

Laughter (1925). Worse would come later when Hemingway mentioned her unkindly in *The Sun Also Rises*.

In 1930, tired of cleaning up after geniuses and their wives, Alice B. Toklas decided to put an end to the popular rue de Fleurus salon and sent notes to everyone announcing: 'Miss Stein no longer requires your presence.' By 1938 the happy period in Paris had come to a cruel end. The lease of rue de Fleurus expired and the couple moved to 5 rue Christine. The move was however seen as positive by Janet Flanner: 'Since Miss Gertrude Stein's collection of pictures practically ranks as one of Paris's private modern museums, it is of interest to report that she and her canvases have moved from her famous Montparnasse salon on the Rue de Fleurus to a remarkable seventeenth-century Latin Quarter flat occupied by Queen Christina of Sweden and still containing her original wall *boiseries* and her reading cabinet. The move was a good thing …'

In 1940 the couple left to seek safety in the rural provinces. *Paris France* describes in a deliberately flat style, quite close to stream of consciousness, and using fanciful punctuation and spelling, her perception of the Paris she had to leave at the beginning of World War II and the provincial France where she and Alice had taken refuge. It touches on deliberately chosen mundane topics such as cooking, village daily life, gossip and fashion, and there is a great deal about dogs.

In the 1920s Gertrude had befriended the historian Bernard Faÿ, who became a frequent visitor in Paris as well as to her former country house at Bilignin. '… he talked out in the garden about everything, about life, and America, and themselves and friendship. They then cemented the friendship that is one of the four permanent friendships of Gertrude Stein's life.' It was to be a very useful friendship indeed. He was a Nazi collaborator, and through his contacts with the Vichy government he helped to protect Stein and Toklas, who would otherwise doubtless have been arrested and deported, as both were Jewish and American. Funds from America stopped coming in and by 1942 they had run out of money. Faÿ came to the rescue, but to keep them afloat, pictures had to be sold. When they were asked what had happened to Madame Cézanne's portrait, the answer was 'we were eating her'. But the bulk of the collection of paintings now at 5 rue Christine was also saved, possibly thanks to Bernard Faÿ. The Paris flat was raided by the Germans in July 1944 but remarkably few things were removed: bibelots, linen and a cushion which Alice had embroidered, representing a Picasso painting. It might have just been a reconnaissance visit, as plans were probably made to come back for the most valuable possessions, but the Allies arrived in August 1944, and Gertrude and Alice were able to move back into a mostly untouched home in December of that year. Some claims have been made that Gertrude was a collaborator and a Vichy sympathiser, as she had translated Marshal Pétain's speeches into English. When Stein died of cancer in 1946, she left her money and collection of paintings to Toklas for 'her use for life'. However the painting collection, which in the meantime had become very valuable, was removed from her flat by the heirs of Michael and Sarah Stein while Alice was absent, and she was later evicted from rue Christine, because she could not afford the rent. Janet Flanner helped her to find another apartment where she remained until her death in 1967. Alice is buried beside Gertrude in Père Lachaise Cemetery in Paris.

In 1935, soon after the publication of Gertrude Stein's *The Autobiography of Alice B. Toklas*, a small group of artists and writers published a 'pamphlet', a *Testimony against Gertrude Stein* through the Service Press at The Hague, in which they expressed their outrage at Gertrude Stein's book, which had brought her international fame. They accused her of indiscretion, of having told stories which should have remained unsaid. For them the book was packed with inaccuracies, caused by her poor command of French as well as her boundless vanity: the editor of *transition*, the literary critic Eugène Jolas, wrote: 'There is a unanimity of opinion that she had no understanding of what really was happening around her, that the mutation of ideas beneath the surface of the more obvious contacts and clashes of personalities during that period escaped her entirely. Her participation in the genesis and development of such movements as Fauvism, Cubism, Dada, Surrealism, Transition [*sic*] etc was never ideologically intimate and, as M. Matisse states, she has presented the epoch "without taste and without relation to reality".' Henri Matisse was one of her most vehement critics, stating that the offensive book was 'more like a harlequin's costume, the different pieces of which, having been more or less invented by herself, have been sewn together without taste and without relation to reality'. The Dadaist writer Tristan Tzara joined the critics, and Georges Braque, doubtless offended by the fact that she had attributed the birth of Cubism solely to Picasso, ignoring his contribution, was particularly damning: 'Miss Stein understood nothing of what went on around her ... she never knew French really well ... she has entirely misunderstood cubism which she sees simply in terms of personalities ... For one who poses as an authority in the epoch it is safe to say that she never went beyond the stage of the tourist.' The Surrealist poet André Salmon contributed: ' ... there is a great confusion of dates, places and persons ...', to which he added her regrettable lack of sense of humour, citing a famous banquet organised for the painter Douanier Rousseau, at which she had misinterpreted the behaviour of some of the guests (including his own). He also confirmed that 'Miss Stein's account of the formation of cubism is entirely false.'

The virulence of these attacks had little effect on Gertrude Stein's reputation, which continued to dominate the Parisian cultural and artistic scene until World War II, eclipsing her lifelong companion **Alice B. Toklas** (1877–1967). Having left San Francisco for Paris in 1907, Toklas moved with a friend to a flat at 75 rue Notre-Dame-des-Champs after a short period staying at Hôtel de l'Univers at 93 boulevard Saint-Michel. She met Gertrude Stein soon after she arrived, and in 1908 went to live with her, staying for the following thirty-eight years. Contemporaries referred to her as Stein's 'secretary', but she was also her literary guide, agent and housekeeper. A shadowy figure managing the practicalities of Stein's life, she ran the house and acted as the hostess who entertained the wives of the visiting male artists and writers: 'Alice sat with the geniuses' "wives",' reported a visitor. Rather ugly, she was described by Sylvia Beach as a 'thin, bird-like woman with a hooked nose, drooping eyelids and a thin mustache'. Janet Flanner thought she looked like a 'gipsy'. The first of Stein's series of 'word portraits', *Ada*, was written in 1910, three years after she met Toklas. The subjects were mostly her famous friends like Picasso and Matisse, but *Ada* is the story of a 'happy young woman', her new partner Alice B. Toklas.

It is fair to point out that Toklas was a writer in her own right. It is also overlooked that she had established a small press, Plain Edition, which published her partner's books. Although Gertrude Stein left much of her estate to Toklas, including their shared art collection, housed in their apartment at 5 rue Christine, Toklas had no legally enforceable rights. In 1964 she was evicted from the flat in rue Christine, which she had shared with Gertrude Stein since 1938, and moved to a small place at 16 rue de la Convention. In her last years Toklas had to rely on charity from friends as well as the small income from her own writing. In serious need of money, she started to produce articles for several magazines and newspapers, including *The New Republic* and the *New York Times*. She also published three books, *The Alice B. Toklas Cookbook* (1954), *Aromas and Flavors of Past and Present* (1958) and a book of memoirs, *What is Remembered* (1963).

Food had been very important for the couple. A visiting friend, Mabel Dodge Luhan, reported that Gertrude '... had a laugh like a beefsteak. She loved beef, and I used to like to see her sit down in front of five pounds of rare meat three inches thick and, with strong wrists wielding knife and fork, finish it with gusto, while Alice ate a little slice, daintily, like a cat.' Throughout their life together, Stein had been the writer, and Toklas had organised the catering. She had not published anything since she was seventeen, but when *The Alice B. Toklas Cookbook* came out in 1954 it was praised by Janet Flanner in the *New Yorker* as 'a book of character, fine food and tasty human observation'. She saw in it much more than recipes, and noted that Toklas was a good writer. 'Though born in America,' wrote Toklas, 'I have lived so long in France that both countries seem to be mine, and knowing, loving both, I took to pondering on the difference in eating habits and general attitude to food and the kitchen in the United States and here.'

The *Cookbook* gives recipes for traditional feasts like Thanksgiving, at which a turkey extravagantly stuffed with mushrooms, chestnuts and oysters was prepared, but it also describes the hard times during the Occupation when food was rationed and scarce, with milk, butter and eggs difficult to find. She and Stein coped by growing vegetables in the garden of their house at Bilignin in the Jura, where they had taken refuge. Anyone interested in traditional French cuisine would find her detailed recipes interesting and easy to follow, and would enjoy the information provided with reminiscences, notes and commentaries. The chapter entitled 'Dishes for Artists', for example, informs us that 'Picasso was for many years on a strict diet'. The chapter 'Murder in the Kitchen' is a witty description of the necessary if unpleasant process of dispatching creatures before cooking them: 'The carp was dead, killed, assassinated, murdered in the first, second and third degree. Limp, I fell into a chair, with my hands still unwashed reached for a cigarette, lighted it, and waited for the police to take me into custody.'

One last chapter includes recipes from their friends Natalie Barney (stuffed aubergine) and the controversial 'Haschich Fudge [*sic*]' made with a mixture of fruit, nuts and spices, to which a 'bunch of *cannabis sativa*' can be pulverised and added. She notes that the cannabis may be difficult to come by, but that it is found growing wild in Europe. The recipe caused some controversy and brought her unwelcome notoriety, as her name was later associated with a range of concoctions called the 'Alice B. Toklas brownies'. In the 1968 film *I Love You, Alice B. Toklas* Peter Sellers plays a respectable lawyer who falls in love with a beautiful young hippie who cooks 'groovy' cannabis brownies.

Toklas's last years in Paris were very difficult, because of poor health and financial problems. Isolated and lonely, she still saw some friends, including Janet Flanner, who was a regular visitor at the hospital where Toklas died at the age of eighty-nine, bringing delicacies from Fauchon. She was buried next to Gertrude Stein in Père Lachaise Cemetery in Paris, and her name is engraved on the back of Stein's headstone.

8

Conclusion

Alas old Paris is disappearing with frightening speed.

(Balzac)

Most of the writers and artists discussed in this book would still recognise the city as they knew it. It looks superficially unchanged nowadays, although those who lived in Montparnasse would probably be shocked at the sight of the tower now looming over their favourite haunts.

Despite having lost its prime place as an international cultural centre, Paris still attracted artists and writers after 1950. Italo Calvino kept a house there between 1967 and 1980, and considered it an ideal place to write. Paris remained popular with Latin American writers including Cortázar, Borges and García Márquez, and a succession of Americans, Jack Kerouac and the Beat Generation, Paul Auster, Norman Mailer, Truman Capote and Gore Vidal. The American essayist Susan Sontag was buried in Montparnasse Cemetery in 2004. She died in New York, but had lived in Paris in 1957.

PHOTO 31   Notre-Dame, damaged by fire in April 2019

According to the architectural critic Ian Nairn, the boulevard Saint-Germain is still a place 'in which it is honourable and decent to be either intellectual or unintellectual', but like so many popular tourist destinations Paris has changed, probably for the worse. Many great Left Bank bookshops have closed and been replaced by what Eric Hazan calls in *A Walk Through Paris* 'commodity fetishism'. The city has gone through a process of gentrification, with much of its working-class and immigrant population pushed to the periphery, and is becoming a tourist attraction, a set piece. The cost of housing, rent and hotels has soared. Paris is now the most expensive city in the world after Singapore, no longer a possibility for 'down-and-outs'. Some projects, like the gigantic proposal to develop the Gare du Nord, are resisted by local residents.

PHOTO 32 The present Shakespeare and Company bookshop

Recent events have brought international concern to the city which suffered horrific terrorist attacks in 2015 and 2016. At the same time there was renewed interest in literary Paris. Following the events, Ernest Hemingway's nostalgic memoir *A Moveable Feast* sold out overnight. International concern rose again more recently in April 2019, when a terrible fire destroyed part of Notre-Dame, the most iconic building in the city, visited, painted and written about by practically everyone.

That too was followed by a renewed interest in literary works such as Victor Hugo's *Notre-Dame de Paris*. The queues waiting to enter the Shakespeare and Company bookshop, now a few steps from the cathedral, show that literary Paris is still alive and well.

French Expressions

abonné(e)	subscriber
agrégation	academic competition to teach at high level
à la garçonne	boyish hair cut, bob
arrondissement	administrative area of Paris
bal musette	dance hall
café-tabac	café also selling cigarettes
Chevalier de la légion d'honneur	public service award, equivalent to Knight or Dame
crémerie	milk bar, café
croix de guerre	award for bravery in wartime
flâner (flânerie, flâneur, flâneuse)	strolling the streets, especially to observe
La Belle Époque	period of high Western culture 1871 to 1914
lecteur, lectrice	assistant language teacher at a university

les années folles	the Roaring Twenties
Paname	popular word for Paris
parisienne	Parisian woman, also suggesting style
plongeur	low-paid position washing dishes
roman à clef	novel with characters based on real people
salon	social gathering at home of fashionable hostess
salon d'automne	annual exhibition of works by artists in Paris
succès de scandale	success of work of art because of link to scandal

Haunts and Locations

ART SCHOOLS, ART DEALERS AND ARTISTS' COLONIES

Académie de la Grande-Chaumière, 14 rue de la Grande-Chaumière (6, ie 6th arrondissement)
Académie des Beaux-Arts, 23 quai de Conti (6)
Académie Julian, 31 rue du Dragon (6)
Académie Vassilieff, 21 avenue du Maine (14)
Bourdelle art school, 18 rue Antoine Bourdelle (15)
Hôtel Drouot, 9 rue Drouot (9)
Institut Rodin, 132 boulevard du Montparnasse (14)
La Cité fleurie, 65 boulevard Arago (14)
La Ruche, 2 passage Dantzig (15)
Le Bateau-Lavoir, 13 rue Ravignan/place Emile Goudeau (18)
Villa Seurat, 101 rue de la Tombe-Issoire (14)

EDUCATIONAL ESTABLISHMENTS

Collège de France, 11 place Marcelin Berthelot and 52 rue du Cardinal Lemoine (5)
École Normale Supérieure, 45 rue d'Ulm (5)

Lycée Condorcet, 8 rue du Havre (9)
Lycée La Bruyère, 31 avenue de Paris, Versailles
Lycée Saint-Louis, 44 boulevard Saint-Michel (6)
Sorbonne (University of Paris) (5)

SALONS

Comtesse Greffuhle, 8–10 rue d'Astorg (8)
Gertrude Stein and Alice B. Toklas, 27 rue de Fleurus (6), 5
  rue Christine (6)
Natalie Barney, 20 rue Jacob (7)
Winnaretta Singer, Princesse de Polignac, 43 avenue Henri
  Martin (18)

CAFÉS, RESTAURANTS, CLUBS AND BARS

Au rendez-vous des mariniers, 33 quai d'Anjou, Île Saint-
  Louis (4)
Brasserie Lipp, 151 boulevard Saint-Germain (6)
Café Balzar, 49 rue des Écoles (5)
Café Cyrano, 3 rue Biot (17)
Café d'Harcourt, 6 rue de Lota (16)
Café de Flore, 172 boulevard Saint-Germain (6)
Café de la Comédie, 157 rue Saint-Honoré (1)
Café de la Mairie, 8 place Saint-Sulpice (6)
Café de la place Blanche (near rue Fontaine) (17)
Café de la Paix, 5 place de l'Opéra (9)
Café de la Rotonde, 105 boulevard du Montparnasse (6)
Café des amateurs (now café Delmas), 2 place de la
  Contrescarpe (5)

Café du départ, rue Gay-Lussac (5) (opposite gates to Jardin du Luxembourg) probably now Le Cercle Luxembourg, 1 rue Gay-Lussac (5)

Café Old Navy, 150 boulevard Saint-Germain (6)

Café Tournon, 18 rue Tournon (6)

Café Wepler, 14 place de Clichy (18)

Chez Emile (now Laterasse), 145 boulevard Saint-Michel (5)

Chez Inez, 15 rue Champollion (6) (now part of the Sorbonne)

Chez Rosalie, 7 rue Campagne-Première (6)

Closerie des Lilas, 171 boulevard du Montparnasse (6)

Fouquet's, 99 avenue des Champs-Élysées (8)

Harry's Bar, 5 rue Daunou (2)

Hôtel Ritz, 15 place Vendôme (1)

La Coupole, 102 boulevard du Montparnasse (14)

La Palette, 43 rue de Seine (6)

La Rotonde, 105 boulevard du Montparnasse (6)

Le Boeuf sur le Toit, (originally at 28, rue Boissy d'Anglas (8)), now 34 rue du Colisée (8)

Le Chat noir, 68 boulevard de Clichy (18)

Le Dingo Bar, (now l'Auberge de Venise) 10 rue Delambre (14)

Le Dôme, 108 boulevard du Montparnasse (14)

Le Falstaff, 42 rue du Montparnasse (6)

Le Jockey, 127 boulevard du Montparnasse (14)

Le Lapin Agile, 22 rue des Saules (18)

Le Lido, 116 avenue des Champs-Élysées (8)

Le Lutétia, 49 rue Linois (15)

Le Montana, 28 rue Saint-Benoît (6)

Le nègre de Toulouse, 159 boulevard du Montparnasse (14) (no longer extant)

Le petit Trianon, 80 boulevard de Rochechouart (18)

Le Pré aux clercs, 30 rue Bonaparte (6)

Le Select, 99 boulevard du Montparnasse (14)

Les Deux Magots, 6 place Saint-Germain-des-Prés (6)

Maxim's, 3 rue Royale (8)

Michaud's (now Le comptoir des Saints-Pères), 29 rue des Saints-Pères (6)

Petit café PLM, 17 boulevard Saint-Jacques (14)

Polidor, 41 rue Monsieur le Prince (6)

Rosebud, 11 rue Delambre (14)

CIRCUSES, DANCE HALLS, THEATRES

Bal Bullier (no longer extant), 31 avenue de l'Observatoire (14)

Bal du Printemps, 74 rue du Cardinal Lemoine (5) (no longer extant)

Bal Nègre, 33 rue Blomet (5)

Cabaret des Quat'z'arts, 62 boulevard de Clichy (18) (no longer extant)

Casino de Paris, 16 rue de Clichy (9)

Cirque Medrano, 63 boulevard de Rochechouart (9)

Comédie française, 1 place Colette (1)

Folies Bergère, 32 rue Richet (9)

Folies Bobino, 20 rue de la Gaîté (14)

Le cirque d'hiver, 110 rue Amelot (11)

Le Monocle, 60 boulevard Edgar Quinet (14)

Le Moulin rouge, 82 boulevard de Clichy (18)

La Petite Chaumière, 2 rue Berthe (18)

Théâtre de Babylone, 38 boulevard Raspail (7)

Théâtre des Champs-Élysées, 15 avenue Montaigne (8)

Théâtre du Châtelet, 2 rue Édouard Colonne (1)

Théâtre de la Gaîté, 31 rue de la Gaîté (14)

Shops

Galerie Au Sacre du Printemps, 5 rue du Cherche-Midi (6)
Galeries Lafayette, 40 boulevard Haussmann (9)
La Maison des amis des livres, 7 rue de l'Odéon (6)
La Samaritaine, 19 rue de la Monnaie (1)
Le Bon Marché, 24 rue de Sèvres (7)
Shakespeare and Company (Beach), 12 rue de l'Odéon (6)
Shakespeare and Company (Whitman), 37 rue de la Bûcherie (5)

Public Spaces

Bois de Boulogne (16)
Bois de Vincennes (19)
Jardin des Plantes, 57 rue Cuvier (5)
Jardin du Luxembourg (6)
Les Halles (1)
Musée de Cluny, 28 rue du Sommerard (6)
Musée du Louvre (1)
Musée du Luxembourg, 19 rue de Vaugirard (6)
Parc Montsouris, 2 rue Gazan (14)

Sporting Venues

Le Vélodrome d'hiver, rue Nélaton (15)
Hippodrome Racecourse Auteuil (16)

Brothels

Alys, 15 rue de Saint-Sulpice (6)
Le Chabanais, 12 rue Chabanais (2)

Le Sphinx, 31 boulevard Edgar Quinet (14)
Suzy, 7 rue Grégoire de Tours (6)

HOSPITALS AND CEMETERIES

American Hospital, 63 boulevard Victor Hugo, Neuilly-sur-
   Seine
Cimetière des Gonards, 19 rue de la porte de Buc, Versailles
Cimetière de Montmartre, 20 avenue Rachel (18)
Cimetière du Montparnasse, 3 boulevard Edgar Quinet (14)
Cimetière du Père Lachaise, 8 boulevard de Ménilmontant
   (20)
Cimetière de Thiais, 261 route de Fontainebleau, Thiais
Hôpital Broussais-Charité, 98 rue Didot (14)
Hôpital Cochin, 27 rue du Faubourg Saint-Jacques (14)

CHURCHES AND CATHEDRALS

Église Saint-Sulpice, 2 rue Palatine (6)
Église de Saint-Honoré d'Eylau, 66 bis avenue Raymond
   Poincaré (16)
Notre-Dame, 6 parvis Notre-Dame (now place Jean-Paul II)
   (4)
Russian Orthodox Church (now Alexander Nevsky
   Cathedral), 12 rue Daru (8)

Chronology

1889   *Exposition universelle* (World's Fair)

1894–
1906   Dreyfus affair

1898   Émile Zola *J'accuse!*

1899   Renault automobile factory founded

1900   *Exposition universelle.* Second Olympic Games, Bois de Vincennes

1902   George Méliès *Le voyage dans la lune.* Debussy *Pelléas et Mélisande* premiere

1903   First Salon d'Automne

1903   First Tour de France. Poiret fashion house launched

1904   *Entente cordiale* between France and England signed 8 April

1905   Separation of Church and State in France

1907   France, Britain and Russia sign *Triple entente*

1907   Picasso *Les demoiselles d'Avignon*

1909   *Cléopatre* at the Ballets Russes

1911   Debussy *Le Martyre de Saint Sébastien*

1912   Debussy *Prélude à l'après-midi d'un faune*

1913   Proust *À la recherche du temps perdu*. Stravinsky *Le Sacre du printemps*

1914   Goncharova designs *Le Coq d'or* for the Ballets Russes. Germany declares war on France 3 August – start of World War I

1918   Bombing of Paris. Armistice signed 11 November

1919   General strike in Paris 1 May. Treaty of Versailles 28 June

1922   James Joyce *Ulysses*. Death of Marcel Proust

1923   Premiere of Stravinsky *Les Noces*. Milhaud *La création du monde* with Ballet Suédois

1924   André Breton *Manifeste du surréalisme*. George Antheil and Fernand Léger with Dudley Murphy *Ballet mécanique*

1925   *Exposition des arts décoratifs et industriels modernes*

1928   Radclyffe Hall *The Well of Loneliness*

1929   Financial crash followed by worst economic depression in US history. Le Corbusier starts *Cité de refuge* social housing project. Luis Buñuel and Salvador Dalí *Un Chien Andalou*

1930   Buñuel *L'Âge d'or*, Breton second *Manifeste du surréalisme*

1931   *Exposition coloniale* (Colonial Exhibition covering French colonies). Republican Government elected in Spain

1932   Launch of transatlantic liner *Normandie*

1933   Gertrude Stein *The Autobiography of Alice B. Toklas*

1935   First International Congress of Writers in Defence of Culture

1936   Italy and Germany recognise Francoist regime in Spain

1937   *Exposition internationale des arts et techniques dans la vie moderne.* Picasso exhibits *Guernica*

1938   Munich Agreement 29 September. Jean-Paul Sartre *La nausée*

1939   War on Germany declared 3 September – start of World War II

1940   German invasion of Paris 14 June

1942   André Breton third *Manifeste du surréalisme*. Albert Camus *L'étranger*

1944   Allied forces land in Normandy (D-Day) 6 June. Liberation of Paris 25 August. Women given right to vote in France

1946   Closure of brothels across France (*Marthe Richard* Law). Fourth Republic (economic reconstruction, and start of independence for many French colonies)

Further Reading

Amine, Laila, *Postcolonial Paris: Fictions of Intimacy in the City of Light*, University of Wisconsin Press, Madison, WI, 2018

Arpaia, Bruno, *The Angel of History*, trans. Minna Proctor, Canongate, Edinburgh, 2007

Auster, Paul, *Hand to Mouth*, Faber & Faber, London, 1998

Baxter, John, *Montparnasse: Paris's District of Memory and Desire*, HarperCollins, New York, NY, 2017

Beach, Sylvia, *Shakespeare and Company*, University of Nebraska Press, Lincoln, NE, 1991

—, *The Letters of Sylvia Beach*, Keri Walsh (Ed), Columbia University Press, New York, NY, 2011

Beaton, Cecil, *The Wandering Years: Diaries 1922–1939*, Weidenfeld and Nicolson, London, 1961

Beevor, Antony & Cooper, Artemis, *Paris After The Liberation 1944–1949*, Penguin Books, London, 2007

Benjamin, Walter, *The Arcades Project*, trans. Howard Eiland & Kevin McLaughlin, Harvard University Press, Harvard, MA, 2002

Benois, Alexandre, *Reminiscences of the Russian Ballet*, trans. Mary Britnieva, Putnam, London, 1945

Benstock, Shari, *Women of the Left Bank: Paris, 1900–1940*, University of Texas Press, Austin, TX, 1987

Bouvet, Vincent & Durozoi, Gérard, *Paris Between the Wars: Art, Style and Glamour in the Crazy Years*, trans. Ruth Sharman, Thames and Hudson, London, 2010

Brody, Paul, *The Real Midnight in Paris*, Barnes & Noble, New York, NY, 2012

Burke, David, *Writers in Paris, Literary Lives in the City of Light*, Counterpoint, Berkeley, CA, 2008

Calvino, Italo, *Hermit in Paris*, trans. Martin McLaughlin, Vintage, London, 2004

Campbell, James, *Paris Interzone: Richard Wright, Lolita, Boris Vian and Others on the Left Bank*, Minerva, London, 1995

—, *Exiled in Paris*, University of California Press, Oakland, CA, 2003

Carco, Francis, *The Last Bohemia: From Montmartre to the Quartier Latin*, trans. Madeleine Boyd, Henry Holt & Co, New York, NY, 1928

Chadwick, Whitney & Latimer, Tirza True (Eds), *The Modern Woman Revisited: Paris Between the Wars*, Rutgers University Press, New Brunswick, NJ, 2003

Cocteau, Jean, *The Journals of Jean Cocteau*, Museum Press, London, 1965

Cohen, Margaret, *Profane Illumination: Walter Benjamin and the Paris of Surrealist Revolution*, University of California Press, Berkeley, CA, 1993

Colette, *The Pure and The Impure*, trans. Herma Briffault, NYRB Classics, New York, NY, 2000

Cossart, Michael de, *The Food of Love: Princesse Edmond de Polignac (1865–1943) and her Salon*, Hamish Hamilton, London, 1978

Drummond, John, *Speaking of Diaghilev*, Faber & Faber, London, 1999

Duncan, Isadora, *My Life*, Liveright, New York, NY, 1995

Flanner, Janet, *Paris was Yesterday, 1925–1939*, Viking Press, New York, NY, 1972

Gallix, Andrew, *We'll Never Have Paris*, Repeater Books, London, 2019

Glass, Charles, *Americans in Paris: Life and Death under Nazi Occupation 1940–1944*, Penguin Books, London, 2011

Goodwyn, Janet, *Edith Wharton: Traveller in the Land of Letters*, St Martin's Press, New York, NY, 1990

Halverson, Krista (Ed), *Shakespeare and Company, Paris: A History of the Rag & Bone Shop of the Heart*, Shakespeare and Company, Paris, 2016

Hanson, Arlen J., *Expatriate Paris: A Cultural and Literary Guide to Paris of the 1920s*, Arcade Publishing, New York, NY, 1990

Hargrove, Nancy Duvall, *T.S. Eliot's Parisian Year*, University Press of Florida, Gainesville, FL, 2010

Hazan, Eric, *The Invention of Paris: A History in Footsteps*, trans. David Fernbach, Verso, London, 2011

—, *A Walk Through Paris: A Radical Exploration*, trans. David Fernbach, Verso, London, 2018

Jolas, Eugène, Braque, Georges, Tzara, Tristan, a.o. *Testimony Against Gertrude Stein*, Servire Press, The Hague, 1935

Kochno, Boris, *Diaghilev and the Ballets Russes*, Harper & Row, New York, NY, 1970

Lewis, R. W. B., *Edith Wharton: A Biography*, Harper & Row, New York, NY, 1975

—, & Lewis, Nancy, (Eds), *The Letters of Edith Wharton*, Scribners, New York, NY, 1988

Marnham, Patrick, *Diego Rivera: Dreaming with His Eyes Open: A life of Diego Rivera*, Bloomsbury, London, 1998

McBride, Henry, *An Eye on the Modern Century: Selected Letters of Henry McBride*, Yale University Press, New Haven, CT, 2000

Mellow, James R., *Charmed Circle: Gertrude Stein and Company*, Henry Holt & Co, New York, NY, 2003

Moore, George, *Memoirs of My Dead Life*, William Heinemann, London, 1906

Nabokov, Vladimir, *Speak, Memory: A Memoir*, Victor Gollancz, London, 1951

Nairn, Ian, *Nairn's Paris*, Notting Hill Editions, London, 2018

Olivier, Fernande, *Picasso and His Friends*, Heinemann, London, 1964

Phelps, Robert, trans. Richard Howard, *Professional Secrets: An Autobiography of Jean Cocteau, Drawn from his Lifetime Writings*, Farrar, Straus & Giroux, New York, NY, 1970

Poirier, Agnès, *Left Bank: Art, Passion and the Rebirth of Paris 1940–1950*, Bloomsbury, London, 2018

Pound, Ezra, *The Letters of Ezra Pound 1907–1941*, Harcourt, Brace & Co, New York, NY, 1950

Proust, Marcel, *Remembrance of Things Past*, Faber & Faber, London, 2000

Putman, Samuel, *Paris Was our Mistress: Memoirs of a Lost & Found Generation*, Southern Illinois University Press, Carbondale, IL, 1970

Radiguet, Raymond, *Count d'Orgel's Ball*, trans. Annapaola Cancogni, NYRB Classics, New York, NY, 2005

Reynolds, Nicholas, *Writer, Sailor, Soldier, Spy: Ernest Hemingway's Secret Adventures, 1935–1961*, Harper Collins, London, 2017

Riley Fitch, Noël, *Walks in Hemingway's Paris*, St Martin's Press, New York, NY, 1989

—, *Sylvia Beach and the Lost Generation: A History of Literary Paris in the Twenties and Thirties*, W.W. Norton & Company, London, 1985

Rivera, Diego, with March, Gladys, *My Art, My Life: An autobiography*, Dover Publications, New York, NY, 1991

Rodriguez, Suzanne, *Wild Heart: A Life – Natalie Clifford Barney's Journey from Victorian American to Belle Epoque Paris*, Harper Collins, New York, NY, 2002

Roe, Sue, *In Montparnasse: The Emergence of Surrealism in Paris, from Duchamp to Dali*, Penguin, London, 2019

Sante, Luc, *The Other Paris*, Faber & Faber, London, 2015

Schack, William A., *Harlem in Montmartre: A Paris Jazz Story between the Great Wars*, University of California Press, Berkeley, CA, 2001

Schouten, Fiona, *A Diffuse Murmur of History: Literary Memory Narratives of Civil War and Dictatorship in Spanish Novels After 1990*, P.I.E., Brussels, Belgium, 2010

Serge, Victor, and Sedova, Natalia Ivanovna, *Life and Death of Leon Trotsky*, Haymarket Books, Chicago, IL, 2016

Shattuck, Roger, *The Banquet Years*, Faber & Faber, London, 1958

Soupault, Philippe, *Last Nights of Paris*, trans. Williams, William Carlos, Exact Change, Cambridge, MA, 1992

Stein, Gertrude, *The Autobiography of Alice B. Toklas*, Vintage Books, New York, NY, 1960

Stravinsky, Igor, *Chronicle of My Life*, Victor Gollancz, London, 1936

White, Edmund, *Marcel Proust*, Viking, New York, NY, 1999

Index